Challenging Moral Particu

Particularism is a justly popular 'cutting-edge' topic in contemporary ethics across the world. Many moral philosophers do not, in fact, support particularism (instead defending 'generalist' theories that rest on particular abstract moral principles), but nearly all would take it to be a position that continues to offer serious lessons and challenges, and that can not be safely ignored.

This collection of new philosophy papers, written by well known philosophers, will find a ready audience within the international academic philosophical community. Given the high standard of the contributions, and that this is a subject where lively debate continues to flourish, it is reasonable to expect that the book will become required reading for professionals and advanced students working in the area.

Matjaž Potrč is Professor of Philosophy at the University of Ljubljana, Slovenia.

Vojko Strahovnik is an Assistant Philosophy Researcher at the Department of Philosophy, University of Ljubljana.

Mark Morris Lance is Professor of Philosophy at Georgetown University, USA.

Routledge Studies in Ethics and Moral Theory

Challenging Moral
Particularism

**Edited by
Mark Norris Lance, Matjaž Potrč,
and Vojko Strahovnik**

 Routledge
Taylor & Francis Group

NEW YORK AND LONDON

First published 2008
by Routledge
711 Third Avenue, New York, NY 10017

Simultaneously published in the UK
by Routledge
2 Park Square, Milton Park, Abingdon, Oxon, OX14 4RN

Routledge is an imprint of the Taylor & Francis Group, an informa business

First issued in paperback 2011

Typeset in Times New Roman
by Taylor & Francis Books

Library of Congress Cataloging in Publication Data
Challenging moral particularism / edited by Mark Norris Lance, Matja Potrč,
and Vojko Strahovnik.
    p. cm. – (Routledge studies in ethics and moral theory ; 12)
    Includes bibliographical references (p.) and index.
    1. Ethics. 2. Individuation (Philosophy) 3. Principle (Philosophy) I. Lance,
    Mark Norris. II. Potrc, Matja. III. Strahovnik, Vojko.
    BJ1012.C4535 2008
    170–dc22   2007021740

British Library Cataloguing in Publication Data
A catalogue record for this book is available from the British Library

ISBN10: 0-415-96377-X (hbk)
ISBN10: 0-415-88787-9 (pbk)
ISBN10: 0-203-93778-3 (ebk)

ISBN13: 978-0-415-96377-0 (hbk)
ISBN13: 978-0-415-88787-8 (pbk)
ISBN13: 978-0-203-93778-5 (ebk)

Contents

vi *Contents*

Acknowledgments

Our thanks go to the authors/contributors of this volume and to the participants of the 2005 Bled Philosophy Conference on particularism, a conference that was the basis from which the collection originates. As always, Bled proved to be a fruitful environment.

We would also like to thank our colleagues and friends, especially Terry Horgan, Danilo Šuster, Maja Lovrenov and Uroš Rošker for all their help and support. In the preparation of this volume Jonathan Dancy offered invaluable advice concerning the structure and content of this collection. Alenka Pogačnik helped with corrections in the manuscript.

We are grateful to *Acta Analytica* (Transaction Publishers), Blackwell and Oxford University Press for kind permission to use some previously published material. 'Contextual Semantics and Particularist Normativity' by Terry Horgan and Matjaž Potrč is a modified version of their previously published paper 'Particularist Semantic Normativity' (*Acta Analytica*, vol. 21:1, 2006 (38): 45–61). 'Ethical Generality and Moral Judgment' by Robert Audi was previously published in *Contemporary Debates in Moral Theory* (J. Dreier (ed.) Oxford: Blackwell, 2006, pp. 285–304). 'From Particularism to Defeasibility in Ethics' by Mark Lance and Maggie Little is partially based on their previously published papers 'Defending Moral Particularism' (in J. Dreier (ed.) *Contemporary Debates in Moral Theory*, Oxford: Blackwell, 2006, pp. 305–21), 'Particularism & Anti-Theory' (in D. Copp (ed.) *The Oxford Handbook of Ethical Theory*, Oxford University Press, 2006, pp. 567–94) and 'Where the Laws Are' (to appear in R. Shafer-Landau (ed.) *Oxford Studies in Metaethics, Vol. II*, Oxford University Press, 2007). 'Particularism and the Contingent A Priori' by Sean McKeever and Michael Ridge is based on the material from their book *Principled Ethics: Generalism As a Regulative Ideal* (Oxford: Clarendon Press, 2006).

Lastly, we would like to express our thanks for all their support and guidance to the Routledge editor Terry Clague and his assistant Katherine Carpenter.

Mark Lance, Georgetown
Matjaž Potrč, Ljubljana
Vojko Strahovnik, Ljubljana

Contributors

Robert Audi is the David E. Gallo chair in Ethics and Professor of Philosophy at University of Notre Dame. He is the author and editor of several books including *Belief, Justification, and Knowledge* (Wadsworth, 1988), *The Structure of Justification* (Cambridge, 1993), *Action, Intention, and Reason* (Cornell, 1993), *Moral Knowledge and Ethical Character* (Oxford, 1997), *Epistemology: A Contemporary Introduction to the Theory of Knowledge* (Routledge, 1998), *The Good in the Right* (Princeton, 2004), *Practical reasoning and Ethical Decision* (Routledge, 2006) and *The Cambridge Dictionary of Philosophy.*

David Bakhurst is John and Ella G. Charlton Professor of Philosophy at Queen's University, Kingston, Ontario. He is the author of *Consciousness and Revolution in Soviet Philosophy* (Cambridge, 1991), and co-editor of *The Social Self* (with C. Sypnowich, Sage, 1995) and *Jerome Bruner: Language, Culture, Self* (with S. Shanker, Sage, 2001). He has also published numerous articles on ethics, philosophical psychology, and Russian thought.

Jonathan Dancy is Professor of Philosophy at University of Reading (UK) and at University of Texas (Austin). He is the author of *An Introduction to Contemporary Epistemology* (Blackwell, 1985), *Berkeley: An Introduction* (Blackwell, 1987), *Moral Reasons* (Blackwell, 1993), *Practical Reality* (Clarendon, 2000), *Ethics Without Principles* (Clarendon, 2004), and numerous articles. He is also the editor of *Perceptual Knowledge, Reading Parfit, Berkeley's Principles of Human Knowledge* and *Three Dialogues between Hylas and Philonous,* and co-editor of *A Companion to Epistemology.*

Brad Hooker is Professor of Philosophy at University of Reading (UK). He is the author of *Ideal Code, Real World: A Rule-Consequentialist Theory of Morality* (Clarendon, 2000), and editor of *Rationality, Rules, and Utility* (Westview, 1993), and *Truth in Ethics* (Blackwell, 1996), *Well-Being and Morality* (with R. Crisp, Oxford, 2000), *Morality, Rules, and Consequences* (with E. Mason and D.E. Miller, Edinburgh UP, 2000; Rowman and Littlefield, 2000), and *Moral Particularism* (with M. Little,

Clarendon, 2000). He has also published many articles, mostly in moral philosophy.

Terry Horgan is Professor of Philosophy at University of Arizona (Tuscon). He is the author of *Connectionism and the Philosophy of Psychology* (with J. Tienson, MIT, 1996), *Austere Realism* (with M. Potrč, MIT, forthcoming), and articles on many philosophical subjects including metaphysics, philosophy of mind, philosophy of psychology, epistemology, philosophy of language, metaethics. He is also editor of numerous collections including *Metaethics after Moore* (with M. Timmons, Oxford, 2006).

Mark Norris Lance is Professor of Philosophy at Georgetown University. He is the author of *The Grammar of Meaning* (with J. O'Leary-Hawthorne, Cambridge, 1997) and of many articles in journals and books covering the topics of philosophy of language, philosophy of mind, metaphysics, epistemology, normativity, and philosophy of logic.

Margaret Little is Professor at Georgetown's Philosophy Department and a Senior Research Scholar at Georgetown's Kennedy Institute of Ethics. She is the editor of *Moral Particularism* (with B. Hooker, Clarendon, 2000) and author of *Intimate Duties: Re-Thinking Abortion, the Law, & Morality* (Clarendon, forthcoming). Her work covers areas of ethics, with particular interests in moral particularism, moral epistemology, motivation, and feminist bioethics.

Sean McKeever is Professor of Philosophy at Davidson College (North Carolina). He is the author of *Principled Ethics: Generalism as a Regulative Ideal*, (with M. Ridge, Oxford, 2006) and of several articles on moral theory, history of ethics, and political philosophy.

David McNaughton is Professor of Philosophy at Florida State University. He is the author of *Moral Vision: An Introduction to Ethics* (Blackwell, 1988), and articles on ethics, on 18th century British moral philosophy, history of philosophy, and on philosophy of religion. He is the founder of *British Society for Ethical Theory*. He is currently working with P. Rawling on a book on deontology.

Nenad Miščević is Professor of Philosophy at Central European University (Budapest) and University of Maribor. He has written and edited several books – including *Rationality and Cognition* (Toronto, 2000), *Nationalism and Ethnic Conflict: Philosophical Perspectives* (ed., Carus, 2000), *Nationalism and Beyond* (CEU, 2001). He has written papers covering philosophy of mind and cognitive science, epistemology, political philosophy, nationalism, metaphysics, and moral philosophy.

Matjaž Potrč is Professor of Philosophy at University of Ljubljana. His books include *Phenomenology and Cognitive Science* (Röll, 1993),

Origins: The Common Sources of the Analytic and Phenomenological Traditions (ed., with T. Horgan and J. Tienson, Memphis, 2002), *Dynamical Philosophy* (ZIFF, 2004), *Practical Contexts* (with V. Strahovnik, Ontos, 2004) and *Austere Realism* (with T. Horgan, MIT, forthcoming). Articles cover metaphysics, moral philosophy, epistemology, philosophy of mind and cognitive science, vagueness, phenomenology, and Slovene philosophical tradition.

Anthony W. Price is Reader in Philosophy at University of London (Birkbeck). His bibliography includes *Mental Conflict* (Routledge, 1995), *Love and Friendship in Plato and Aristotle* (Oxford, 1997), and articles 'Plato: Ethics and Politics', 'On Criticising Values', 'Plato, Zeno, and the Object of Love', and 'The So-Called Logic of Practical Inference'.

Piers Rawling is Professor of Philosophy at Florida State University. He is the editor of *The Oxford Handbook of Rationality* (with A. Mele, Oxford, 2004) and author of articles covering ethics, decision and game theory, logic, philosophy of language, philosophy of science, rationality and reasons. Currently he is working with D. McNaughton on a book on deontology.

Michael Ridge is Professor of Philosophy at University of Edinburgh. He is the author of *Principled Ethics: Generalism as a Regulative Ideal*, (with S. McKeever, Oxford, 2006) and of several articles on moral theory, social and political philosophy, and history of moral philosophy.

Vojko Strahovnik is an Assistant Philosophy Researcher at the Department of Philosophy, University of Ljubljana (Faculty of Arts). He is the author of *Practical Contexts* (with M. Potrč, Ontos, 2004) and the author of several articles on ethics, epistemology and Slovene philosophical tradition.

Pekka Väyrynen is an Assistant Professor of Philosophy at the University of California, Davis. His publications and research interests fall mainly in the areas of ethics, rationality, and epistemology.

1 Introduction

Challenging moral particularism

Vojko Strahovnik

I

Moral particularism grew out of the work of John McDowell and especially of Jonathan Dancy. It has been on the philosophical stage for more than two decades now. In recent years its various aspects, as well as its theoretical and practical consequences have been debated within moral theory. Especially important landmarks of this process were the publication of a collection of papers *Moral Particularism* (in 2000, eds. B. Hooker and M. Little) and Jonathan Dancy's recent book *Ethics Without Principles* (2004).

The debate on particularism went through some noticeable shifts during this time with a range of views emerging concerning the central claims of particularism and how to understand them properly. In addition, there has been vigorous debate around specific areas of particularism. At the same time insights from particularism began to affect other fields of philosophical debate. At the 2005 Bled Philosophy Conference on particularism (out of which this collection grew and which gathered some of the major figures in the field) themes from normativity in general, semantics, aesthetic, epistemology, ontology and philosophy of science were discussed alongside the themes from moral philosophy.

The acceptability of a principled approach to morality, the question whether universal, exceptionless moral principles govern morality, still lies at the heart of the debate between particularism and generalism. As Sean McKeever and Michael Ridge usefully put it recently: despite a diverse range of views under this label 'all particularist positions can be characterized by a negative attitude towards moral principles' (McKeever and Ridge 2005a). Jonathan Dancy understands moral particularism as the claim that 'the possibility of moral thought and judgment does not depend on the provision of a suitable supply of moral principles' (Dancy 2004: 73). The particularist approach holds that sound moral thought need not consist in the application of moral principles to cases, and that the morally perfect person is not to be regarded as the person of principle. At the other extreme there is the subsumptivist generalist position – the moral status of an act is determined by its falling under a general moral principle. During the years in which particularistic moral theory developed several arguments were put forward in its favour. These involve arguments from reasons and normativity in general, from moral epistemology, from the practical import of moral principles and rules and the nature of moral judgment, arguments appealing to counter-examples to principles, to the complexity of morality, and arguments from moral phenomenology.

This volume addresses these developments in the debate on particularism. Papers cover a wide range of topics, dealing with the question about the appropriate kind of ethical generalities, action-guidingness, predictability and explanatory roles that moral principles should play, the possibility of defeasible moral principles, and default reasons. They also address questions of moral knowledge, semantic normativity, response dependence of moral concepts, holism of value and ethical dimensions of humour. In what follows papers are briefly summarized emphasizing central problems that they address and their interrelatedness.

II

In 'Moral Particularism and the Real World' Brad Hooker presents four challenges to particularism. He identifies holism of reasons as a central tenet of Dancy's particularism and goes on to introduce a distinction between ultimate reasons and derived reasons, the former being normatively basic and invariable, and the latter clearly variable. If holism is going to support particularism it must pertain to ultimate reasons. An argument from holism to particularism about moral thought must include an (independent) argument against the possibility of true informative moral principles. Hooker is sceptical about Dancy's arguments in support of holism of moral reasons and casts some doubt on the distinction between reasons, enablers, disablers, intensifiers, and attenuators. Even given such complex normative structure there still remains the possibility that one could find *true subjunctive conditionals* capturing it, therefore falling short of particularism. Hooker also claims that the epistemic priority of particular cases and expendability of general moral truths is merely an unsupported and implausible assumption made by both particularism and intuitionism. Fine-tuning of the starting moral principles is offered as a strategy for avoiding problems with apparent exceptions involving valence shifts and silencing of basic morally relevant features (e.g., justice, harm, benefit).

At the end of the paper Hooker offers a modified argument[1] against particularism building upon considerations regarding the social function of morality. An essential aspect of morality enables *predictability* of other's behaviour, giving us some assurance that other members of a certain group will not attack us, break promises or lie to us. Moral practice needs principles and rules. One possible way out for particularists would be to argue that the notion of a *default reason* (features of acts that are always morally relevant, unless something goes wrong) is sufficient for reliability and predictability.

But Hooker pushes the particularist to face a dilemma. Either she opts for the notion of default reasons that is close to the general reasons and could be somehow captured by moral principles, thus making her position much less interesting than it appeared at the beginning. Or again she may stick with a less strict notion of default reasons, making her position more radical and interesting, but at the same time much less plausible in virtue of failing to meet the predictability demand.

Papers by Robert Audi, Margaret Little – Mark Lance, and Pekka Väyrynen deal with different kinds of ethical generalities and the roles they play in moral theorizing and moral practice. These authors address issues about moral theory, different kinds of particularism, defeasibility of moral principles, explanation and moral guidance. They test the ground for a suitable kind of moral generality that would fit between the two extremes: radical generalism and radical particularism.

In 'Ethical Generality and Moral Judgment' Robert Audi singles out tensions between the inexact, subtle and elusive nature of ethical issues and the search for highly general and clear moral principles or rules. The right kind of moral generalities situated somewhere between absolute generalism and extreme particularism should meet the relevant theoretical demands and be of use as a practical guide in our everyday moral thinking. Audi proposes a version of moderate Rossian intuitionism that he labels moderate particularism. He differentiates among five kinds of particularism: (i) epistemological, (ii) conceptual, (iii) genetic, (iv) methodological, and (v) normative. Moderate particularism rejects normative particularism and retains the idea of invariability of basic moral reasons. Audi states that vagueness and tradeoff concerns generate problems for any attempt to formulate highly general and exceptionless ethical principles, and he demonstrates this for the cases of Kant's and Mill's ethical theories. He refutes specification and conditionalization strategies as a proper way to avoid these problems, and turns to Ross and to the distinction between prima facie and absolute duties. Rossian principles exhibit '*generality as universal applicability*', since prima facie duties merely identify universally morally relevant features of our actions (always stating good moral reasons, but not always conclusive ones). Audi proposes several distinctions pertaining to the theory of moral reasons and uses these as tools to create a 'holism-friendly' picture of reasons that is at the same time consistent with the invariability of basic moral reasons. His proposal comprises the distinctions between: (i) *deliberative relevance* of a consideration and its *normative relevance*; (ii) considerations (or reasons) below or above the threshold of *ordinary discernibility* in the context of decision; (iii) *intrinsic valence of a feature* and its *overall normative power* in a given context; (iv) *holism concerning final duties* and *holism regarding judgments of prima facie duties*. Moderate particularism avoids the subsumptivist view of moral knowledge. Another possibility to capture the relevant kind of moral generality, namely that of virtue ethics, is also considered but such areatic generalism is rejected showing itself as less plausible when being compared to deontological intuitionism. Audi concludes that radical particularism is an incomplete answer to the vagueness and tradeoffs problems in ethics, and opts for the prospects of moderate intuitionism/particularism.

Next, in 'From Particularism to Defeasibility in Ethics' Margaret Little and Mark Lance debate the relationship between contextualism (or holism) about reasons and particularism. They argue that the full-fledged recognition of exceptions to moral generalizations does not mean that one must accept a picture of morality as being free from any important kind of generalities. The sharp divide between generalism and particularism is a consequence of strict and narrow views about the nature of explanation. According to these views *genuine explanatory reasons* must be governed by universal exceptionless principles. An alternative model of explanation figuring exceptions is offered. The theoretical space between subsumptivism and invariabilism on the one side and between particularism on the other proves to be richer than it would seem at first sight.

Lance and Little defend *deep moral contextualism*: right- or wrong-making, and good- or bad-making features of actions vary with context in ways that preclude codification by exceptionless principles. Their contextualism is broad in scope (it encompasses much of morality) and deep as it does not require 'surface' variability to be redeemed at a deeper level of exceptionless principle. The main drawback of strong moral particularism, such as that of Dancy, is an implausible and inadequate explanation of why and how a certain feature of an action can contribute to its overall moral status. Explanation of why something is a reason for something else (in moral reasoning) must be somehow connected to generality. Lance and Little stress the importance of the difference between adducing reasons for a conclusion and between a particularist narrative. '*The former requires commitment to some sort of generalization – just what the pure discernment theorist denies of familiar factors such as lying and promising.*' Features of such acts as promise-keeping, lying, inflicting pain, being kind are building blocks of everyday morality that entertain an *intimate* connection with their moral import. Those are genuinely explanatory features for the moral status of acts and may be captured into defeasible generalizations.

Defeasible generalities are introduced through the notion of privileged conditions. If we want to single out a connection between a particular descriptive feature of such acts as 'causing pain' and between the negative moral import of this feature that is neither necessarily universal nor pervasive or usual, we can do this by saying that defeasibly, causing pain is wrong-making. When a defeasible generalization faces an exception something has gone astray – the context has relevantly changed in respect to privileged conditions. There are several types of such defeasibility dynamics, such as the paradigm/riff, justificatory dependence, and idealization/approximation. Moral understanding is the understanding of the structure of moral privilege and exception. One must understand the nature of a certain feature in privileged conditions and when outside of such a context, the relation of this last context to the first one, the required compensatory moves, and the acceptability of various deviations.

In his 'Usable Moral Principles' Pekka Väyrynen proposes a new type of moral generality that he calls '*hedged moral principles*', examining the role such principles could play in providing moral agents with adequate *moral guidance*. Hedged moral principles identify moral reasons and at the same time they include reference to normative bases of those moral reasons. Such principles are sensitive to 'undermining defeater' of reasons (consequently they are sensitive to exceptions), and at the same provide explanation about why a certain reason is a reason in the particular case. With this proposal he addresses the particularistic argument that a moral person should not be a 'person of principle' and that adherence to moral principles could lead one into making bad decisions and following poor moral judgments (Dancy 2005). Väyrynen calls this the claim for 'principles abstinence', and singles out two particularist arguments for it, the first being an argument from holism of reasons and the second resting on a supposition that moral principles are poor moral guides. Hedged moral principles are good candidates to avoid this second criticism. Väyrynen starts arguing for this by identifying some characteristics of moral guidance by principles (such as robust reliability of our strategy for acting rightly; acting *for* the right reasons; accessibility and availability of principles to ordinary conscientious moral agents; the possibility of direct or indirect contribution of these principles to the strategy for acting). His argument proceeds in two main steps: (i) acceptance of moral principles leads to moral reasons and shapes an appropriate responsiveness to them; and (ii) via reason responsiveness principles can contribute non-trivially to reliably acting well and thus they supply an adequate moral guidance. Väyrynen concludes that hedged principles provide generalism with such moral guidance and that this guidance is at least as good as an account of moral guidance by the particularist.

A paper by Michael Ridge and Sean McKeever and a reply by Jonathan Dancy deal with the modal status of basic moral facts and the epistemic status of our knowledge of them.

In 'Particularism and the Contingent A Priori' Ridge and McKeever question the plausibility of the *a priori status of basic moral facts* such as those offered by particularists. For a particularist, basic moral facts are facts about reasons – 'facts about what is a moral reason for what' (Dancy 2004: 141). Given the holism of reasons these are facts about particular cases and they are thus *contingent*. A particularist could avoid entering troubling waters if she held that such contingent facts are knowable a posteriori, but Ridge and McKeever argue that given the irreducible nature of moral properties defended by particularism, such a picture of moral knowledge would imply a special moral sense for directly perceiving moral reality. The latter is implausible, however, and it is also explicitly rejected by

Dancy[2] (Dancy 2004: 143–46). So it seems that the particularist is forced to defend the a priori knowledge of contingent moral facts. In *Ethics Without Principles* Dancy indeed defended this position, using a distinction between *positive* and *negative dependence* of knowledge on experience introduced by Giaquinto (1998). If we take a piece of moral knowledge:

The fact that F is a reasons for me to φ.

then surely the knowledge of the fact that F (e.g., that my action would cause pain or that she needs my help) is a posteriori, but the knowledge of the relation that this fact stands in with the right-hand side of the belief is not a posteriori (since the knowledge of the fact that F is not a ground for the belief in question), and such cases of moral knowledge merely negatively depend on a posteriori knowledge (Dancy 2004: 146–48). Ridge and McKeever reject some other defences of contingent a priori knowledge (Kripke, Hawthorne) as unsuitable for the purposes of particularism, revealing a serious challenge for particularism in her defending that 'deeply contingent a priori knowledge that is not the result of any discernable method nevertheless forms the basis for a whole branch of human knowledge'. They point to some disanalogies between cases of knowledge discussed by Giaquinto and the moral case and go on to claim that the aposteriori character of knowledge of the fact that F must 'leak through' to the moral belief. At the end of the paper, the authors argue that in the example of our judgments assessing relevant similarity – offered by Dancy as another case of a priori contingent knowledge – it is not clear at all that one is dealing with a priori knowledge. This additionally undermines Dancy's position.

In 'Are Basic Moral Facts both Contingent and A Priori?' Dancy responds to the arguments put forward by Ridge and McKeever. First he entertains the idea that one could view basic moral facts as (in a certain sense) necessary, but abandons this easy way out for particularism as unclear. He then considers the charge made by Ridge and McKeever that the apparent a posteriori character of knowledge of *facts* that are reasons turns also our moral knowledge that those facts *are reasons* into a posteriori knowledge. By introducing a distinction between two competing understandings of the a posteriori, he defends the position according to which a posteriori knowledge is knowledge that can be acquired via empirical means alone as being the relevant conception when dealing with basic moral knowledge. According to this conception one can gain knowledge of facts *p* and *g* via empirical means alone, but this is not necessarily the case for knowledge of the relation between these facts. The same can be said about the moral case, involving knowledge of basic facts about the situation one is in and knowing what is a reason for what. Basic moral knowledge is not entirely empirical. Given the example above Dancy, contrary to Ridge and McKeever's analysis, claims that knowledge of the fact that F is neither a ground, an enabling condition, nor a presupposition for the moral belief. For example, the fact that she is in trouble (F1) is a ground for the fact that I ought to help her (F2), but the first fact is not a ground for the '*normative meta-fact*' (F3) that F1 is a reason for F2. According to Dancy, F3 *entails* both F1 and F2. At the end of his paper Dancy again defends the analogy between moral knowledge as a form of judgment and our judgments about e.g., relevant similarities (cf. Dancy 2004: 148).

Terry Horgan and Matjaž Potrč in 'Contextual Semantics and Particularist Normativity' outline the basics of contextual semantics. They argue that *truth is semantically correct affirmability under contextually variable semantic standards.* Truth is often a matter of indirect correspondence between thought/language and the world. It involves contextually operative standards for semantic correctness and the actual distribution of genuine objects, properties and relations in the world. Using such a notion one is able to make sense of truth for numerous sentences that seem to be unproblematically true, while at the same time quantifying over entities that should not be countenanced within the appropriate minimalist naturalistic ontology (besides there being no available procedure to paraphrase them or identify them with unproblematic entities). Semantic standards for correct affirmatibility sometimes vary from one occasion to another by virtue of situational factors influencing the operative settings of *contextually variable semantic parameters.* Contextualist semantics fits naturally with the view that the pertinent semantic standards are particularist rather than being systematizable as exceptionless general principles. Horgan and Potrč go on to address some problems for such an account of truth and normativity, especially the so-called 'learnability argument'. They point to the role that *ceteris paribus* principles and semantic skills play in addressing this argument. They express some doubts that semantic normativity conforms to completely general principles and further that it needs to conform to such principles in order to be learnable and masterable by humans.

In the paper entitled 'When the Plot Thickens: Dancy on Thick Concepts' Nenad Miščević deals with the subject of *thick moral concepts* and argues for a specific response-dependent view of these that is readily available to the particularist. Thick concepts are of central importance for particularism, playing the role of 'morally shaped intermediaries' between the lower (natural and purely descriptive) level and the thin moral layer. They put the lower lever into a 'practical shape' that is convenient for enabling us to make overall moral judgment in thin terms (Dancy 2004: 84–85). This important claim and Dancy's claim that such concepts *involve responses of observers* (Dancy 1996) are heavily undermined by his acceptance of anti-dispositionalist views.

Miščević outlines a sketch of what it is for thick moral concepts and properties to be response dependent and presents Dancy's arguments against dispositionalism, arguments that are based on moral phenomenology and motivation. Since thick concepts inseparably include an appeal to appropriate attitude-responses they are best viewed as response-dependent. Arguing from Dancy's commitment to treat moral talk realistically, the same move is proposed toward response-dependence for thick moral properties. Since these are seen as central for morality this pushes Dancy towards accepting a response-dependence account of morality. Miščević proposes a version of a response-dependence account of thick moral concepts and argues that these concepts are structurally similar to pejoratives. Ordinary, or naïve, thick moral concepts are not openly response-dependent; their phenomenology is objectivist. So one should build *response-dependence* only into a *theoretical account* and an explanation of the nature of such concepts and the properties they refer to. A particularist should embrace the proposed response-dependence account. But in this case problems with proper generalities (due to an analogy with color and other secondary qualities) would re-emerge, forcing the radical particularist into rethinking the role of soft or *ceteris paribus* generalities.

In analogy with the holism of reasons, a particularist could talk about holism of (moral) value. What is valuable in one situation or in one context could switch valence or lose value entirely in another. Additionally the complex wholes are subject to organicity, i.e., their value is not necessarily identical to the sum of the values of their parts (Dancy, 2000b: 137–41; 2004: 165–89). Papers by David McNaughton – Piers Rawling and Anthony Price address the issues related to these views.

In 'Holism about Value' McNaughton and Rawling deal with competing interpretations of the *holism of value*. They begin with the Moorean version of value holism, i.e., with Moore's account of organic wholes, according to which the value of a whole can differ from the value of (the sum of) its parts considered in isolation. According to Moore a value *on the whole* is a sum of the values of the parts together with their value *as a whole*. McNaughton and Rawling point to the '*intentional problem*' related to Moore's method of isolation, i.e., the difficulty of considering a particular thing in (absolute) isolation (e.g., punishment in isolation from the crime). A second kind of problem arising out of the isolation test is the problem of over- and under-generalization. Another worry about Moore's account is raised by Jonathan Dancy, who argues that it 'divorces' value from reasons by forcing us to accept the implausible view that sometimes a part must contribute a value to the whole that it itself lacks. Contrary to Dancy, McNaughton and Rawling propose a different interpretation in terms of emergent properties of the whole. Parts only have their intrinsic values and the surplus value is attributed to the newly emergent properties of their combination (as in the case of justice emerging out of the combination of crime and punishment for it). A Moorean may accept the latter interpretation, retaining the link between reasons and value(s), thus avoiding Dancy's objection.

Against Dancy, McNaughton and Rawling argue that his version of the holism of value incorporates unintelligible notions of 'uncontributed value' and 'context-free' value. They propose their own version of value holism that departs significantly from both Moore and Dancy. Rejecting the *isolation method* and consequently *organicity*, they claim that 'parts can only be evaluated in a way relevant to the whole of which they are a part if they are evaluated *in situ*'. There is no uncontributed value around and the value of the whole is simply the sum of the values of its parts (considered as parts of the whole). Such a view is holistic since one cannot determine the value of the whole given the sum of its parts considered in isolation and, *vice versa*, the value of the parts (in that whole) cannot be determined independently of the whole. Regarding the relationship between reasons, values, and action, they defend a notion of the 'value as an end'. You have an 'overall reason to perform some act if and only if this act of yours and its consequences would be valuable'. Actions originate in states of affairs (which have further states of affairs as their parts) and the value of those states of affairs that we are concerned with when acting is their value as an end. McNaughton and Rawling then address some worries raised by T. Scanlon regarding teleological accounts of value.

Anthony W. Price in 'Particularism and Pleasure' discusses particularistic structure of normativity (discerning between reasons, enablers, disablers, intensifiers and attenuators) in respect to the favouring and good-making relation. He stresses that in making distinctions between reasons and other 'forms of relevance' we must be sensitive to context, and that one could often view what seems like an intensifier as a genuine reason, or a part of a more complex reason. On the whole, Price accepts the intuitive appeal behind the mentioned distinctions. The fact that reasons are left 'pretty general' allows them to vary in their favouring contribution, hence we should name such position '*variabilism*' in preference to particularism. Price goes on to consider a generalist move to discriminate between primary (invariable) and secondary (variable) reasons.[3] Against this, a particularist could argue from examples, additionally singling out the fact that some variant reasons are simply good reasons in a particular case without necessarily appealing to some further, evasive and mysterious invariant ground. Price investigates the case of enjoyment (and pain) and searches for a stable resting point for our intuitions regarding different cases. He considers Aristotle's view that the value of pleasure depends upon the nature (worthiness) of its object. Embracing this move would lead particularism down the road of viewing value as determinate and tied to concrete cases. Price sees two alternatives for distinguishing cases of innocent pleasure from the non-innocent ones where the valence of pleasure gets reversed: (i) Pleasure is good by default, but it can become a bad-making feature when its object is bad as it is the case with sadistic pleasure. Here pleasure plays the role of a reason and its '(non-) innocence' plays the role of enabler or disabler of the default positive value. (ii) Human activity is 'naturally a good, unless something corrupts it' and the pleasure arising out of the activity enhances its value when this activity is 'uncorrupted' or attenuates its value when one enjoys acting badly. Price claims that neither alternative is without shortcomings. In (i) it is not at all clear that the nature of one's pleasure could not also be a reason (or part of a reason) for choosing a particular action. The same could be said in (ii) about enjoyment – it can function as an intensifier but also as a reason. Price suggests that the particularist should opt for the first option.

In 'Laughter and Moral Ambiguity: Particularist Reflections on the Ethical Dimensions of Humour' David Bakhurst discusses the subject of *humour* and proposes some new insights that a particularistic approach could bring into the debate. Ethical dimensions of humour deserve careful attention, sensitivity, and reflection that may be provided by the particularist model. He sets the debate with a fictional figure Ernest who opposes humour, recognizing its frequent connection with cruelty and humiliation. Joy, delight, and amusement that accompany humour and laughter generate supplementary problems, since they often originate out of situations that would instead deserve our moral condemnation (cruelty, mistreating, lewdness, manipulation, racism). How can one meet the seriousness of Ernest's commitment to the condemnation of laughter aimed at (a depiction of) morally dubious behaviours, treating them as simply wrong and not funny? One may point out to Ernest three possible considerations regarding such cases: (i) questions of the involved harm; (ii) the absurdity and unreality of many depictions; and (iii) the difference between the depiction and the depicted. Neither would convince Ernest that nothing is wrong with 'offensive' humour. One can never be sure that no one is in fact harmed or offended by a certain joke. Moreover should one be offended or upset? Also, not every kind of humour is openly absurd and unreal; in fact many situations that we find funny are quite realistic. Furthermore, depiction of a certain situation and our laughter directed at it are not unaffected by the wrongness of what is depicted. Ernest insists that by laughing at such jokes we simply display our 'failure of moral sensibilities'. At this point Bakhurst proposes to look at the issue as a complex intertwining of several factors (e.g., different kinds of laughter, contextual background, consideration of what a particular case of laughter expresses, intentions of persons involved). Such complexity calls for *sensitivity* and *good judgment*. One can very well agree with Ernest about some morally dubious instances of humour and at the same time resist the temptation to use these as a foundation for general principles dealing with these issues. Since thick concepts have variable valence, one can allow that sometimes cruelty or lewdness are the features contributing to the funniness of a particular joke, without having a negative moral valence. Nevertheless, critical reflection and attentiveness to moral considerations must always lurk in the background, and it seems that particularism is well equipped to do the job.

I hope that this collection offers sufficient material to grasp the heart of the debate to the readers that are unfamiliar with the topics of particularism. Those already acquainted with the area will get some interesting insight into the development during recent years.

Notes

1 cf. the 'bad' part of the argument in Hooker's 'Moral Particularism: Wrong and Bad' (2000b: 15–22).
2 'To recognise an instance of favouring, more is required than just gazing at it in a receptive frame of mind' (Dancy 2004: 142).
3 cf. R. Crisp's distinction between ultimate and non-ultimate reasons in his 'Particularizing Particularism' (2000: 36–37); and Hooker's distinction between ultimate and derived reasons (in this volume).

2 Moral particularism and the real world

Brad Hooker

The term 'moral particularism' has been used to refer to different doctrines. The main body of this paper begins by identifying the most important doctrines associated with the term, at least as the term is used by Jonathan Dancy, on whose work I will focus. I then discuss whether holism in the theory of reasons supports moral particularism, and I call into question the thesis that particular judgements have epistemological priority over general principles. Dancy's recent book *Ethics without Principles* (Dancy 2004) makes much of a distinction between reasons, enablers, disablers, intensifiers, and attenuators. I will suggest that the distinction is unnecessary, and I will argue that, even if there is such a distinction, it does not entail moral particularism. In the final two sections, I try to give improved versions of arguments against particularism that I put forward in my paper 'Moral Particularism: Wrong and Bad' (Hooker 2000b: 1–22, esp. pp. 7–11, 15–22).

The issue

Whenever an action is *morally required*, of course there is some moral reason to do it. Likewise, whenever an action is *morally wrong*, there is some moral reason not to do it. The same is true for other so-called thin moral properties, properties such as *being morally bad, being morally vicious*, etc.

I am not here committing myself on whether the reason for action comes from the thin moral property. A so-called buck-passing theory of (e.g.) goodness or wrongness holds that the goodness or wrongness of something does not add to the reasons agents have with respect to that thing. Rather, on the buck-passing view, the reasons come from the facts that make something good or wrong.[1] But these are not matters to be investigated here. For, whether or not buck-passing theories of thin moral properties are correct, we can agree that whenever an action is *morally required*, there is some moral reason to do it, and whenever an action is *morally wrong*, there is some moral reason not to do it.

At least for the purposes of discussing Dancy's particularism, I want to grant that we cannot articulate true informative principles that identify for each situation which acts would be wrong. In other words, at least for the sake of argument here, I accept that moral wrongness is determined by competing moral reasons in a way that cannot be illuminatingly captured in a general principle. To reject Dancy's particularism, one need not think that we can articulate true informative principles that identify for each situation which acts would be wrong. One need accept merely the kind of moral pluralism that W. D. Ross championed. According to Rossian moral pluralism,

1 There is a plurality of moral duties that can be stated in general principles.
2 There is no deeper normative principle that underlies and provides justification for them.
3 The different duties may conflict.
4 The duties do not come in a strict order of priority that resolves all conflicts between them.
5 There is an ineliminable need for the exercise of *judgement* in order to resolve some conflicts.

The term 'duty' as in 'your duty in this case is to take care of your mother' might seem to suggest a conclusive (or 'all-things-considered') judgement about what you morally ought to do. In the above statement of Ross-style pluralism, the term 'duty' is *not* meant to suggest that. On the contrary, (3) states that duties can conflict. Where duties conflict, you must do what goes against at least one of the conflicting duties.

Ross wanted to distinguish between (a) the correct moral input to the question what, all things considered, it is morally right to do in the situation and (b) the correct answer to the question what, all things considered, it is morally right to do in the situation. Ross used the term 'prima facie duties' to refer to moral inputs. Ross used the terms 'duty proper', 'duty *sans phrase*', and 'all-things-considered duty' to refer to the correct answer to the question of what, all things considered, it is morally right to do in the situation.

Prima facie – or, to use better terminology, pro tanto – duties are considerations that count morally in favor of or against acts. In any situation in which there is one or more pro tanto duty in favor of an act and none against it, the act is right all things considered.[2] Pro tanto duties identify moral pros or moral cons and these retain their force even when they conflict. Ross thought no pro tanto duty was necessarily stronger (i.e. stronger in every conceivable case) than any combination of other pro tanto duties. We need good judgement, Ross believed, to decide which such duty is the most important in the case at hand.

Dancy's view goes considerably beyond Ross in denying the role of principles. Ross thought that the pro tanto duties come in the form of principles, even if the resolution of their conflicts cannot always be captured in illuminating principles. Dancy's holism, in contrast, holds that there are no properties that, whenever they occur, must always be moral pluses, and no properties that, whenever they occur, must always be moral minuses. On this view, any feature of an act that counts as a moral plus in one context may not count as a moral plus in another context.

Dancy's main argument in his earlier book *Moral Reasons* (1993) was that holism about reasons gives us moral particularism, or more generally particularism about reasons for action. Dancy now admits that holism does not *entail* particularism, though he often suggests in *Ethics without Principles* that holism *supports* particularism. Dancy defines holism and atomism as follows:

> *Holism* in the theory of reasons: a feature that is a reason in one case may be no reason at all, or an opposite reason, in another.

> *Atomism* in the theory of reasons: a feature that is a reason in one case must remain a reason, and retain the same polarity, in any other (Dancy 2004: 7).

Some clarifications are in order. The first, and perhaps most important, is that atomism is a theory about ultimate reasons, not a theory about derived reasons. Suppose your friend is in Rockdale and taking the bus is the only legal way for you to get there tonight. The conjunction of these two facts might provide a reason for you to take that bus. The reason to take the bus would be that doing so is the only legal way for you to be together with her tonight. But, obviously, we would be referring here to derived reasons. The reason to take the bus to Rockdale derives from, presumably, the immediate or long-term benefit to you or to her of your being together. The following seems to me the way to understand the situation. You have an ultimate reason to take the bus to Rockdale, and there are further reasons derivable from that ultimate one.

Ultimate reason for taking this bus to Rockdale:
    that at least one of you and your friend would benefit.
Derived reason for taking this bus to Rockdale:
    that you and your friend would be together tonight.
Doubly derived reason for taking Rockdale bus:
    that your taking this bus is the only legal way for you to get to Rockdale tonight.

Now one important fact about derived reasons, which is stressed by Philip Stratton-Lake in forthcoming work, is that derived reasons don't really add normative weight to the case for what the ultimate reasons support. If the derived reasons did add normative weight to the ultimate reasons, then there would be a danger of double (or even triple and more) counting. Once we have it that you or your friend would benefit from your taking the bus to Rockdale, the reason you have for taking the bus to Rockdale is not increased in weight or number by the fact that taking the bus would put you and your friend together tonight or by the fact that your taking the bus is the only legal way for you to get there.

Nevertheless, let us for a moment consider the derived reasons. The feature picked out by a derived reason can switch normative polarity. For example, the feature some acts have of putting you together with your friend is a reason in favor of such acts in some cases. But this feature might switch polarity in other cases. Likewise, the feature some acts have of putting you on the bus to Rockdale is a reason in favor of such acts in some cases, but hardly in all.

That *derived* reasons can switch polarity is obviously true. So atomism would be completely implausible if it claimed that derived reasons cannot switch polarity. In order to be even vaguely plausible, atomism must focus on ultimate reasons. Atomism thus claims that a feature that is an *ultimate* reason in one case must remain an ultimate reason, and retain the same polarity, in any other case. Likewise, in order for holism to be more than an obvious truism, holism must claim that even a feature that is an *ultimate* reason in one case may be no reason at all, or an opposite reason, in another case.[3]

Derived reasons are conditional. Are ultimate reasons? Even if ultimate reasons are conditional, does this entail particularism? I will come back to this issue in the section on enablers and disablers.

Here is the second clarification I want to make about holism and atomism. Dancy seems to construe atomism in the theory of reasons as holding that *any* feature that is a reason in one case must remain a reason, and retain the same polarity, in any other. Does he likewise construe holism as insisting that *any* feature that is a reason in one case can be no reason at all or even an opposite reason in another case?

To fend off those who claim that there might be a few features that don't lose or switch their normative polarity case to case, Dancy wants to say that moral particularism is not committed to so strong a claim as that *any* feature that is a reason in one case can be no reason at all or even an opposite reason in another case. Suppose that indeed moral particularism is not committed to so strong a claim as that *any* feature that is a reason in one case can be no reason at all or even an opposite reason in another case. Then presumably there are varieties of particularism that admit there are some features that don't lose or switch their normative polarity case to case.

I still have not said exactly what particularism must affirm. Dancy's *Ethics without Principles* (2004: 1, 5, 7) defines particularism as follows:

> *Particularism*: the possibility of moral thought and judgement does not depend on the provision of a suitable supply of moral principles.

Dancy's *Moral Reasons* (1993: 56) characterized particularism as 'the claim that we neither need nor can see the search for an "evaluative outlook which one can endorse as rational as the search for a set of principles"'. But

Dancy went on to claim in that book that his form of particularism holds that 'the moral relevance of a property in a new case cannot be predicted from its relevance elsewhere' (1993: 57, 61).

Two points of clarification are in order. First, Dancy meant so-called properties *other than thin moral properties*, such as rightness or goodness. Particularism does not deny that the moral relevance of thin moral properties can be predicted. Second, Dancy's claim about prediction is apparently about moral thought. But Dancy seems inclined to a metaphysical thesis that would support his claim about moral thought. This metaphysical thesis is that whether a property (other than a thin moral property) counts morally for or against an act that has that property depends on the circumstances, to the extent that the very same (non-thin) property that in some circumstances counts morally in favor can in other circumstances be morally neutral or even morally negative. The particularism set out in Dancy's earlier book thus embraced metaphysical holism about non-thin properties.

There is a difference between the doctrine that moral thought does not need principles and the doctrine that the very same property that in some circumstances counts morally in favor can in other circumstances be morally neutral or even morally negative. One is a doctrine about moral *thought*. The other is a doctrine about moral *properties*. Even if these two doctrines fit together nicely, there are differences between them. So it matters which of these two doctrines we take to define moral particularism, as I shall now illustrate.

From holism to particularism?

Since holism, as Dancy defines it, is a doctrine about properties, then, in so far as holism is supposed to support particularism, the route presumably goes from holism via particularism-construed-as-a-doctrine-about-moral-properties. Only after that intermediate step does the route reach the conclusion of particularism-construed-as-a-doctrine-about-moral-thought. In fact, I think the argument must be even more complicated. In the argument from holism to particularism-construed-as-a-doctrine-about-moral-thought, there needs to be a step from particularism-construed-as-a-doctrine-about-moral-properties to the denial that there are true informative general moral principles, and only then to particularism-construed-as-a-doctrine-about-moral-thought.

I am not saying that there cannot be some other argument concluding in moral particularism-as-a-doctrine-about-moral-thought that does not have, as an intermediate step, the denial that there are true informative general moral principles. But I do not know of an argument that *starts with holism* and concludes with particularism-as-a-doctrine-about-moral-thought but does not have as an intermediate step the denial that there are true informative general moral principles.

Three questions about the relation of Dancy's holism to his particularism present themselves. First, is holism about theoretical reasons (reasons for belief) correct? Second, if theoretical reasons are holistic, must practical reasons (reasons for action or sentiments) be holistic? Third, if practical reasons must be holistic, does this entail that there are no true informative general moral principles?

Holism about theoretical reasons?

Dancy suggests that holism with respect to theoretical reason is virtually universally accepted (Dancy 2004: 74). Suppose I have a visual experience as of something red in front of me. Normally, this visual experience is some reason for me to believe that there is something red in front of me. But consider a different context, one that is abnormal. Suppose I believe I have recently taken a drug that makes blue seem red to me. In this case, I have no reason at all to believe that there is something red in front of me.

As indicated in my 'Moral Particularism: Wrong and Bad' (2000b: 14), I'm hardly confident that all theoretical reasons are holistic in the way Dancy supposes they are. Furthermore, I cannot believe that holism with respect to theoretical reason is virtually universally accepted. There are plenty of epistemological foundationalists, and at least some of these accept atomistic theoretical reasons.

Even if all theoretical reasons are holistic, must all practical reasons be holistic?

We already know that there are important differences between theoretical and practical reasons. Couldn't one of the differences between them be that one kind of reason is holistic but the other atomistic?

Dancy's answer starts by pointing out that ordinary practical reasons, i.e. non-moral, non-aesthetic practical reasons, are holistic (Dancy 2004: 75). He claims that the fact that someone wants power may be a reason to give it to him, or may be a reason not to give it to him.

My reply is that someone's desiring power cannot by itself be an *ultimate* reason either to give it to him or not to give it to him. There is a derived reason to give him power if he would use the power for good ends. And there is a derived reason against giving him power if he would use the power for bad ends.

More generally, ultimate practical reasons that are not moral or aesthetic are reasons to benefit oneself, and these seem to me not particularistic in the relevant sense. Of course, often there are stronger moral reasons to do something other than benefit oneself. Nevertheless, it is a true informative general principle of practical reason that one always has at least some reason to do what would benefit oneself.

So I reject the antecedent of the conditional that, if non-moral practical reasons are holistic, so are moral reasons. Of course, rejecting the antecedent of the conditional does not entail rejecting the conditional's consequent. But rejecting the conditional's antecedent kills using the conditional in a *modus ponens* argument.

Although Dancy does not reject the antecedent of that conditional, he does confront the idea that the conditional is mistaken. That is, he confronts the idea that *moral* reasons might be atomistic even if all other practical reasons are holistic. He has two objections to this idea. The first is that 'straight off it just seems incredible that the very logic of moral reasons should be so different from that of others in this sort of way' (Dancy 2004: 76). The second is that 'nobody knows how to distinguish moral from other reasons' (76).

But why couldn't the logic of moral reasons be so different from that of other practical reasons (Little 2000: 276–304, esp. pp. 294–95)? Perhaps moral reasons need to be predictable, stable and mutually recognized, in ways that other practical reasons do not need to be. And perhaps this is because many moral reasons are associated with particularly important co-operation and co-ordination, and enforced by important sanctions. We need to be at least fairly confident that others will behave in certain ways, even when inconvenient for them or contrary to their aggressive or acquisitive instincts. In addition, we need to be able to predict what kinds of act other people would blame us for, or resent or punish. Our assurance that other people will behave in certain ways and our ability to predict how they would react to our behaviour will be helped enormously if we know they are committed to certain rules. These facts are among the grounds for thinking moral reasons need to be tied to rules in a way that other kinds of practical reasons need not.

I will come back to points about predictability. First, I need to complete my assessment of Dancy's argument from holism.

Reasons, enablers, disablers, intensifiers, attenuators

The main thrust of Dancy's *Ethics without Principles* is his development of the distinction between contributory reasons, enablers, disablers, intensifiers and attenuators. This distinction was there in his earlier book *Moral Reasons* (1993: 56–58), but its role is much greater in *Ethics without Principles*.

A contributory reason is a feature that favors or disfavors an action, an emotion, etc. Dancy gives the following example:

1 I promised to do it.
2 My promise was not given under duress.
3 I am able to do it.
4 There is no greater reason not to do it.
5 So: I do it.

Dancy holds (1) to be a contributory reason. He holds that (2) and (3) are not contributory reasons but instead enabling conditions for (1) to be a reason to do the act. He takes (4) to be neither a reason nor an enabling, disabling, intensifying or attenuating consideration but rather a verdict on the relation between the reason identified in (1) and any competing reasons.

Dancy's (2) above seems to me too simple. My promise has to have all of the following features, if it is to be morally binding and thus give me a moral reason to do the act in question:

- The promise was not extracted from me by a threat to infringe someone's (e.g. my) moral rights.
- My promise was not made while I was literally insane.
- My promise was not the result of someone's having misrepresented or withheld facts from me that I had a right to know.
- Keeping the promise would not require me to infringe anyone's moral rights.
- The person to whom I made the promise has not cancelled it.

Dancy thinks that, even if my list is correct, it is a list of enabling conditions for promises to generate reasons for action, rather than either a list of reasons or a list of parts of reasons. I take the conditions in my list instead to be *parts* of a complete specification of the reason. So Dancy thinks that the reason in play here is 'that I promised'. My view is that the reason in play, properly understood, is the much more complex 'that I promised when the promise was not extracted from me by threat to infringe someone's moral rights, was not something I said while literally insane, was not the result of someone's having misrepresented or withheld facts I had a right to know, was not a promise that would require me to infringe anyone's moral rights, and has not been cancelled by the person to whom I made the promise'.

Dancy has an argument for his view:

> [T]hose who recognize that their promise was deceitfully extracted from them often feel some compunction in not doing what they promised, even though they themselves recognize that in such circumstances their promise does not play its normal reason-giving role. I think their attitude would be different if what plays the reason-giving role were not that one promised but that one 'freely' promised (where to be free a promise must not be extracted by deceit) (Dancy 2004: 39).

I admit that those who recognize that their promise was deceitfully extracted from them often feel some compunction in not doing what they promised. Dancy can hold that the reason coming from a promise can be enabled either by the promise being given freely or by the promise not being given freely. How can I, who hold that the reason for action imposed by promises is more complicated, explain why those who recognize that their promise was deceitfully extracted from them often feel some compunction in not doing what they promised?

First, people's feelings are not always a reliable guide to moral reality. People can feel obligated when they really are not obligated.

Second, relevant uncertainty can arise. Suppose Jones made a promise because of Smith's having misrepresented or withheld facts from Jones. Then there might well be dispute or uncertainty about whether those facts were ones that Jones had a right to know. Or suppose Jones made a promise because Smith made a threat. Then there might be dispute or uncertainty about whether the threat that elicited the promise was a threat to infringe someone's moral rights. Because of uncertainty about what she had a right to know or about whether the carrying out of a threat would have infringed someone's rights, Jones might rightly be worried about breaking a promise made as a result of deception or threat.

A good test case here is one where it is absolutely clear to the promisor that her promise was made as a result of the other party's withholding of information that the promisor had a right to know. Another good test case is one where it is absolutely clear to the promisor that her promise was made as a result of the other party's threatening to infringe someone's moral rights. In such cases, the promise is not morally binding and imposes on the promisor no good reason for action. If some people would nevertheless feel compunction about breaking such a promise, I think they are naïve.

Let me now turn to Dancy's (3) above. He thinks that 'x has a reason to φ' implies 'x can φ'. I am not so sure about that. But rather than debate that matter here, I want to make the following points. Certainly, if 'has a reason to' does *not* imply 'can', then (3) is not a necessary condition for me to have a reason to keep the promise. On the other hand, if 'has a reason to' *does* imply 'can', then (3) merely points to a restriction on the domain of things for which one can have reasons. This restriction may be one that we take for granted and so usually don't mention. Nevertheless, we could build something like (3) into our complete specification of the relevant reason. Before I go further into the idea of a complete specification of the relevant reason, let me say something about Dancy's intensifiers and attenuators.

His example of an intensifier is a case where 'that she needs help' is a *reason* for helping her, and 'that no one else is around to help her' is an *intensifier* (Dancy 2004: 41). For Dancy, the fact that no one else is around to help her is not an additional reason to help her, but rather an intensifier of the reason constituted by the fact that she needs help.

There are lots of ways of understanding this example other than Dancy's distinction between reasons and intensifiers. For example, the strength of the reason to help someone could be understood as partly a function of how much the expected difference to the beneficiary would be. The expected difference is a function of the possible benefits times their probabilities. Now contrast two cases where the amount of benefit at stake is the same, but in one case I am the only one who can provide that benefit and in the other case there are others who might provide help if I don't. Suppose, for the sake of simplicity, that, in the case where there are others there who could help, there is a 50% chance someone else will help if I don't. Here is a table representing the situations.

		Value of possible benefit to her of being helped	Probability of this possible benefit's coming about	Expected value of this possible outcome	Expected difference my helping would make
No one else there to help	I help	10	1	10 x 1 = 10	
					10
	I don't	10	0	10 x 0 = 0	
Others there who might help	I help	10	1	10 x 1 = 10	
					5
	I don't	10	0.5	10 x 0.5 = 5	

On the picture presented in this table, the reason provided by 'that she needs help' comes in different strengths. And this can be explained without separating out the reason from intensifiers.

In fact, I think a similar structure is true for many different kinds of moral reasons. Just as the strength of a reason to benefit someone depends at least in part on what the expected difference to the beneficiary would be, the strength of a reason to keep a promise depends in part on the size or seriousness of the promise, and the strength of the reason not to harm someone depends in large part on the quantity of harm.

I will be briefer with Dancy's comments on attenuators. He supposed attenuators to be structurally like intensifiers, except that attenuators work in the opposite direction. That the trouble she is in is her own fault attenuates the strength of the reason to help her (Dancy 2004: 42).

We could reply to Dancy's thesis about attenuators in exactly the same way we could to his thesis about intensifiers. That is, we could say that of course moral reasons have built into them sensitivity to a number of different factors. The reason to help others is sensitive not only to the expected difference to the potential beneficiaries but also to their culpability or desert.[4]

Alternatively, we might think that the better way to handle Dancy's example about the culpable agent who needs help is that here a second reason comes into play. On the one hand, there is a reason to help that is sensitive to the expected difference to the beneficiary coming from our action. On the other hand, there is a reason to support people's getting what they deserve. To the extent that the potential beneficiary in Dancy's example is at fault, perhaps she deserves the trouble she has. So perhaps what he has described is an example where reasons of kindness are offset by reasons of justice.

Likewise, I think that, for some examples where Dancy would say there is a reason plus an intensifier, we would want to say there really are just two different reasons. Is the fact that someone now has less benefit than she deserves an intensifier of our reason to help her, or is it a second reason to help her? I will come back to this issue in a later section.

The main point of Dancy's thesis, that reasons are separable from *enablers* and *disablers,* is that a feature can be a reason in one situation and yet, though that same feature is present in another situation, not be a reason there. The main point of his thesis that reasons are separable from *intensifiers* and *attenuators* is that the very same reason can be present in two different situations but have different strengths, because of something external to the reason itself.

His distinction between, on the one hand, reasons and, on the other hand, enablers, disablers, intensifiers, and attenuators enables him to distinguish between (a) what considerations favor or disfavor an action and (b) the facts that enable or disable considerations to act as favorers or disfavorers, and to what degree (*Ethics without Principles*, p. 99). He thinks reasons are what can count morally in favor of an action. He thinks enablers and disablers determine whether the action has something counting morally in its favor. And he thinks intensifiers and attenuators determine to what degree the action has something counting in its favor.

At a number of different places in *Ethics without Principles*, Dancy objects to the attempt to capture at least part of morality in terms of subjunctive conditionals (Dancy 2004: 20, 38, 42, 50, 52, 64, 98, 99, 127, 172, 191). To go back to our old friend, an example of a subjunctive conditional is:

> *If* you were to make a promise to someone to do something, and that promise were not extracted by a threat to infringe someone's moral rights, and the promise were not made while you were literally insane, and the promise were not the result of someone's having misrepresented or withheld facts that you had a right to know, and keeping the promise would not require you to infringe anyone's moral rights, and the person to whom you made the promise had not cancelled it, and you could do what you promised, *then* there would be a moral reason for you to keep the promise, and the strength of the reason would be sensitive to the seriousness of the promise.

Such subjunctive conditionals seem to Dancy too crude since they fail to distinguish reasons from enablers, disablers, intensifiers, and attenuators. According to Dancy, even if we refine our subjunctive conditionals as much as we like, 'the eventual result will not serve one of the main supposed purposes of principles, namely that of telling us why we should do the action, that is, what makes the action right' (Dancy 2004: 127).

This objection supposes that, although the true subjunctive conditionals tell us *the conditions under which* we have reasons and *how strong* those reasons are, what we instead want to know is more narrowly merely what the reasons are. I cannot agree. If a subjunctive conditional is true, why wouldn't we want to know the whole subjunctive conditional, rather than merely a part of it? If we admit that there are true subjunctive conditionals in morality – i.e. true principles – I cannot see why we wouldn't very much want to know what they are.

I have one more important point to make about Dancy's argument from the distinction between reasons and enablers, disablers, intensifiers, and attenuators to his particularism. Suppose Dancy persuades us that enablers, disablers, intensifiers, and attenuators are *not* parts of reasons but instead separate morally relevant features. Being persuaded of that would not foist upon us moral particularism. Suppose reasons, enablers, disablers, intensifiers, and attenuators *can all be captured in true subjunctive conditionals*. Then, the thesis that there are no true general moral principles is false. What Dancy needs in order to move from the distinction between reasons and enablers, disablers, intensifiers, and attenuators to moral particularism is the thesis that reasons, enablers, disablers, intensifiers, and attenuators cannot be captured in true moral principles.[5]

Epistemological expendability

Before I turn to arguments against particularism, let me deal with another argument of Dancy's in favor of particularism (Dancy 2004: 155–57). The argument takes its point of departure from what I think is a bad mistake made by W. D. Ross and his contemporaries. This point of departure is the idea that we first make true moral judgements about particular cases, and then by intuitive induction we come to believe general principles.

I tentatively accept that, were this account of the acquisition of principles correct, it would give some support to Dancy's particularist claim that our moral thought does not really need principles. If we begin by making true moral judgements about particular cases before we believe any moral principles, there is at least something of a puzzle about why, epistemologically, we need moral principles. If we regularly can make, and make do with, particular moral judgements in advance of forming any general moral beliefs, why aren't general moral beliefs epistemologically expendable?

Here I can but repeat what I said in reply in my paper 'Intuitions and Moral Theorizing' (Hooker 2002). I flatly deny that moral knowledge always does start off with judgements about particular cases. Moral knowledge, for virtually all of us, starts with learning such general moral truths as that there are moral reasons against hurting others, harming or taking others' possessions, breaking one's promises and lying.

Dancy's argument that moral principles are epistemologically otiose begins with the assumption that we do make moral judgements about particular cases before believing general moral principles, and therefore without recourse to them. I cannot see what that assumption has going for it, except the backing of such clever people as Ross, Broad, Carritt and Dancy. Appeals to authority, however, are not enough, at least in this case. The epistemology of everyday moral judgement does not lead to particularism; quite the opposite, I think.

Counter-examples to particularism

Insofar as particularism is committed to the denial of true moral principles, moral particularism is vulnerable to counter-example. I went through a number of these in my paper 'Moral Particularism: Wrong and Bad'. I went through a further seven counter-examples to particularism in my 'Intuitions and Moral Theorizing' (2002). Dancy, however, focuses on counter-examples coming from Ross, McNaughton and Rawling, and Crisp.

Ross's list of prima facie (or as we now call them, pro tanto) duties was as follows (in Dancy's words, 2004: 120):

1 duties grounded in previous acts of one's own: (1a) fidelity, (1b) reparation
2 duties grounded in previous acts of others: gratitude
3 duties of justice
4 duties of beneficence to others
5 duties of self-improvement
6 duties of non-maleficence to others.

As against duties grounded in previous acts of one's own and duties grounded in previous acts of others, Dancy writes, 'no action will be right simply because it is a response to previous acts of others, or indeed of one's own' (Dancy 2004: 120). Well, of course the *bare* fact that an act is a *response to previous acts of others or of one's own* is not enough to ensure that there is something morally in favor of the act. The response needs to be one of fidelity rather than infidelity, gratitude rather than ingratitude, reparation rather than further injury. Ross seems entirely right that the fact that an act is one of fidelity or reparation or gratitude is always a moral plus.

As against (4) and (5), Dancy complains,

> [T]here are many acts that would benefit others that I have no parti-
> cular duty or reason to do, and in many cases the act would not even be
> for the better. If someone does not deserve a benefit (or rather 'unde-
> serves' it), giving her that benefit is not something one has a prima facie
> duty to do; and the same *mutatis mutandis* applies to those who, by
> their own acts, have lost a certain immunity to harm (Dancy 2004: 120).

There are two ways a Rossian could respond to Dancy's suggestion that benefiting others does not always have positive moral polarity. One possible

Rossian response would be to refine the duties of beneficence and non-maleficence so that they concern not all benefits and harms to others, but only *deserved benefits* and *undeserved harms*. The idea is that a concern for justice could be imported into the duties of beneficence and non-maleficence. Fred Feldman and Shelly Kagan have recently been exploring such options.[6]

The other way Rossians could respond to Dancy's objection is to claim that beneficence, non-maleficence and justice should be kept as separate duties and to hold that such duties can conflict.

Now, I admit that we normally don't think of ourselves as having some reason to benefit the wicked. But this might well be because there are so many better things to do with our time, attention and energy. There are many deserving people who need help, and our attention is rightly devoted to them. But consider the following.

Imagine that there is only one person left on some isolated island or planet. We could benefit this person, e.g. by helping him get out of some deadly pit, but this person is a murderer. Suppose we could help him without endangering ourselves or others. Suppose also that helping him would require the very most minimal effort, and that this effort could *not* be redirected to benefit others instead. Suppose all we have to do to get him out of the deadly pit is push a button right in front of us. In this sort of case, we might hold that there is at least some slight moral pressure to help him. Justice would not be served by such an action. And justice in this case might well be more important than beneficence. Still, the point is that beneficence would have at least some weight here.

I have just outlined two possible Rossian responses to Dancy's suggestion that benefiting others does not always have positive moral polarity. Let me now turn to the anti-particularist idea that justice always has positive moral polarity. Dancy has three replies to the suggestion that reasons of justice (or rather injustice) always have the same moral polarity.

Dancy's first reply is that sometimes, e.g. in certain aspects of family life, 'the question whether what one proposes to do would be just or unjust "does not arise"' (Dancy 2004: 121). So, 'the role of justice as a reason can vary according to context'. But this seems a weak reply. Of course there may be areas where justice does not arise. There are areas where other moral considerations do not arise too. That is not news, and not an answer to the point that justice always counts on the same side *whenever it does arise*.

Dancy's second reply is to claim that *justice* is not fully a thick moral concept. Rather, *justice* is somewhere between thin concepts such as *morally right* and thick concepts such as *honest*. I concede that this concept may not be as thickly descriptive as some other moral concepts. Relatedly, what counts as just may be more contestable than what counts as honest or kind. Still, justice does always have positive moral polarity, and is clearly thicker than concepts such as *morally right*, *morally wrong*, etc. In any case, I don't think we need to rely on justice as our sole counter-example to Dancy's particularism. As I've argued elsewhere and above, there are other counter-examples.

Dancy's third response aims not at any particular counter-examples but rather at the whole idea that his particularism is vulnerable to counter-example. He contends that showing that there *are* some true general moral principles, some invariant moral reasons, does not show that there *must* be some, or that we *need* invariant reasons and general principles.

But if there are true general moral principles, then to the extent that a moral theory fails to contain or imply them, that theory is inaccurate or at least incomplete. If there are true general moral principles, then, since particularism directs our attention away from them, particularism is misleading. So, if there are true moral principles, even if only about pro tanto duties, then moral particularism is an incomplete and misleading theory.

But suppose Dancy replies that, even if there are some true moral principles, moral agents don't need them and moral practice can get along quite well without them? In the next section, I will rehearse some of the reasons that moral practice does need principles.

Social effects

Imagine a society of particularists – by which I mean a society of people who don't believe or use general moral principles, even principles about what counts morally in favor of actions and what counts morally against. What would the consequences be of pervasive belief in and use of particularism? I will explain why I think the consequences would be terrible. If I'm right, then moral practice needs principles in order to avoid these terrible consequences.

Act-consequentialism is often accused of being a poor decision procedure because of lack of information about likely consequences, lack of time to gather the information, and people's typical lack of impartiality such that they overestimate the expected benefits to themselves and underestimate the expected costs to others. But at least act-consequentialism as a decision procedure would tell people to try to be impartial as between their welfare and the welfare of others.

Contrast act-consequentialism as a decision procedure with particularism as a decision procedure. Act-consequentialism as a decision procedure would tell agents to focus on the good at stake and to be impartial in calculating that good. Presumably, particularism is more pluralistic than act-consequentialism. Particularism might well tell agents to focus on more different kinds of considerations. And particularism might well fail to insist on impartiality in assessing the good.

Beyond that, we know that particularism tells agents to make the best decision in the circumstances. But that isn't much of a guideline! Hence, as Michael Ridge and Sean McKeever argue in *Principled Ethics* (2006), moral particularism as a decision procedure provides far too much scope for special pleading and rationalization of self-serving action. In the real world, particularism is unlikely to lead people regularly to make correct moral decisions. On the contrary, because I think that, with particularism as a decision procedure, people would persuade themselves that what they wanted to do was, in the particular circumstances, morally allowed, I think that people's use of particularism as a decision procedure would regularly have terrible consequences.

The Ridge–McKeever objection to particularism as a decision procedure is primarily that it will lead people to make many incorrect decisions. My earlier paper on particularism (Hooker 2000b) argued that particularism is not only wrong but also bad. By 'bad' I meant that public awareness of people's commitment to particularism would undermine confidence in people's ability to predict how others will act. These two objections are related but not the same.

To be more specific about my own objection, my earlier paper contrasted a conscientious particularist and a conscientious Rossian generalist on the question of trustworthiness. I contended that the Rossian generalist would be somewhat more trustworthy. The Rossian generalist holds that there is at least one moral reason in favor of keeping a promise that was not the extracted by threat to infringe someone's moral rights, was made while the promisor was sane, was not the result of someone's having misrepresented or withheld facts that the promisor had a right to know, was not a promise that would require the promisor to infringe someone's moral rights, and was not a promise that has been cancelled by the promisee. The particularist, in contrast, holds that there might be no moral reason to keep such a promise. I suggested that the particularist could therefore be expected to be less predictable and less reliable. Let me call this the predictability argument against particularism.

As I indicated in my earlier paper, in this argument I tried to abstract from the question of whether particularism or generalism would get the correct answer about when to break promises. So I wrote that my argument

> does not beg the question against particularism by assuming the particularist is going to make more moral mistakes than the Rossian generalist. My argument was that, whether or not particularism is likely to lead agents to make moral mistakes, the Rossian generalist seems in the circumstances more likely than the particularist to keep the promise (Hooker 2000b: 21).

I now think I misformulated my predictability argument. I meant to abstract away from the question of whether particularism gets the correct answers. In order to abstract away from this, I granted for the sake of argument that particularism did get the correct answer. Actually, I had in mind that I could abstract away from the issue of whether particularism or generalism gets the correct answers by supposing they both do. But if they both get the correct answers, then they must get the *same* answers. In that case, the particularist can be expected to reach the same conclusions as the generalist. And in that case we can predict the particularist's answers by predicting the generalist's answers. So if they both get the right answers, the answers must be the same, and they must be equally predictable. In that case, my argument about differential predictability collapses.

Hence, I had better assume that the particularist and the generalist reach different answers. Now, if my argument grants that they reach different answers, I cannot assume they both reach the right answers.

Well, should we assume that the Rossian generalist's answers are more often right than the particularist's? If we do, then we have indeed begged the question against the particularist here. So, what if we grant instead that the particularist's answers are more often right? If we grant this, then we have granted particularism the upper hand.

We have seen that my predictability argument against particularism needs not to assume that both particularism and generalism get the correct answers. Nor should this argument rely on an assumption about which of the theories gets the answers right more often than the other. Let the argument from predictability be run without any assumption about which theory gets the answer right more often.

So now suppose you find yourself choosing between living in a society of conscientious particularists or in a society of conscientious Rossian generalists. Suppose you are certain the respective members of both societies would try hard to reach the correct moral conclusions on the basis of their respective moral theories. You are also certain that members of both societies would do what they conclude morality requires. You don't know, however, which society would get the right moral answer more often.

Now, how much would you be able to predict the particularists' decisions? You know that they will do what they conclude morality requires. Do you know anything more about their decisions? Precious little! They don't, for example, believe that there are general reasons of fidelity, reparation, gratitude, beneficence, non-maleficence, or even perhaps justice, even overridable ones. If literally all you know about someone's morality is that she will do what she believes morality requires of her, how confident can you be about predicting what other properties her acts will have? In order to be able to predict someone else's behaviour, you need to know more specific information than simply she will do what she believes she is required to do.

Does predictability really matter that much? If belief in theory *A* makes people less predictable than they would be if they instead believed theory *B*, does this by itself suggest that theory *A* is more likely to be true than theory *B*? I admit that in general the answer is no. However, in the special case of choosing between moral theories that are otherwise equally plausible, a difference in how predictable people who accepted these theories would be does seem, at least to me, to count in favor of the theory whose adherents would be more predicable agents.

Default reasons

I admit that to some extent Dancy's notion of default reasons can come into play here. Default reasons are supposed to be considerations with a default valence. Unless some disabler is present, these default reasons will count in an invariant way. But where disablers are present, the consideration that is a default reason serves as no reason.

In order to enable us to predict how people will behave, default reasons need to be very like reasons that appear in general principles. That is, they need to appear in principles that identify considerations as normally reasons, and that indicate what the potential disablers are. Of course, if we know people's general moral principles, and if we know they are conscientious moral agents, we presumably have at least some information about how they are likely to behave.

But Dancy claims, 'a default value is not the same as a normal value – a value that a feature has in most contexts, or in normal contexts in some other sense of "normal"' (Dancy 2004: 185–86). Presumably, he likewise holds that default reasons are not necessarily reasons *in most contexts*. (See Dancy's rejection of true principles of relevant similarity: Dancy 2004: 95, 131.)

So suppose our particularist agents are committed to default reasons but insist that these are *not* necessarily reasons in *normal* contexts. As far as we know, then, particularists might think that these default reasons obtain only in extremely abnormal contexts. And suppose that our particularist agents believe that there are no true general principles identifying all the disabling conditions for default reasons. On these assumptions, I cannot see that appeal to the existence and use of default reasons can defuse my objection that thoroughgoing particularist agents are too unpredictable.

I accept, however, that there are ways of developing the idea of default reasons such that, were a particularist agent committed to default reasons, the particularist agent would be adequately predictable. This point seems to me but one instance of an important general point: the more radical particularism is, the more exciting but the less plausible it is. Of course this is a conflict that many of the most interesting theories face.[7]

Notes

1 Philip Stratton-Lake and I discuss the buck-passing theory in 'Scanlon versus Moore on Goodness', in Stratton-Lake and Hooker (2006).

2 See the bottom of Ross's *The Right and the Good* (1930) p. 19. For criticism of Ross's account, see J. Dancy (2003a), 'What Reasons Do'. In a reply to Dancy (Hooker 2003), I tentatively proposed this revision of Ross: A feature of an action would be a reason for action or a part of a reason for action if and only if this feature's presence would determine what the agent ought to do if the agent were choosing between an act with this feature and an act without it and the two alternative actions had exactly the same other features as far as possible. That was inadequate as it stands, because of the special case of features that count as

reasons for action only if there is some other reason in play. I should have added a qualification about that special kind of case. Perhaps, I should also have restricted the account to *moral* reasons and *moral* oughts.

3 For previous discussion of the distinction between ultimate and derived reasons, see my 'Moral Particularism: Wrong and Bad' (Hooker 2000b: 12–13), and Roger Crisp 'Particularizing Particularism' (Crisp 2000: 23–47, esp. 36–39).

4 See Feldman (1992: 182–85); Feldman (1997: 164–69); and Kagan (1999: 298–314).

5 A number of critics of particularism have made this point. The most extended development of it that I know of is in Michael Ridge and Sean McKeever, *Principled Ethics: Generalism as a Regulative Ideal* (2006).

6 See the references in note 4.

7 I thank Anna Bergqvist, Roger Crisp, Jonathan Dancy, John Horty, Richard Kraut, Margaret Little, Doug MacLean, Sean McKeever, Francesco Orsi, Micheal Ridge, Mark Sainsbury, Valerio Salvi, Daniel Star, Christine Swanton, Tim Williamson, Paul Woodruff and Susan Wolf for helpful comments on a previous draft.

3 Ethical generality and moral judgment

Robert Audi

Ethics is commonly considered a realm of inexact standards, unpredictable exceptions, 'grey areas', and subjectivity. Even those who believe in moral rules tend to think that they admit of exceptions or should be stated with qualifiers such as 'normally', 'for the most part' and 'other things equal'. Aristotle formulated a major point underlying this view when he said, regarding the mean between excess and deficiency, that it is 'relative to us' (*Nicomachean Ethics* 1107a). The influence of this point in his presentation of the 'Golden Mean', especially taken together with Aristotelian virtue ethics in general, has been enormous. The point does not depend on virtue ethics, though any virtue ethicist is likely to accept it and to hold that what we ought to do on a given occasion depends on what virtue requires in the circumstances. To say this, however, is not only to relativize obligation to circumstances, as nearly every moral theorist would, but, in effect, to inter- pose the complex and controversial concept of virtue between circumstance and action. Is there a better alternative that enables us to determine our obligations more directly?

In seeking to avoid excessive relativity, it is natural for philosophers to search for basic principles. For many philosophers, and particularly for those constructing an ethical system, only principles that are both clear and highly general will suffice. Quite apart from any theoretical concerns, it is also natural for moral agents to seek clarity and generality in ethics. Ethical generality facilitates the teaching of ethics to children, the guidance of moral decisions, the justification of moral judgments, and the formulation of laws and social policies. Examples of general moral principles abound; recall those corresponding to the prohibitions of lying, stealing, and killing that are expressed in the Ten Commandments. Among those put forward by philosophers, there are probably none more widely cited than Kant's cate- gorical imperative or Mill's principle of utility (though, to be sure, in vary- ing formulations). The central question I want to pursue is what kind of generality moral principles may exhibit.

If there is any position in the history of ethics that stands out for its attempt to capture both ethical generality and the kind of relativity to context that Aristotle described, it is the intuitionism of W. D. Ross. He formulated general principles, but treated each as in a sense admitting of an indefinite range of exceptions; he also gave special emphasis to – and perhaps treated as in some way basic – singular moral judgments, those to the effect that a particular person (including oneself) should do a particular deed. On the first count, he is a kind of generalist, on the second, a kind of particularist. My aim here is to explore the varieties and prospects for both kinds of position in ethics. A moderate Rossian intuitionism, and especially the kind of generality it embodies, will be my main focus.

Types of ethical generality

It is doubtful that there is any philosophically interesting notion of ethical generality that can be specified in a purely formal way. Mere universality, at least, in the sense of having the form of 'All *F*s are *G*s', will not serve. Consider the principle that all lies not excusable by considerations of confidentiality, self-protection, non-injury, self-development or impact on human welfare are wrong. This is universal, 'perfectly' general, and arguably true; but it is not a good moral guide. There is too much lack of clarity about the nature of the exceptions and indeed about how trade-offs among them might be accommodated, say where self-protection would be well served by a given action but confidentiality breached. There may be other problems, but the vagueness and the trade-off problems, as I will call them, are serious and recurring difficulties in any plausible ethical framework. The systems of Kant and Mill each have resources one might use to deal with these problems. Exploring their systems in detail would be a major task that is impossible here, but let me make just a few points to suggest why these systems do not readily solve the problems.

In the case of Kant, let us focus on the intrinsic end formulation of the categorical imperative: 'Act in such a way that you always treat humanity, whether in your own person or in the person of any other, never simply as a means, but always at the same time as an end' (1961: 96).[1] Even if we ignore the controversy concerning how to interpret this imperative, we must grant that there can be a trade-off between treating one person as an end and treating someone else as such (say, where one's time and resources are limited); and it might be argued that treating some people as ends might conflict with avoiding treating others merely as means, as where the only way to save a large number of people is to sacrifice one. It is true that once we have a proposed moral principle, the universality formulation of the imperative commends itself as a *test* of its adequacy; but even then, there remain problems concerning what counts as *rational* universalizability.[2]

As to Mill, he was specific enough in *Utilitarianism* to enable us to make a more explicit appraisal of his success with the two problems of special interest here, the vagueness and trade-off problems. On one interpretation of his principle of utility, it says that an act is obligatory if and only if it has at least as much utility as any alternative available to the agent, where utility is understood in terms of contribution to the happiness of sentient beings, measured by the ratio of pleasure to pain caused by the act, with quality as well as quantity taken into account.[3] Difficulties with this formulation are well known, and here I make no attempt to appraise its ultimate plausibility. For our purposes, it is enough to note two points.

First, the principle has significant vagueness. This holds regarding the notions of pleasure and pain, the concept of the *quality* of a pleasure, and the *scope* of the reference to sentient beings – for instance, concerning how animals figure in the calculation (for instance, how various species count in relation to pain and pleasure), and concerning how readily an agent should be able to perform an action in order for it to count as available: roughly, as a genuine alternative. (I leave aside the question how far into the future consequences matter for moral decision – I assume that, strictly speaking, it is for ever and that vagueness is perhaps not a problem here, whatever may be the difficulties of calculation.)

Second, as to the trade-off problem, there is the difficulty of weighing quantity against duration of pleasures and pains; and Mill himself recognized the further difficulty of measuring quality against quantity. He proposed a formula for dealing with it; but he left us with an indeterminacy.[4] He did not even address the point that moral reflection reveals a greater obligation to reduce pain rather than enhance pleasure, other things equal. This point is unavoidably vague, but is highly plausible and widely taken into account in moral thinking.

Mill was aware of the sorts of difficulty I have described. His response, above all, was to suggest that in practice we can usually be guided by what he called 'secondary rules', such as the rule that one should not lie. We do not need to appeal to the principle of utility except when we encounter a conflict between duties that we have under two or more secondary rules.[5] There is much plausibility in the idea that usually we can be guided by secondary rules. These are, however, vague; and as Mill would grant, reliance on them does not free one from the trade-off problem.

Are there any moral principles that are at least largely immune to these problems? One might hope to frame some that are so definite as to avoid the vagueness problem by their clarity and so selective in their requirements as to put them beyond the trade-off problem. This aim would force us to set aside certain kinds of principle that might be true, say that one should never do an absolute injustice. A word like 'absolute' is significantly vague to begin with and conceals such trade-off problems as occur in wartime, where collateral harm to innocent people is inevitable and must be weighed against the value of victory. Qualifiers like 'absolute' and 'unconditional' conceal rather than solve our problem.

We might hope, however, to frame exceptionless, fully general principles by anticipating the relevant conditions in which the kind of obligation in question does not apply (or is overridden) and building them into its content. Call this a *conditionalization strategy*. With this strategy in mind, consider a reply to the claim that we need not always do what we promise to do (as where we miss a dinner appointment in order to prevent a serious accident). 'To any relatively trivial promise there are a host of tacit conditions, all of which will normally be satisfied, which promiser and promisee must and do understand, and when, as occasionally happens, such a condition is not satisfied, the promiser treats his obligation as annulled' (Donagan 1977: 93).[6] I have four points about this tacit conditionalization strategy.

The first point concerns the content of promises. It is essential to keep in mind that *what* we promise to do is what we specify in saying 'I promise to ...' (the specification may be indirect, e.g. where we say 'yes' to 'Do you promise to ...?'). Most commonly this is an action, though we may only indicate a range of actions, as where we promise our support for a project. We do sometimes cite conditions that must obtain before the obligation 'takes effect', for instance in promising 'to pay a bill *if* he doesn't'. But here we make a *conditional promise*; this is not putting conditions *on fulfilling* a promise. I could promise to defend you *if* your life is threatened even where I see nothing whatever as a condition for my defensive action in case the threat materializes.

Second, though promising takes place against a background of understanding of *excusatory conditions* – the kind whose presence absolves one of moral guilt for non-performance – normal contexts of promising do not require that there be a definite list of these assumed to be absent, nor can we in general specify them *all* even with effort. Third, it would not be morally advisable for us to try to internalize the suggested excusatory list standard even if we could; for then we would be loath to believe we had been promised anything significant unless the excusatory conditions (or others warranting non-performance of the promised deed) were specified or – as is quite unlikely – clear enough not to need specification. Finally, the occurrence of excusatory conditions does not *annul* the promise in question; otherwise there would be no obligation, or a different kind of obligation, to explain the non-performance to the promisee by appeal to such a condition. I conclude that the tacit conditionalization strategy fails as an attempt to show that some (sound) moral principles are absolute (and in that sense perfectly general), and that if it is improved by allowing a blanket clause such as 'so long as nothing of greater importance requires non-performance', it would still only conceal the kinds of problem we are addressing.

It might seem that some acts are utterly impermissible. This would imply that there are absolute generalizations of narrow scope. Isn't it always wrong to torture an infant? We recoil at the mere thought of this. But is it impossible that an infant be afflicted (perhaps by brain manipulation) with a condition curable only by torture? In that case, the kind and amount of torture relative to the kind of life we can secure for the child becomes crucial. This is a trade-off problem. We might now try the principle that it is always wrong to torture an infant *for fun*. But here another problem arises:

'for fun' is not part of an act-description but an indication of motivational underpinning. Adding it to a report of what someone does tells us *why* the agent did it; it is explanatory of the action, not an indication of a different or further act. If the action is not absolutely wrong, does *it* become wrong if performed for a reprehensible reason? This is doubtful. A permissible act can be performed with shameful motivation.

Perhaps we may say, however, that there are some absolute conditional obligations, for instance, *given* the regrettable necessity to torture an infant, to avoid doing it for fun (this is not avoiding an 'act' of doing-it-for-fun, but avoiding torturing an infant in any case in which one *would* be doing it for fun, something one may well be able to anticipate). But what if the only way one could bring oneself to torture the child, and thereby meet one's regrettable obligation, is to cause oneself to be motivated in such way that one does it for fun? There are many questions here. I will not pursue them now. Enough has been said to make it clear that the suggested *specificity approach* to achieving moral generality without serious vagueness or difficult trade-off problems is not promising.

Apparently, the vagueness and trade-off problems are unavoidable in ethical theory. Ross saw that, and his strategy was to integrate a kind of particularism (a term to be clarified shortly) with the highest level of ethical generality he thought it reasonable to seek. He did this by appeal to Aristotelian practical wisdom as our only good resource for dealing with the trade-off problem and, regarding the vagueness problem, with the presupposition of Aristotle's judicious point that one must not demand more precision than the subject admits. Ross seems to me to have been on the right track on both counts. The next section will briefly set out his position on ethical generality. We can then consider some important challenges to it.

The Rossian integration between the particular and the general

Ross took obligatoriness (actual duty, in his terminology) to be a consequential attribute of action: roughly, to belong to an act in virtue of certain of its other properties. Among the most important are the grounds of obligation he cited in his famous list of prima facie duties in chapter 2 of *The Right and the Good* (1930).[7] He also used the word 'resultant', and he treated obligatoriness – *final duty*, as I shall call it – as a 'toti-resultant attribute', on the ground that it belongs to an act in virtue of its 'whole nature', whereas being a prima facie duty is a 'parti-resultant attribute' (see e.g. ibid. 122–23). His view was that its whole nature is something we can never know for certain; and it is apparently at least partly for this reason that the most general moral principles he proposed are phrased in terms of prima facie rather than final duty. We have prima facie duties of fidelity (requiring promise-keeping and avoidance of lying), of reparation, gratitude, justice, self-improvement, beneficence and non-injury.

Ross's principles are general not in the sense that they specify types of acts that *must* be performed on pain of moral failing – call that *generality as exceptionlessness* – but roughly in the sense that there is *always* a moral reason to observe them – call that *generality as universal applicability.* In being defeasible, they are, to be sure, not 'absolute' but *prima facie,* as is apparent where one duty is overridden by another. Here 'prima facie' is not epistemic: its force is not to indicate that what may seem to be a duty is not one, though Ross saw that this is true. Its force is to indicate that what *is* a duty-if-not-overridden can be overridden and thereby fail to be a (final) duty. Universal applicability, moreover, does not mean bearing on conduct for all persons at all times, but rather having such bearing *given* a person's satisfying the grounding conditions. If I promise nothing, I have no promissory obligation; but *given* my promising, I have a prima facie obligation in any kind of situation. To be sure, there may always be someone I can benefit, so the prima facie duty of beneficence may apply to me at all times and places regardless of what I do.

On the plausible assumption that obligatoriness is a consequential property, one might think that Ross stopped short of the strongest form of generality he might have captured: the kind expressed by principles that are universal in scope but, unlike the principle of utility and the categorical imperative, specific as to the act-type they demand. A rationale for this idea might be that, *given* an exercise of practical wisdom in which we determine our final duty in a context of moral decision, we may retrospectively formulate such a generality by describing the situation in sufficient detail. If I can see that nothing overrides my obligation to keep a promise, surely I can frame a generalization listing the relevant considerations – obviously finite in number since I take them all into account in a reasonable amount of time. Surely, it may seem, I can frame an informative principle to cover the type of action in question. But is this so?

Granted, if we know that we have a final duty to *A*, we may infer that in exactly similar circumstances anyone would have this final duty. But similarly, if we know that a Modigliani sculpture is graceful, we may infer that any sculpture exactly like it will also be graceful. This is an aesthetic generality of quite limited significance. In particular, it does not by itself help us significantly to *identify* what counts toward beauty in sculpture or how to create it in a non-imitative way. Let us explore how far some major ethical theorists have gone in enabling us to formulate significant moral generalizations.

Suppose, as Mill, Kant and apparently Ross as well believed, we always have duties of beneficence (for at least most of us, there is virtually always something significant we can do to help others). To be sure, one might (as Ross and others have taken Kant to do) regard promissory duties as invariably overriding those latter duties; and one might, as Mill presumably did, think that in some cases it can be obvious that utility is best served by keeping one's promise. But even supposing one can know that one's promissory duty overrides any duties of beneficence one has, putting such an overridingness clause in one's guiding moral principle gives it generality at the cost of both vagueness and a tacit acknowledgment of the trade-off problem. It would not do to try to teach the duty of beneficence to our children by saying that one should do good deeds for others unless one has a stronger (an overriding) conflicting duty, for instance to keep a promise.

Ross would say that we can never know whether such overridingness obtains, and even that we cannot know the related (and arguably equivalent) proposition that no other duty overrides the promissory one, say a duty of justice or non-injury. For one thing, there is commonly injustice to which we should attend; for another, whether we may cause injury in keeping a promise (even injury to the promisee) may be difficult to predict. I do not share Ross's rigorism about knowability. I believe we often know what our final duty is. Still, even on the assumption that we do know a singular moral judgment to be sound, this is *because* we presuppose something which is both highly vague and itself presupposes that there are possible trade-offs.

Should we conclude, then, that (as Ross may have thought) the kinds of prima facie principle he articulated are the most general ones close enough to action to be a practical guide to moral judgment? I believe that conclusion would be too strong. What counts as a practical guide to judgment is, in a certain way, relative to the capacities and experience of the agents whose guidance is in question. Moreover, the Rossian principles themselves are not equally applicable to everyday action. Even a young child can tell right off that saying a certain thing would be a lie; and the promising rule applies to deeds that, having been promised, have antecedently entered consciousness and so, when the time comes to keep the promise, can commonly be re-identified without reflection.[8] But some kinds of injury are not readily identifiable. Some psychological damage, for instance, is highly injurious, but not readily perceptible.

As to the duties of justice, some of these may, even for morally sensitive agents, be as difficult (or as easy) to identify in practice as are acts that treat someone 'as an end', in a broadly Kantian sense. Some moral agents are extraordinarily perceptive and have great facility in moral reasoning; some situations straightforwardly demand a given action which, like pulling a drowning child from deep waters, any normal person can see to be obligatory.

What is practical for one agent, or for one kind of situation, need not be practical for another; and even if we can find clear cases of the generally impractical at one end of the moral spectrum and clear instances of practical ones at the other, we cannot determine, a priori, just what contents will or will not yield practical moral principles across all moral agents and in all contexts of moral decision. There may be moral principles far more general than Ross's that are practical for some agents in some contexts, perhaps including *principles of action* like the categorical imperative and *principles of character* such as the injunction to be just, honest, loyal and kind.

To be sure, principles of character may be argued to count as moral principles only insofar as they 'point' to action. But virtue ethicists would deny this; and, more important for the issue here, these principles are in any case capable of being both general, and, in some cases, practical. It should be added that directly guiding moral decision is not the only function a moral principle can have. It can also unify and provide understanding of less general principles, as may be held for the categorical imperative and the principle of utility.[9]

To say that there can be true moral principles that are both of great generality and have potential value in guiding action is not to posit any principles that bypass the vagueness and trade-off problems. Suppose (as Ross apparently thought) these problems are inevitable. Was Ross right in thinking that we may at least bring to the effort to surmount these problems the kinds of prima facie principle he articulated? Or are practical moral problems so particular that even Rossian principles may not apply to them in the way he thought? One way to frame the question I have in mind is to ask if there is any ethical generality at all *before the fact*, i.e. apart from a context in which judgment is to be made. This brings us to the sense in which Ross was a particularist and to questions about whether we should prefer a version of particularism that is inconsistent with his ethical generalism.

Five types of particularistic intuitionism

I have so far represented Ross as formulating the most general moral principles that he considered both true and sufficiently practical to represent the moral standards, or at least moral presuppositions, of mature moral agents as such, i.e., conceived as 'plain men' not committed to an ethical theory. Since the principles are highly general, one might wonder in what sense Ross could be regarded as a particularist at all. His intuitionism may at least be considered epistemically particularistic. Specifically, he held that at least some intuitions about concrete cases are epistemically more basic than, or in any event indispensable to, intuitive knowledge of the corresponding generalizations. Indeed, in the course of moral development, it may be only when one thinks of a deed concretely and sees that it is wrong that one can see (or be justified in believing) that all deeds of that kind are wrong.[10] This is doubtless the kind of thing C. D. Broad had in mind in holding that experience of fittingness in particular cases is required before one can 'rise', by intuitive induction, to general knowledge of the kind of case in question (1930: 282).

In calling Ross's intuitionism particularist, I use a term that applies to many domains, but my concern here is mainly with the notion of duty. I have already suggested that Ross's intuitionism is an *epistemological particularism*, which (putting it in more general terms) is roughly the view that cognitions (including intuitions as a special case) regarding duty in a concrete instance, such as a situation in which one must aid an injured person, are epistemically prior to cognitions regarding duty in general, particularly to knowledge or belief of a general principle of duty. Intuitive induction is one kind of epistemic process in which knowledge of something particular yields knowledge of something general that the particular instantiates.

A related view is *conceptual particularism*, roughly the position that cognitions concerning such concrete cases are conceptually prior to cognitions concerning duty in general. On this view, one can acquire (or at least possess) the concept of duty only on the basis of acquiring (or at least possessing) the concept of, say, a duty to do a good deed for someone who has gone to great trouble to help one paint a garage. It is from one's understanding of such a concrete duty that one acquires a concept of duty as such. This is not the view that *knowledge* of particular truths about a case of duty yields knowledge of something general about duty; that epistemological point, which an epistemological particularist like Ross is likely to accept, could hold where the former kind of knowledge embodies a general concept of duty. Conceptual particularism requires that one have a concept of a particular duty as a basis for a concept of duty in general.

Conceptual particularism should be distinguished from an empirical thesis we might call *genetic particularism*, the position that in the normal order of learning of concepts and propositions, exposure to concrete cases is prior to understanding general deontic concepts and general principles of duty. This view does not entail conceptual particularism, since the *content* of what one learns initially through exposure to concrete cases can be conceptual and general: a child who genuinely learns what it is to have a duty to keep a particular promise may at some level be both acquiring the concept of a duty to keep *promises* (this is conceptual learning) and learning that promising implies such a duty (this is propositional learning). Ross, like Broad and others, was apparently a genetic as well as an epistemological particularist. But it is not clear that he held conceptual particularism, and in any case a moderate intuitionism can hold the former two views and not the third.

Genetic particularism does not entail that any specific method of moral thinking is preferable to the others, but it naturally goes with a kind of *methodological particularism*. This is the thesis that moral reasoning, whether about individual cases calling for moral judgment or in theoretical matters, should give some kind of priority to reflection on particular cases, such as those in which one person owes reparation to another or does an injustice to another.[11] This view can take various forms, depending on the kind of substantive priority that a proponent assumes, say temporal or, more likely, epistemological. I mention this view for the clarity it adds by contrast with the other kinds of particularism. Many intuitionists have implicitly held some version of it, but as a methodological view it might be held by non-intuitionists and is not of major concern in evaluating substantive particularist views or in determining the respects in which sound moral principles can be general.

A fifth kind of (ethical) particularism – *normative particularism* – is more controversial among intuitionists. I refer to the view that the deontic *valence* of a consideration (such as one's having promised to do a deed), i.e. the consideration's counting for or against the action in question (or neutrally) is determinable only in particular cases and is not invariant across different cases. This differs from the counterpart ontological view on which the valence of any element is *determined* by factors that vary from case to case. It is clear that different sorts of thing can underlie an injury or an injustice; our question is whether the valence of, say, injury or lying varies, not whether the basis of what has the valence can vary.

A stronger normative particularism has it that even the *relevance* of a consideration to determining duty is ascertainable only in particular cases.[12] If this view is sound, then not only could lying count negatively or positively in different cases; in some it could also be irrelevant. Ross was not a normative particularist in either sense. He held, regarding the grounds of basic prima facie duties, an *invariant valence view*: the valence of, say, an action's being an injury of another person is always a prima facie reason against it. Let us explore this view.

Moderate intuitionism and normative valence

A moderate intuitionism can (with Ross) maintain epistemological and genetic particularism, leave open conceptual particularism, and reject normative particularism in favour of the invariant valence view. It is natural to call this position a *moderate particularism*, by contrast with the strong particularism that endorses all four particularist theses. But at least the invariance thesis, as in a sense generalist, may seem inappropriate for any particularist view and perhaps even for ethical intuitionism as such. Let us explore this.

Suppose I promise to pick a friend up at a certain crowded place at ten and I discover just as I am about to drive off that a third party intends, when I get there, to detonate a powerful bomb he has concealed in my car. Is my promising to pick up my friend even relevant to deciding whether to do so, much less a consideration favoring it? We might also imagine the man who promised Macbeth to kill Lady Macduff and her children. This is a morally outrageous act. Does he have even a prima facie obligation to do it? Should we not adopt a thoroughly contextualist view here, as a strong particularist would?[13] A great deal can be said on this issue. I have space for only a few of the major distinctions a moderate intuitionism can bring to bear.

First, it is essential to distinguish the *deliberative relevance* of a consideration, roughly its relevance to making a decision regarding what to do, from its *normative relevance*, its valence (positive or negative) in relation to the action(s) in question. My promise to pick up my acquaintance is not deliberatively relevant; I would be at best foolish to bring it into my thinking about whether to do something that would kill dozens of innocent people. It does not follow that it has no normative relevance. To say so would be like saying that because it makes no sense to wait for a penny in change at the cost of missing one's flight, the penny has no value. Granted, to *say* that a promise like the one in question has normative relevance is odd. But that may be owing to the pragmatic point that it is highly misleading to call a consideration normatively relevant when in the circumstances any normative weight it has is far below the threshold of deliberative relevance. That it is misleading or even in some way wrong to assert a proposition does not imply that it is untrue.

A further point supporting the normative relevance view (and indeed the invariant valence view) is that despite how obviously my promissory obligation is outweighed, it is important to offer my friend an explanation of my non-appearance. This bespeaks a normative factor that was overridden rather than eradicated. The case of Macbeth's hired killer is perhaps more complex than the other example. It is not clear that he would owe Macbeth an explanation if he failed; still, that could be not because he had no such prima facie duty but because it is massively overridden by a duty not to cooperate with someone who would have one kill innocent people (other negative duties toward such a person may also come in). Nonetheless, the man's feeling such a duty would be a positive element in his character; compare him with a man who would be quite willing to do the killing but accords no weight to the promise and instead breaks it in order to perpetrate an exactly similar killing for which he is paid more. The best explanation of the even more negative assessment of the second agent is that, with the first, the promise retained some moral weight despite its outrageous object; in acknowledging that weight, the first man showed himself likely to be at least one step closer to reformation than the second. The first needs a moral transformation that may include everything except whatever element of fidelity is implicit in his sense of fiduciary duty; the second may need a complete moral transformation.

Another point emerges if we imagine the bomb case differently. Suppose I later discover that I can get the bomb defused in time to pick up my friend up a bit late. I should then do this rather than not appear at all. This point also suggests that a positive reason has been overridden in a way that generates a duty of substitution, rather than that in the context the promise had no force at all. The promise remains as a ground on which one should try to build something, even when it is clear that one should not do the promised deed.

This brings us to a second major distinction that must be observed here. Just as we can distinguish considerations above and below the threshold of deliberative relevance, we can distinguish considerations above and below the threshold of ordinary discernibility in the context of decision. A flashlight beam is not visible in bright sunlight; promising to pick up my friend at ten is not readily discernible as a reason to do so in the special case in question. But just as we can conceive removing the sunlight, we can conceive removing the bomb; and there seems no better reason to say that the presence of the bomb changes the force of the promise than to say that the presence of the sunlight changes the brightness of the flashlight.

Indeed, suppose I am certain that the very same people (including my friend and me) will be killed by a different terrorist if I do *not* pick up my friend at ten. For those to whom promising is a serious matter, it may seem better to keep the promise than not: at least I fulfill one more obligation before the end. I say 'may seem' because in this case I allow myself to be *used*, and there is prima facie reason to avoid *that*. To get a good analogy to the flashlight we may have to remove this element. In principle, however, a consideration's being below the level of ordinary discernibility does not entail its being below the threshold of deliberative relevance (and conversely). A similar point might apply in mathematics. Given a clearly cogent proof of a theorem, competent testimony that it is a theorem may add so little to one's justification as to seem negligible; but given a plausible attack on the proof, such testimony might become an important reason to retain belief of the theorem. Deliberative relevance varies with changes in context.

These points about promising should not be allowed to create the impression that it is easy to say just what constitutes a promise. The notion has an element of vagueness. For instance, can one promise under duress, as where one is forced at gunpoint to say 'I promise to vote for you'? I am inclined to say that so speaking in response to a *threat* does not suffice for promising, but that if one is forced to promise something because (say) one has a debt of gratitude, then (in at least some cases) one's promise can be genuine.[14] Imagine that, in gratitude, I owe you a great deal and you are a good candidate. If you insist, I presumably may promise to vote for you. Granted, I might have stronger moral reasons to vote for someone else. But suppose the only other candidate is equally good (hence not better) and that I have in mind another way to discharge my debt of gratitude to you. Even if I prefer the other way of discharging my debt, I am not free to choose that and vote for the other candidate, but should keep my promise. Genuine promises seem to retain weight not only when massively outweighed but also in some cases when they are infelicitously made.

A third distinction pertinent here is between the intrinsic valence of a consideration and its overall normative role in the context of a given decision or action. A major case in point is *Schadenfreude*, roughly taking pleasure in the suffering of another. Can the prima facie duty of beneficence, for instance, provide any reason at all to give someone an opportunity to take pleasure in sadistically beating another person? Plainly, this is the wrong kind of pleasure. Does the invariant valence view allow us to say this, at least if it endorses promotion of pleasure for someone as a (prima facie) reason for action? (It may, of course, deny that beneficence is manifested in promoting just any kind of pleasure.) The view does allow this.

To see how, we might focus on the closely related case of pain. Is it not at least in part because of the invariant badness of pain (at least of the kind in question) that the pleasure in question *is* the wrong kind? That an act produces pain is a reason to abstain from it. Moreover, we may plausibly hold that the overall state of affairs, someone's taking pleasure in paining another, has a negative value vastly outweighing the positive value of the pleasure in question. This point may allow us to say, in some cases, that whatever positive value promoting pleasure may have is below the threshold of deliberative relevance and perhaps even below that of ordinary discernibility.[15]

The fourth distinction relevant here is between a kind of *holism regarding judgments of final duty*, roughly the view that where two or more conflicting considerations bear on a prospective action one can discern one's final duty only in the light of an overall assessment of them, and *holism regarding judgments of prima facie duty*, which is roughly the strong particularist view that the same point applies to judgments of prima facie duty. Moderate intuitionism (including Ross's, apparently) is committed to the first but not the second kind of holism.

Holism regarding final duty might be called *bottom-up holism*: the identity and interrelations of the particular elements having a constant valence are the main basis of the overall judgment. On this view, final duty is compositional. Holism regarding prima facie duty – a position that goes with a normative particularism – might be called *top-down holism*. On this view, only the overall assessment of the whole – roughly, of the act in its full context – can indicate the valence of the elements in question, such as promising, lying, and injury. Suppose one faces a conflict of duties, with considerations of fidelity and familial beneficence favoring an expenditure for one's children and considerations of both rectification and beneficence favoring an incompatible expenditure for a special charity. Determination of final duty can be a holistic matter involving a huge variety of considerations even if the relevant prima facie duties are grounded in factors having a constant valence.

A constant valence, moreover, does not entail a constant *weight*. Promising, for instance, can invariably be a normative reason to do the thing in question even if some promises provide better reason for action than others and even if, as circumstances change, the overall weight of a promise in the context of decision can change. A change in weight tends to carry with it a change in moral significance; other things equal, the less weighty a consideration, the less significant. Moral significance is perhaps a threshold concept, like discernibility; and just as a consideration may be below the threshold of ordinary discernibility without being irrelevant or without its appropriate moral valence, it may be below the threshold of moral significance relative to a given decision without irrelevance or a change in its appropriate valence. Moral significance, like its close relative, deliberative relevance, does vary with context. Both notions help to show that one can be a holist about final duty and not about prima facie duty.[16]

A nice analogy to express the idea of holism about final duty is the role of a dab of paint in the whole artwork: 'Natural features carry their contribution to an action's moral status in the way that a given dab of paint on the canvas carries its contribution to the aesthetic status of a painting: the bold stroke of red that helps balance one painting would be the ruin of another' (Little 2000: 280).[17] This is true, but, aesthetically, much depends on what aspect of the paint we consider, just as, morally, much depends on the aspects of an action in a social context, say that of being the making of a promise or of causing pain. Color can be invariant. The paint can retain its color regardless of the painting to which it belongs; but its effect on one may be good, on another bad. Similarly, the pain caused by a slap on the face is bad, and there is reason to avoid causing it, whether the context is an angry attack or a needed reversal of a dangerous drowsy condition that threatens a car accident. But the one can be inexcusable as an assault and the other morally right as a protection necessary in the context. A major difference is that there is no sound generality giving a particular color or shade invariant aesthetic positive or negative significance, whereas there are sound generalities giving certain kinds of acts invariant moral positive or negative significance. The aesthetic domain is not rule-governed in the way the moral realm is, but both are organic in that the value of the whole is not necessarily the sum of the values of the parts or aspects.[18]

It would be misleading, however, to say that in the slapping case the *contribution* of something prima facie wrong and intrinsically bad is to make something larger right and good, as if some element or aspect of the pain or the causing of it were transmitted to the whole and perhaps mysteriously transformed in the process. We must distinguish in such cases between the contribution of a part or aspect to a whole and its *effect* on that whole.[19] The effect of the pain that the slapping causes is to induce wakefulness; but the pain does not contribute to wakefulness, as the pleasures of conversation may contribute to the enjoyment of a dinner.

To be sure, for a strong coherentist theory of justification, *any* kind of justification is a holistic matter. For coherence is never linear, but always determined by how all the relevant elements (usually taken to be numerous and most commonly conceived as cognitions) fit together. One may, however, embrace a coherence theory of the acquisition and functioning of concepts – *conceptual coherentism* – without holding *epistemological coherentism*, which is roughly the view that the justifiedness of beliefs and other cognitions (including intuitions) is grounded in the mutual coherence of the relevant items.[20] We apparently do not acquire concepts one by one, and understanding any of them is essentially connected with understanding certain others. But it does not follow from this conceptual coherence constraint that there are no considerations which, even by themselves, provide us with prima facie justification.

Indeed, just as it is doubtful that we can account for justified belief without giving experience *some* role in generating prima facie justification, it is doubtful that we can even be in a position to decide what action is our overall duty without giving some role to independently accessible considerations, such as fidelity and veracity, generating prima facie duty. Note, too, that appeal to such considerations always has some measure of both explanatory and excusatory power. If, for instance, we wonder why someone said something evasive, some degree of explanation can be provided by saying that it avoided lying. Similarly, if I fail to keep a promise, say to preserve a confidence, I may excuse – or at least mitigate – the prima facie wrong by saying that I was asked direct questions and would have had to lie to preserve it. The invariant valence view explains such points better than alternative views.[21] This is not to imply that every non-performance of a duty *calls* for excuse or mitigation; it may be quite clear (as in the terrorist case) that a promise should be broken. A type of duty, such as a promissory one, can have an invariant valence without all its non-performances needing excuse or mitigation. The point here is that *performing* it can always provide some mitigation (or at least a morally relevant counter-consideration) where a wrong has been done.

It should be plain from a number of points made in defending the invariant valence view that it does not imply a *subsumptivist conception* of our knowledge of singular moral judgments, the idea that these judgments are knowable only as applications of generalizations, such as Rossian principles of prima facie duty. This conception may also arise from the correct point that in many cases, before we can answer the commonly encountered question of what, overall, we should do, we must be able to see that two or more conflicting (prima facie) generalizations apply to our options. But the applicability of several generalizations to a case does not imply that one's final obligation therein is determined by applying a further, reconciling generalization. That point holds even if such a generalization is in principle formulable after the fact.

Moral character as an element in ethical generality

Moral generality need not be understood along Rossian lines. I have already indicated that a virtue theorist might take the bearing of moral traits to be the basis of any general moral standards with significant practical application. It is noteworthy, in this connection, that in specifying the grounds of prima facie duties, Ross emphasized certain virtue notions. The duties to keep promises and avoid lying are called duties of fidelity; and there are also aretaic duties of gratitude, justice, and beneficence. It is difficult to find virtues so closely linked to the duties of self-improvement, reparation, and non-injury, but what we need to discover here can be seen from the other cases.

The suggested view might be called *aretaic generalism*: the only basic kinds of ethical generalizations that are significant and useful are certain kinds in which virtue is central, such as 'We ought to be honest'. Applying this to promises and lying, one might hold that the basic moral reason not to break promises or lie is that such conduct bespeaks infidelity to one's word. We could even go so far as to say that the latter is our primary moral reason for the relevant act, and the fact that an act is a lie is only a derivative moral reason: operative only when the act is suitably connected with a virtue.[22] This would account for varying valence on the part of the latter kind of reason. In the game of contraband, for instance, the point is to lie and get away with it, and so lying is not even prima facie wrong in this context.[23] I have two sorts of question here.

First, if it is true that certain virtue concepts (and perhaps other 'thick' moral concepts) carry invariant valences, how is that to be explained? Deontologists like Ross and presumably Kant will likely respond with either or both of two points. One is that virtues may be viewed as above all internalizations of moral principles (where this involves, of course, a sense of how to deal with trade-off problems). The other, which is suggested by Ross's emphasis on intuitive induction as a basis of moral understanding, is that moral concepts are basically tied to certain act-types, and understanding what constitutes a virtue is at least in good part a matter of seeing what types of act are appropriate to expressing it: keeping one's word, helping others, making reparation for harming others, and so forth. Arguably, if there were not basic moral reasons to perform acts of these kinds, there would not be the associated virtues. There is much more to be said on this issue.[24] My point here is simply that a great deal of argument would be needed to show that the strategy in question provides as good an account of the relevant data as a deontological intuitionism like Ross's.

The second point concerns concrete cases. It should be granted that when a person does something wrong, we can, given information about the context and motives of the deed, find terms connected with virtue that apply to the act or the agent or both. The language of virtue is immensely rich, and it can also apply in cases of fulfillment of moral obligation. But this does not show that the moral reasons operating in the context are *grounded* in the relevant virtues. The point is compatible both with the view (which an intuitionist like Ross might well hold) that virtues are internalizations of moral standards of a Rossian kind and with the axiological view that both aretaic (virtue) reasons, such as 'It is dishonest', and deontological ones, such as 'It is a lie', are grounded in (even if not only in) values, such as the kinds essential in human flourishing.

A related point should be made about the intriguing case of a game in which lying is part of the point. It is essential to distinguish here between two kinds of overrider, those that apply to an entire series of acts of a certain kind and those that apply to a single one. Consider the moment at which we agree to play the game. This agreement overrides the obligation not to lie for the entire game; it is a *diachronic* (temporally extended) *overrider* of indefinite scope. By contrast, the need to break a promise to do a single thing given a sudden stronger obligation to put out a fire is a *synchronic overrider*. The plausibility of the example seems to me to rest at least partly on our picturing the individual acts of lying. These are unexcused by any overrider at the time; there is no synchronic overrider. Their apparent disconnection with anything outside the game may also contribute to the impression that there is no overrider at all. But should anyone think that there would be no prima facie moral reason not to lie to someone who is not in the game, who happens to ask the relevant questions about the contraband, who cares about the answer, who knows nothing of the rules or spirit of the game, and who could be given the information without detracting from the game? I doubt it.

Final duty and overall moral judgment

So far, I have defended the invariant valence view and affirmed the kind of ethical generality that goes with it. But it may be reasonable to claim something more specific. Suppose that (all) moral properties are consequential on (supervene on, in one sense of 'supervene') some finite set of natural ones and that the relevant natural ones and their grounding relations to the moral ones are discernible by ordinary kinds of inquiry. Then, given a sound moral judgment in a case of conflicting obligations, it would seem that one can in principle formulate a generalization that non-trivially applies to similar cases. For the overall obligatoriness one discerns will be based on natural properties, each of which one can in principle discriminate and appeal to in framing a generalization. Still, this kind of generalizability in principle is not a necessary condition for one's forming a justified judgment (or one constituting knowledge). One can achieve a sound result whether or not one generalizes on it or is even able to do so. It could be, for instance, that overall obligation is *organic* and that, given the sense in which it is, there is no guarantee that in every case of sound moral judgment we can specify just what properties are its basis. Recall the example of a painting: we can justifiably believe a painting to be beautiful even though we would need both new observation and reflection even to begin to point to the elements in it that render it beautiful. Even if prima facie obligation is entailed by certain natural properties (a view that intuitionists commonly hold), overall obligation apparently requires a more complicated account.

One might question whether final obligation *is* consequential on natural properties. Consider having a final obligation to tell the truth, where this obligation prevails over a conflicting obligation to protect a friend. What might be the natural base of the relational normative property of (moral) *prevalence* or *being weightier*? As a moral pluralist, Ross would insist that there is at best no one dimension, such as the hedonic, determining the finality of the duty of veracity. There is no reason to doubt, however, that a counterpart prevalence will occur in any exactly similar case of conflicting duties. This does not entail that final duty is consequential on natural properties, but how are we to explain this generalizability except on the assumption that final obligation *is* grounded in natural properties of the relevant case? I see no good alternative explanation.

It is, moreover, at least in the spirit of a rationalist intuitionism to say that *if* we could formulate and understand all of the relevant variables, we might thereby achieve knowledge of the resulting – presumably consequential – final duty. Suppose, however, that there simply is no closed list of relevant natural properties. If not, then first, the consequential character of final duty is difficult to establish, since the overall basis of the duty may be inaccessible, and second, the epistemic organicity of final duty is to be expected, since one should not expect knowledge of final duty to be determined in any quantitative way by fewer than all of the variables underlying it. Such consequentiality may yet hold. Compare again the beauty of a painting: should we not consider it consequential on such elements as the colors and shapes and their relations because we cannot close the list of relevant factors? Responding to all of the relevant properties does not entail an ability to list them.

Suppose, by contrast, that in some cases we can formulate and understand all of the variables relevant to determining the finality of a duty. The generalization we could then articulate might be (and, on sufficient reflection, could be seen to be) self-evident or otherwise a priori. One might now plausibly argue that the comparative weights of the relevant duties in the kind of case in question are an a priori matter. This not only would not undermine the idea that final duty is consequential on natural properties, but would in fact extend the scope of intuitionist moral principles beyond the range anticipated by Ross and other intuitionists. Although there would still be no a priori hierarchical ranking that places some general duties, such as those of fidelity, over others, such as those of beneficence, some judgments of final duty could be instances of more specific comparative moral principles; and there would then be more such principles available to us in proportion to our skill at generalizing on the use of practical wisdom.[25]

A further point concerning the epistemic resources of the intuitionism I am defending is that in many cases of a singular judgment settling a conflict of duties, there is the possibility of reaching a reflective equilibrium between this judgment and various moral principles and other singular judgments. This equilibrium may contribute to the justification of that judgment, as well as provide, in some cases, justification for a second-order belief that the judgment is justified. It may even make the difference between a judgment with only some degree of justification and one sufficiently well justified to be both a good guide for action and a candidate for knowledge. Here, then, is one way a judgment that begins as a tentative assessment can graduate to the status of justified belief or even knowledge.

There is another aspect of the question of how general practically useful moral principles can be. It concerns possible conflicts, and hence apparently the need for trade-offs, between moral and non-moral values. This problem can affect any plausible ethical theory. To be sure, Kant treated ethical considerations as basic in the theory of practical reason and regarded the categorical imperative as grounding absolute moral obligations. But suppose for the sake of argument that it does ground some absolute obligations. This does not entail that there is no possibility of anyone's ever rationally doing something that morality does not permit. Even apart from the (disputed) possibility of doing this knowing the act is morally impermissible, one can rationally hold a mistaken view, such as the view that a deed is permissible, and rationally holding this belief can render rational an action based on it.

Regarding consequentialist theories, if (as I shall assume) they ground all reasons for action in whatever they posit as having intrinsic value, then unless (implausibly) a utilitarian view considers *only* one quite specific kind of value to be basic, something like an incommensurability problem can arise. Consider a hedonistic utilitarianism. Even if, contrary to the view of Mill and others (almost certainly including Aristotle), no one kind of pleasure is better than any other, there would still be difficulties in weighing promotion of pleasures against reductions of pains. The trade-off problem is apparently inescapable in ethics. Radical particularism is in part a response to it, but its resources are inadequate to the task.

On the basis of this explication and partial defence of a moderate particularism and the kind of ethical generality it provides for, I conclude that a Rossian intuitionism is a plausible basis for an account of ethical generality. There is a significant kind of ethical generality: some moral principles are both wide in scope and useful in day-to-day moral thinking. The application of general principles must, however, be balanced by attention to concrete cases understood in the light of a multitude of facts about them. Moral knowledge can occur at either level. Some of it is quite general, some highly particular. At either level, moreover, certain kinds of consideration play an important role in our moral attitudes and judgments. Ross and other intuitionists have apparently been right in taking certain kinds of element to have a constant valence; but those intuitionists (and other moral theorists) who take the valence of such elements to vary with context are surely correct in emphasizing that moral judgment must be highly sensitive to particular facts that differ from one case to another.

There is, then, a holism concerning final duty that constitutes common ground between Rossian intuitionists and ethical theorists who believe in a stronger particularism. On either kind of view, I believe that we can find more room for a rationalist moral epistemology than is generally realized. Once it is seen how to eliminate mistaken assumptions that neither Rossian intuitionism nor rationalism need endorse, we can clear away some of the major obstacles in the way of a rationalist account of the foundations of ethics. There is much to commend a fallibilist, intuitionistic moral rationalism that countenances both ethical generality and moral intuitions about concrete cases as prima facie justified inputs to ethical theorizing.[26]

Notes

1 Some translators use 'merely' rather than 'simply', and I follow their practice as preferable in capturing the relevant notion as expressed in English.

2 For extensive critical discussion of how to interpret and appraise Kant's categorical imperative (in more than one formulation), see Parfit (forthcoming).

3 One can also formulate the principle in terms of *expected* utility; but there is no need to add that complication explicitly. We can assume that a utilitarian will in any case have a theory of excuses; hence if one does something wrong, one may be excusable provided one was justified in taking the utility of the act to be optimal.

4 Mill spoke of 'the rule for measuring it [quality] against quantity, being the preference felt by [all or almost all?] those who in their opportunities of experience, to which must be added their habits of self-consciousness and self-observation, are best furnished with the means of comparison' (Mill 1863: ch. 2). He left indeterminate whether a simple majority suffices here or whether a stronger consensus is needed. Sidgwick's version of utilitarianism does not encounter this problem. He says, e.g. that 'by Greatest Happiness is meant the greatest possible surplus of pleasure over pain ... of course, here as before the assumption is involved that all pleasures are capable of being compared quantitatively with all pains ... so that each may be at least roughly weighed in ideal scales against any other' (Sidgwick 1907: 413). As Sidgwick's use of 'roughly' suggests, however, the vagueness problem is not eliminated; and although Sidgwick's formulations are superior to Mill's on some points, trade-off problems also remain.

5 The view is also expressed by Mill in ch. 5 of *Utilitarianism*. It is among the passages in that book that lead to a reading of him as representing rule-rather-than-act-consequentialism. For a defense of the former and a detailed contrast between it and the latter, see Hooker (2000a).

6 The principle Donagan is defending by such a tacit conditionalization strategy is that it is '*impermissible for anybody to break a freely made promise to do something in itself morally permissible*' (Donagan 1977: 92–93).

7 For Ross's list of prima facie duties see *The Right and the Good* (Ross 1930: 20–21). A difficulty with the list as a candidate for a comprehensive self-sufficient set of moral principles is that some of its elements employ moral terms, e.g. 'wrongful'. I have indicated a strategy for dealing with this problem (Audi 2004: ch. 5).

8 Since one can promise to do something rather indefinite, say give psychological support, it is not always the case that when the time comes to perform, one need not reflect on what one promised but only remember it.

9 This unifying and explanatory function of certain comprehensive moral principles is explicated in Ross (1930: ch. 3).

10 Ross says, of 'insight into the basic principles of morality', that it is not based on 'a fairly elaborate consideration of the probable consequences' of certain types of acts; 'When we consider a particular act as a lie, or as the breaking of a promise ... we do not need to, and do not, fall back on a remembered general principle; we see the individual act to be by its very nature wrong' (Ross 1939: 172–73). Speaking approvingly of Aristotle, Ross said of right acts that, while first 'done without any thought of their rightness', when 'a certain degree of mental maturity' was reached, 'their rightness was not deduced from any general principle; rather the general principle was later recognized by intuitive induction as being implied in the general judgments already passed on particular acts' (ibid. 170).

11 Methodological particularism and other kinds are distinguished by Walter Sinnott-Armstrong (1999). A strong version would hold that adequate moral reasoning *must* properly attend to particular cases.

12 Jonathan Dancy holds both forms of normative particularism (e.g. 1993: 60–62, 66–68).

13 For Dancy, 'The leading thought behind particularism is that the behavior of a reason ... in a new case cannot be predicted from its behaviour elsewhere. ... I borrow a book from you, and then discover that you have stolen it from the library. ... It isn't that I have *some* reason to return it to you and more reason to put it back in the library. I have no reason at all to return it to you' (Dancy 1993: 60). One might think this view is supported by an argument of Sidgwick's: '[A] promise to do an immoral act is held not to be binding, because the prior obligation not to do the act is paramount ... otherwise one could evade any moral obligation by promising not to fulfill it, which is clearly absurd' (Sidgwick 1907: 305). But notice that not only does he implicitly recognize some promissory obligation by calling the prior, conflicting obligation *paramount*; he also says the former is not *binding* rather than, e.g. eliminated or never generated by promising in the first place. The validity of his reasoning, moreover, requires only that prior obligations *outweigh* any promissory obligation arising from the promise (where 'prior' means roughly 'antecedently existing' rather than 'having priority' – that reading would make his point trivially true).

14 cf. Hooker's claim that a promise extracted under duress has no force (Hooker 2000b: 9).

15 I discuss the problem of *Schadenfreude* and the related organicity of intrinsic value in some detail elsewhere (1997: ch. 11; 2004: ch. 4).

16 cf. Dancy: 'Since I recommend a particularist understanding of the rightness or wrongness or the action [public executions of convicted rapists if the event would give pleasure both to the executioner and to the crowds], I recommend a particularist approach to the rightness or wrongness of any resulting pleasure' (Dancy 1993: 61). This is not quite to deny that one can be a holist about final duty and not about prima facie duty, but Dancy seems to think it at least unnatural to hold the former without the latter view. I cannot here do justice to the richness of his discussion of the overall question of particularism. For a later statement of Dancy's views, see his 'The particularist's progress', in Hooker and Little (2000) (which also contains many other positions concerning particularism).

17 I hasten to add that Little's intention is apparently to use the analogy to support the view that 'the very "valence" of a feature is context-dependent' (Little 2000: 280). As I see it, however, valence is like color in that it need not change in order for the element in question to have different effects in different contexts.

18 I explore the nature of organic unities and the non-additivity view just stated in some detail elsewhere (2003).

19 My view here contrasts with that of Jonathan Dancy in his critical study of Moore (2003b).

20 I develop this distinction elsewhere (1997: ch. 4), where I defend a moderate foundationalism that incorporates what I consider the most plausible elements in epistemological coherentism.

21 If coherence is the only standard we bring to holistic moral assessment of an action, we cannot adequately distinguish between right and wrong. Wrong-doing can be supported by as coherent considerations as doing what is right. This is not the place to assess the prospects for a coherence theory of justification, but detailed critical treatments are offered in Audi (1997: ch. 4) and Plantinga (1993). Ross is clearly a foundationalist about the grounds of duty, and a moderate intuitionism is most plausible when placed within a carefully qualified foundationalism regarding prima facie duty.

22 In defending a Rossian account of the kinds of moral principles he formulates and in the moral concepts he works with as at least as basic as virtue notions, my

view contrasts with that of David McNaughton and Piers Rawling in their wide-ranging 'Principled Ethics' (2000). See, e.g. pp. 267–73.

23 For instructive discussion of the contraband example (and of the views of Dancy, from whom it comes), see McNaughton and Rawling (2000).

24 I have discussed this issue in some detail elsewhere (Audi 1995).

25 For discussion of the resources of Rossian intuitionism regarding comparisons of duty, see McNaughton (1996).

26 Earlier versions of this paper were given at the University of Helsinki and Wake Forest University. I benefited from the discussion on both occasions, and would also like to thank Derek Parfit for helpful comments on an earlier draft.

4   From particularism to defeasibility in ethics

Mark Norris Lance and Maggie Little

1 Introduction

A number of theorists have recently urged that the moral principles so prized by many are in fact irreducibly strewn with exceptions.[1] Lying is always wrong-making – well, not when playing the game Diplomacy, in which lying is the point of the game, or again when confronted with the Nazi concentration camp guards, to whom the truth is not owed. Pleasure is always good-making – well, not when it is the pain enjoyed by the sadist, delighting in his victim's agony.[2] It is always wrong-making not to take competent agents at their word; well, not in the S&M room, where 'no' precisely does mean 'yes'.

The claim proffered is not simply that the wrongness of the lie or goodness of the pleasure are in these instances *outweighed* by other considerations, or again that the exceptions can be expunged if only we refine our principles carefully enough. The claim, instead, is that the 'moral valence' these features carry to their respective situations have themselves switched from their more familiar mode, and in ways that cannot be helpfully codified. The fact that something is a lie does not always count against it; the fact that something would bring pleasure is not always a count in favor; and there is no specifying in genuinely explanatory terms the conditions under which they do. Moral considerations, on this view, are *radically* context-dependent.

Of course, much debate has ensued on whether this is the right picture of morality.[3] But a separate question is what would follow if it were. According to many, the answer – for better or for worse – is moral particularism. As its name implies, moral particularism is a view that stands opposed to certain roles for generalizations. More specifically, it is the view that explanatory or theoretical moral generalizations play no essential role in moral understanding.[4] According to particularists, moral understanding is the exclusive province of particular judgments, perceptions, skills and syntheses of individual considerations. While moral generalizations may still stand as useful rules of thumb or helpful heuristics, they do not provide true explanatory generalizations illuminating the structure of morality, for morality cannot be thusly illuminated. In the view of many, this is the view implied by thorough-going contextualism: to accept such a view in ethics is to believe that morality – and our understanding of it – is not a domain governed by laws.

We disagree. In a series of recent papers, we have argued that thorough-going moral contextualism is true, while moral particularism, thusly defined, is false.[5] Indeed, our primary purpose has been to diagnose why the two positions are so often thought to be one. In our view, a central culprit is the widespread assumption that generalizations must be exceptionless if they are to do genuine and fundamental theoretical work: on such a view, the irreducible presence of exception must mean the absence of explanatory generalization. Such an assumption can arise from a number of different sources – from conceptions of the nature of reasons, explanation, theory, or laws, or again from broad metaphysical assumptions; our goal has been to challenge it nonetheless.

The wedge we have employed in driving distance between contextualism and particularism has been the notion of a 'defeasible generalization'. There is, we believe, an important kind of generalization that is both fundamentally explanatory and fundamentally porous – shot through with holes. We have been developing a semantics and epistemology of such generalizations in an attempt to show that it is possible for them to play explanatory roles without being reducible to, replaceable by or ultimately beholden to exceptionless generalizations. Such a view makes room, we believe, for moral contextualists to accept plausibly necessary ties between reasons, explanations, concepts and generalizations, to embrace moral theory as a significant enterprise, and to recover much more natural accounts of moral dispute and moral learning.

In this article, we summarize the account and its application to ethics.[6] Rather than arguing for thorough-going contextualism, our goal is to argue that its lesson has been misinterpreted. In showing why such contextualism does not imply particularism, though, we believe light may be shed not only on the moral landscape as it is seen by contextualists, but on the nature of reasons, principles, laws and explanation; given this, the route we travel may be of interest even to those less inclined to contextualist impulses.

We start by getting clearer on the form of contextualism that is at play.

2 Deep moral contextualism

Virtually every moral theorist working today agrees that context matters in certain ways, and that principles are not the whole of the moral story. In some cases the points are modest. We are reminded, for instance, that theory does not apply itself, that one must exercise judgment in determining how a theory applies to a particular case, that the application of moral concepts is itself already a complex skill that requires moral understanding, and of course that moral perception, like any other perception, is essential to the enterprise and not usefully characterized as following a set of rules.

Others advance a slightly more ambitious form of contextualism, aimed at rejecting the idea that the relations amongst various moral principles or duties can be codified. W. D. Ross provides a famous example. According to Ross, there are a range of moral duties, expressed in terms of thick moral concepts, which are relevant to the right and the good. When these duties conflict, as they can, there is, Ross urged, no algorithmic method for reaching an ultimate verdict; what is required, instead, is a sort of moral discernment, skill, or wisdom that is not itself capturable as the application of a principle. Depending on the context, justice can trump mercy, or mercy trump justice; there is no setting out in cookbook fashion when they do.

But if Ross was a contextualist when it came to such 'combinatorial' matters, he was a staunch principlist when it came to the individual duties themselves. For Ross regarded the central moral concepts set forth in these duties – fidelity, promise-keeping, and the like – as each having constant 'moral valence'. That an act causes pain, or that it is an instance of lying, is always a reason to avoid it, even if one that, in appropriate circumstances, is overridden by other considerations. Causing pain or lying may not always be wrong, all things considered, but causing pain and lying are always and invariantly wrong-*making*.

It is just here that more ambitious contextualists part company. Such contextualists argue that the considerations that in one context count as good- or bad-making, right- or wrong-making, can in another context count in just the opposite way – or no way at all – and all in ways that can't be concretely cashed out. It is not just that the moral contribution made by these considerations gets outweighed by others, as when the pain of a measles shot is justified by the utility it brings; rather, the moral valence of the consideration – its positive or negative contribution to overall moral status – itself depends irreducibly on the background context in which it appears. Not only can't one codify how the moral weight of a given feature stacks up against other moral considerations, it needn't have any moral weight to begin with, and certainly none of any given direction.

Now of course, most everyone thinks there are *some* sorts of considerations whose import varies with context: the utilitarian agrees that wiggling one's thumb can contribute disutility in one context and utility in another. More interesting moral contextualists claim, though, not just that incidentals can vary in this way, but that valence can switch *at the level of explanation*. The ambitious contextualist urges that a consideration can itself function as a *reason* – a full, complete, and genuine reason – while acting fully otherwise in another circumstance, and again in a way that cannot be helpfully codified. Such a view, then, is meant to come squarely up against the traditional view that explanation must involve subsumption under exceptionless generalization.

Variance at the level of explanation is in fact crucial to understanding the claim here. Some have argued that debates over moral contextualism are nothing more than a tempest in a teapot. After all, it will be said, even ambitious contextualists (or at least most of them) agree that the moral supervenes on the natural – two situations cannot be alike in every natural respect and differ in their moral features. This means that given a sufficiently powerful language there must be *some* exceptionless generalizations that express the moral as a function of the natural. Such 'supervenience functions', as we might call them, may of course be enormously complex – indeed, possibly irreducibly infinite – but that's just a difference in degree, not kind. Moving to the other end of the spectrum, even the most committed contextualist, it will be said, will admit that there is *some* level of abstraction where moral generalizations are safe from exception, if only principles such as 'pursue the good' or 'do the right thing.' This means, it seems, that they are not rejecting such principles, just squabbling over their concreteness. Ambitious contextualists, in short, don't reject exceptionless moral principles; they just relocate them.

Such an argument is mistaken. Acknowledgement of mere supervenience functions, for one, does not go far toward acknowledgement of principles. As John McDowell points out, supervenience can be admitted so readily because doing so admits to so little: it doesn't mean that there are any useful patterns to the way in which the dependencies line up.[7] While situations can't differ in their moral properties without also differing in their natural properties, this does not imply that a given moral difference (say, the difference between being cruel and not) need always be found in the same natural differences. Instead, stringing together the situations in which an action is cruel may yield groupings that would simply look gerrymandered to anyone who does not have independent competency with the moral concepts. (The action performed by the 167-pound man on Murray Avenue in Pittsburgh at 2:04 pm on Thursday, *or* the action performed by the cleverest woman in Vladivostok in the 19th century, *or* . . .) On such a picture, the complicated sets of properties mentioned in supervenience functions will not constitute anything recognizably explanatory; they are too disjointed – 'too indiscriminate', as Jonathan Dancy puts it – to serve (Dancy 1999b: 26).

Similarly for abstraction. It's certainly true that no one will abjure the existence of exceptionless heady abstractions in morality. At the limit, we can *invent* a predicate whose application entails invariant moral import (we could dub 'lighing,' say, as the term to pick out those cases of lying that are wrong-making). But this doesn't yet mean we have on hand anything explanatory or procedurally useful. If its classification as such simply reflects judgment of its immoral nature definitionally, no substantive explanatory work will be done by the generalization that lighings are wrong. Similarly for very abstract concepts: 'do the right thing' or 'choose well, Grasshopper' offer little substantive guidance. Such predicates may all still be useful – say, in marking off moral from pragmatic or again legal reasons, in summarizing or regimenting our views; but expression of the generalization won't serve as a check on one's specific intuitions. Ambitious moral contextualism, then, is a contentful rather than empty claim: it claims that variance of moral import can happen at the level of genuine explanation.

Amongst those who recognize the possibility of genuinely multi-valent moral reasons, differences arise over their claimed breadth and depth. Breadth has to do with how many of the putative moral principles function in an exceptionless manner. 'Narrow' contextualists will think that there are exceptions to a few putatively significant moral principles, or again that it is only certain sorts of principles – say, connections between non-moral descriptions and moral verdicts – that resist principled formulation. Broad contextualists, in contrast, believe, that many or all important principles turn out to be exception-filled, and that valence-switching applies at the level of thick moral concepts. More specifically – for everyone, again, can agree that one use of 'justice' and 'cruel' is to refer to invariant summary concepts – they believe that the substantive conceptions of justice and cruelty offered (and contested) by theorists, by reference to which we understand, specify, or fill in the summary concepts, are richly riddled with exceptions.

Depth, in turn, concerns whether one sees the absence of exceptionless principles as a sort of surface phenomenon. Some argue, for example, that while competent every day moral reasoning need not, and typically should not, involve principles, there is a more basic level of moral theory that is governed by exceptionless principles. 'Surface' contextualists believe that some such fundamental, exceptionless layer must exist to account for the contextual variability of moral reasoning at the surface level. 'Deep' con-textualists, in contrast, believe that exceptions go down to the explanatory ground: there is no need to vindicate variation on the basis of exceptionless principles. Sometimes, one gains in explanation by moving from a surface characterization of the phenomenon, to a characterization in more funda-mental terms. But by the same token such ascent sometimes *lessens* expla-natory potency. Sometimes the real work of illuminating, rather than mere regimenting, is done by the thick, rich, and messy world of the multi-valent.

We ourselves are both deep and broad in the contextualism we endorse.[8] Virtually any substantial moral generalization, operating at any but the summarizing level, we would claim, will hold in some contexts and not in others; and contextual variability need not be vindicated by a deeper level of exceptionless generalization. Rather than arguing for the claim, though, we want to explore what would follow if ambitious moral contextualism were true. According to Jonathan Dancy, one of the most prominent voices advocating the importance and ubiquity of exceptions, the answer is moral particularism.

3 Moral particularism

Jonathan Dancy has provocatively argued that morality is without princi-ples. Dancy urges, as above, that a consideration can itself function as a reason – a complete and genuine reason – while acting otherwise in another circumstance. To be sure, there must be further differences to be found if a consideration that counts in one case as a reason does not in another; but it's a mistake, Dancy argues, to think that those differences must then be mentioned as part of what makes the action wrong. We must distinguish reasons from enablers, defeaters, intensifiers and the like. Further, Dancy urges, none of this is likely ever to be helpfully codified – to state in finite form the conditions under which a reason is enabled, or an enabler defeated.

Dancy's deepest basis for thinking such codification unlikely is that he thinks it unnecessary. It is a profound mistake, he believes, to think that reasons function by virtue of subsumption under principle. And the reason he believes it a profound mistake is because, more specifically, he thinks it unnecessary to regard reasons as backed by *any* sort of generalization. The considerations that are good- and bad-making, right- and wrong-making, need not be backed by any sort of theoretical generalization in order so to count.

Instead, he argues that considerations function as reasons when they stand in a particular metaphysical relationship he dubs 'resultance'. One of the ways we explain in everyday life, he urges, is by pointing to such a relationship. That White is winning in a given position is a result of the passed pawn on the Queenside; that the painting is beautiful is a result of its colors' pensive juxtaposition. Such examples, he agrees, make it tempting to accept a *constitution* theory of resultance, according to which what it is for this object now to be *G* is constituted here by its being *F.* In the end, though, the relationship is simply hard to say much about: it is, he argues, a primitive but thoroughly familiar relationship.

This isn't to say that all properties are moral equals. Some properties, Dancy argues, are 'moral defaults'. Metaphorically put, they come to a situation already 'turned on'; more formally, they are properties that need no *enabler* in order for them to function as reasons of a certain direction, though they may, of course, be 'turned off' in all manner of contexts by the presence of defeaters or underminers. The central claim is one of explanatory asymmetry: there are some properties with a default valence – one which itself needs no explanation; it can, like any import, shift to another, but its doing so demands explanation. One thus may need to explain why pain is, in this case, good-making, but not why in another it is bad-making.

Dancy's epistemology, in turn, is a thoroughly discernment-based account. He advances a form of moral discernment which, far from mystical, involves training into a skill. To achieve moral knowledge can be a complex task, involving attention to whether disablers are present and the like. The account of knowledge and explanation is, broadly put, not one of subsumption but of narrative. As with describing a building, we characterize the situation in ways that will get others to interpret and see it as we do (Dancy, 1993: 112). According to Dancy, the lesson of all this is clear:

'Reasons do not function in virtue of generalizations; they are about the ways things add up here' (1993: 106).

This is certainly a view that will leave some uneasy. It is not just that Dancy's epistemology is radically anti-theoretic, it's that Dancy's view of reasons, and hence of explanation, seems untenable. To understand something as a reason, according to Dancy, is not a function of uncovering any sort of generalization; rather, apprehending that a consideration is a reason is a form of discrete discernment – a nuanced, skilled form of discernment, to be sure, but discernment nonetheless, a matter of seeing how things add up here. But this seems to get the idea of reasons, in general, and of explanation, in particular, deeply wrong. Reasons and explanation are not something that *could* be, as Dancy puts it at one point, 'stubbornly particular' (1993: 104). They have *something* to do with generalization, even if the connection is not a deductive one.

To see, let's think for a moment about resultance. Taken abstractly, there are any number of different sets of facts that could be right as the resultance base of something's being, say, a winning position for White. We could mention the position of the passed pawn; then again, we could say the position's strength is constituted here by the complex fact of the entire tree of legal game continuations, or any number of levels in between. Similarly, in the case of the painting, we could say that the beauty is constituted by the distribution of red and green, or again that it's constituted by the distribution of molecules, or atoms or atomic particles across a given region.

What allows us to pick from amongst these various possible levels the one that is the favored, *explanatory* relationship? How do we go about determining the level at which resultance is said to hold? The answer, for Dancy, is that resultance is a primitive metaphysical relation. He takes our intuition about which level of description is the one that 'really' counts and dubs it as pointing to a special metaphysical relationship.

For many, though, there is more of an answer that can – and should – be given. Whatever the details, something counts as explanatory when it serves a particular *epistemic function*, namely, when it can serve in particularly robust ways (with 'robust' interpreted differently by different theorists) as the basis of an inference to the conclusion. This is what ties the idea of something being a reason to something that can serve in *reasoning*. But to play *this* role requires hooking in to generalization. To be committed to the propriety of any inference (whether explanatory or not) *is* to be committed to its propriety in some set of other contexts.

Thus, imagine that Smith, a moral novice, is told by Jones, the moral expert, that the action they just witnessed is bad *because* it is cruel. Imagine further that, when Smith again witnesses cruelty and thinks it a basis for believing, or perhaps presuming, or at least hypothesizing (all epistemic attitudes) it bad-making, she is met with absolute and utter befuddlement by Jones: 'Why ever would you think *that* a reason?' Surely, one loses touch with what is meant by 'reason' in the face of such a reaction. As Alan

Goldman puts it, the difference that stands as a reason can't just be a 'one-off' (Goldman 2002).

There is, of course, a difference between simply counting as a reason to believe that something is good and counting as a reason that *makes* the thing good.[9] That a morally wise person endorses an action gives some reason to regard it as good, but is hardly part of why it would *be* good. Genuinely good-making considerations are those reasons that are part of a true explanation of why the thing is good, in contrast to an explanation of why it was permissible of someone to believe it good.

But the point is not to say that all good-making considerations are merely reasons for *S* to believe that an action is good, but that they must at least be able to *serve* as a reason for *S* to come to that conclusion. And it's very difficult to see how Dancy's reasons could do so. Here's why. In order for one to move in reasoning from *P* to *Q*, one must be able to ascertain *P* in a way that is epistemically prior to ascertaining *Q*. But for Dancy, *P*'s standing in a relation of 'reason-for' to *Q* is a stubbornly particular, brute metaphysical fact. *P* is a reason for *Q* *in this very context*, and nothing is thereby implied about whether it is a reason in any other. So in order to 'infer' *Q* from *P* – assuming that one's inference is meant to track the Dancyng[10] reason-for relation – she would already have to know that she was in 'this very context'. But that requires knowing that *Q*, since the truth of *Q* is essential to the identity of this particular context. So there is really no reasoning going on, simply recognition of the total facts of the situation, even if some of those are relational facts such as that *P* is a metaphysical 'reason for' *Q*. Apprehending that a consideration is a 'reason' is a form of discrete discernment, of seeing how things add up here; and one comes to it, along with recognition of the right-hand-relatum, in a holistic epistemic grasping. Dancyng 'reasons', we conclude, are reasons in name only.

This is not to deny that discernment is a crucial piece of moral episte-mology. (Indeed, there may well be some concepts, or features of situations that are only ever morally relevant insofar as they function as a piece of a holistic discernment of what to do.) Nor are we claiming that good- and bad-making features must always function inferentially: once one has the concept of harm or again cruelty, one can discern them in a case at hand. Rather, our claim is that if harm is genuinely explanatory of the cruelty of a given action, or again if the cruelty is genuinely explanatory of the wrong-ness of a given action, then there must be some significant range of cir-cumstances in which some sort of (non-deductive) inference from harm to cruelty, or again cruelty to wrongness, is a good one.

On our view, then, there is a key difference between explanation and dis-cernment. There is a crucial difference between adducing reasons for a conclusion, and merely providing an audience enough of a narrative to allow them to discern that truth on their own. The former requires com-mitment to some sort of generalization – just what the pure discernment theorist denies of familiar factors such as lying and promising.

Nor is this to deny that there is such a thing as a relationship of resultance. Rather, it's to say that we get to classify any candidate as standing in such a relationship only in virtue of the candidate's epistemic relevance. Similarly with the categories of defaults, enablers, disablers, and underminers. It is not that such distinctions make no sense, or that one can't regard them as properly 'metaphysical' at the end of the day; the point, rather, is that the criteria for counting as a member of such a class must concern its ability to play an epistemological role (a role the proper spelling out of which calls for much further work).

In short, by severing reasons and explanation from generalization, we believe that Dancy removes them from the sort of epistemic space that underwrites their nature as such.

We want to argue that there is a different lesson that can be taken from deep contextualism. We agree that exceptions are ubiquitous, that the very task of trying to find strict explanatory generalizations is founded on fallacy. We believe, though, that the right lesson to take is not to eschew explanatory generalizations, but to change our picture of what they must look like to do the work they need to do. The exceptions pointed to by deep contextualists can, instead, be marks that the explanations in question are ones offered by defeasible generalizations. Let's take a look.

4 Defeasible generalizations

When we reflect on the sorts of explanatory generalizations deployed in various theoretical enterprises, a notable feature emerges: disciplines from epistemology to biology, from ethics to semantics, are rife with generalizations that seem explanatory even while they are porous – shot through with exceptions that cannot be usefully eliminated. Defeasibly, matches light when struck; in standard conditions, lying is wrong-making; other things being equal, fish eggs develop into fish; for the most part, pain has a negative valence; *ceteris paribus*, people mean what they say. Those drawn, as we are, to contextualist impulses will be skeptical of finding any tractable, concrete, helpful way to fill in the conditions in which the effects actually occur (of demarcating all the circumstances in which, say, fish eggs don't turn into fish). Such generalizations aren't, that is, mere enthymemes – statements that could be filled in by spelling out tacit conditions without loss of explanatory import. Yet the statements don't thereby seem empty – claiming simply that such effects *can* happen, or do unless they don't.

Neither do such generalizations seem well captured as statistical claims that the asserted connection holds with high frequency. For one thing, the interpretation is just factually unavailable with many central examples, such as the claim about fish eggs – which, as it turns out, only rarely succeed in turning into fish. More deeply, statistical generalizations, while important in life, are not robustly explanatory. Except in areas like quantum mechanics, which are ruled by genuinely statistical laws, statistical generalizations are contingent ones. But the above generalizations seem to mark some sort of explanatory, *intimate* connection between fish eggs and fish, appearances and reality, lying and wrong-making, even if they countenance exceptions.

Put metaphorically, the point of such generalizations seems to involve isolating a connection that is, for one reason or another, particularly 'telling' of something's nature.[11] Sometimes when we issue a generalization to the effect that something has a certain feature, what we really want to say is not that such a connection always, or even usually, holds, but that the conditions in which it *does* hold are particularly revealing of that item's nature, or of the broader part of reality in which the item is known. We are taking as *privileged*, in one way or another, cases in which the item has the feature specified.

Let's look at a simple example: defeasibly, matches light when struck. Only defeasibly, for there are all manner of conditions – wet, overly cold, overly hot, overly lacking in oxygen, etc. – in which matches do not light when struck, and little hope that we could specify in finite form the list of suppressed premises. Nor is the claim a simple statistical generalization. In certain circumstances – say, for those who live in watery Atlantis – the exceptional cases are far more locally common and far more salient than the non-exceptional. Rather, the generalization marks the nature of matches: more specifically, the connection between striking and lighting marks precisely the difference between seeing something as of the artifact kind 'match' and seeing it as of the natural kind 'phosphorus and crushed glass-tipped stick.' Of course, which artifactual categories one bothers to maintain has an indirect dependency on statistical frequencies: denizens of Atlantis presumably wouldn't bother demarcating something as this particular artifact, or invent matches in the first place. The point, though, is that if they were to have *this* concept, they would have the concept of something that defeasibly works in a way that it rarely works 'around here'.

More specifically, the artifact kind, where deployed, is circumscribed by marking some conditions – however frequent or rare they may contingently be – as *privileged,* and to see the behavior of matches in general as understandable by reference to departures from those conditions. Very roughly put, to understand the defeasible connection between striking and lighting that governs the concept match (to understand matches in a practical sense) is to know what conditions are privileged, to understand the various ways in which conditions can vary from the privileged ones, and to understand the differences those deviations make. It is to understand, for instance, that matches don't light when wet, unless again they are in the presence of a particularly heavy concentration of oxygen, but even then not if the temperature is near to absolute zero, and on and on. One will not be able to spell out exhaustively what privileged conditions consist in, nor the set of possible departures. But someone with a broad understanding of matches will have a good practical understanding of privileged conditions and deviations in the relevant domain – as evidenced by the fact that they generally succeed in their attempts to light matches, don't waste their matches by making attempts when there is no hope of success, etc.

To understand such generalizations, then, requires a practical grasp of a particular similarity relation among worlds – a grasp of the modal geography of worlds near to the privileged one. Our practical understanding of privileged conditions functions to give us a baseline set of conditions in which the generalization holds directly, to allow us to single out as salient the ways in which another situation may be non-privileged, and, finally, to understand what compensatory adjustments are asked for by the ways in which we there depart from privileged conditions.

It is important to emphasize this last. If all we knew were what happened in the privileged conditions – conditions, note, we often don't inhabit – we would have no idea whatsoever of the import something carried elsewhere. The generalizations would simply be a description of what exceptionlessly happens in a highly circumscribed and often unusual scope of possible worlds, with no relevance whatsoever outside that scope; life beyond the privileged conditions would be a black box.[12] The claim, then, is not simply that some circumstances are privileged, but that our understanding of the property's import *everywhere* (everywhere of relevance to the theoretical domain in question, that is) is informed by how one's situation stands in *connection* to those circumstances.

Here's another example to illustrate. Defeasibly, soccer is played with 11 players on a side. Only defeasibly, for there are all manner of variants – 20-on-20 little league games, 5-on-5 pick-up games – and no codifying the variants that might so count. Here, the privileged conditions are taken as defining the game, but not in the sense of defining rigid necessary and sufficient conditions for anything to count as soccer; rather, the rules of FIFA soccer define a *paradigm* that admits of all manner of riffs.

But consider the details of *how* one riffs on the paradigm of FIFA soccer. Suppose we play 5-on-5 soccer; we are likely also to make the goal smaller. Why? Because in the relevant sense a 5-on-5 game with smaller goals, despite two rule changes rather than one, is *more like* paradigmatic soccer than 5-on-5 with normal goals. With fewer players on the field, it is much easier to get into position to have an open shot on goal; the goals are typically shortened to compensate in order to maintain similarity in the *difficulty of scoring*.

Notice what is happening abstractly here. The paradigm or set of generalizations that obtain in the privileged conditions – here the rules of FIFA soccer – characterize an epistemic center. A large space of games, both privileged and non-privileged, are then understood in terms of their relations to this privileged center. What appeared formerly as a mass of unconnected instances of sport comes into unified focus when seen in terms of their relations to the particular paradigm, allowing defeasible generalizations play the sort of unifying role that is typical of explanatory generalizations. FIFA soccer is paradigmatic soccer; 5-on-5 soccer with normal goals is still soccer, but defectively so; kickball is not soccer at all, but rather a riff on baseball.

Understanding a defeasibility claim, then, involves not just learning to look at what happens in the space that is privileged, but learning to find one's way around an entire map of a terrain that is centered on the privileged space.

5 Typology of privilege-deviation

Put at this level of abstraction, our claim about the relation between defeasible generalizations and privileged conditions is perforce highly schematic. A more substantive view begins to emerge with a more precise understanding of the notion of privilege. It turns out that there are a number of distinct types of privilege, each with its own structure of compensatory relations to the non-privileged. Sometimes, the distinctions will correspond to different disciplines within which defeasible generalizations function, but often as not we will see a variety of privileging types within a single discipline.

One type, as we noted above, is paradigm-riff. Soccer is a good example; here is another. Most people would be willing to define a chair, functionally, as something to sit on. A moment's reflection, however, reminds us that there are any number of exceptions to this generalization – ornamental chairs made intentionally frail, for instance. Moreover, it is hard to see how we could say once and for all what counts – whether the object at the Museum of Modern Art is a chair, or a work of art, or both. Nonetheless, it seems right to think there is an intimate connection between the concept 'chair' and the function of holding people in repose; and we might intuitively think to put the point by saying something like 'ceteris paribus, chairs are things we can sit on'.

Such a claim is not a statistical one. A very opulent, or orthopedically challenged, society might in fact have more ornamental than functional chairs lying about. Nor are we saying that there's anything defective about the exceptions (they're no good to sit on, to be sure, but that doesn't keep them from being fabulous – and fabulously sought-after – chairs). What we mean, instead, is that all chairs in the privileged class are fit for sitting, and that the relation between privileged and peripheral chairs is something like that of theme and variation. The ornamental chair is a riff on the theme of chair; and one can't understand a riff without understanding the theme to which it stands as variation. (This is of course close to what Wittgenstein had in mind as a family resemblance: our point is that conceptual families, like their human counterparts, are rarely egalitarian.) The privileging move here, then, is about what has, as it were, conceptual priority: to understand something as an ornamental chair one must understand the notion of chairs that are for sitting on, but not vice versa.

In this case we had a single concept, the extension of which was given via some notion of acceptable variation from a paradigmatic theme. Ornamental chairs are still chairs, though they are so by way of similarity to a different sort of chair. But paradigm-riff privileging often comes in a richer form. Consider irony. An ironic use of a sentence is a speech act in which what is meant is roughly the opposite of that which is usually meant by the utterance of that sentence. ('Well, George W. Bush sure proved a wise and peace loving leader.') But irony is not simply a species of ambiguity, in which a sentence said in one tone of voice has one meaning and in another the opposite. For irony to function as it does, it must wear its reversal of semantic valence on its sleeve. It presents itself explicitly as being a non-standard use. Not, again, in a statistical sense: we could, in principle, turn into a society of Oscar Wildes, using irony more than literal speech. The point is that these speech acts nonetheless function by *carrying a trace* of 'standard' use. Utterances of *P*, we might put it, *always* have the property of defeasibly meaning *P*, even when used ironically to mean not-*P*. To use a sentence ironically is thus to use it in a way that can be understood only as derivative upon literal uses. Irony is essentially a riff on literal use, but a riff whose character as a riff is essential to it. (Compare kitsch in art.)

Sometimes, the privileged/non-privileged relation is constituted by a form of justificatory dependence. To illustrate, imagine having a perception as of a red cup. Having such a perception typically has a positive epistemic valence vis-à-vis the belief that there is a red cup; put into our language, defeasibly, appearances that *P* are justifying of beliefs that *P*. But sometimes, of course, having the appearance pushes in the direction of not believing its content – as when you know the evil demon is playing with your eyesight in a particular way. Epistemological contextualists will argue that there is no spelling out once and for all, in any relatively concrete terms, the conditions under which the perceptual experience is justifying. Nonetheless, it seems natural to think there is some sort of intimate connection between appearance and justification. For when appearances *are* unreliable – when seeing as *P*, or appearance that *P*, is not justifying of *P* – one's knowledge of this fact itself must rely on justification provided by contexts in which one *can* rely on appearances (as when, say, we see the evil demon at work). Cases in which one is justified in taking one's appearances at their word stand as epistemically unproblematic; it is cases in which one is not so justified that demand explanation – and an explanation precisely that appeals to cases of the former type.

Appearances, then, can mislead, but the relation between an appearance that *P* and a justified belief that *P* is deeper than the connection between, say, a justified belief that *P* and a justified belief that *Q* – *even* when *P* and *Q* happen to be tightly evidentially related; and this is so, even if given one's own background beliefs, the second actually holds more often in your vicinity than the first. For while the belief that *P*, may in fact provide evidence that *Q*, it's of the essence of an appearance that *P*, that it is defeasibly connected to justification of *P*. Appearances, we might put it, are necessarily *defeasibly trustworthy*. They carry this feature – the property of being defeasibly trustworthy – as a trace even into situations in which their justificatory import changes from trustworthy to non-trustworthy.[13]

Sometimes, the justificatory dependence embedded in the privileging move is more specific yet: a counter-valence story must also make essential reference to something that has gone wrong. Think again about the epistemic case. Amongst the exceptions we can encounter to being able to take appearances at face value, some are cases in which we can nonetheless reach, as it were, as much justification as those in privileged conditions. If we have available a clear translation manual, we can make adjustments that preserve justification (think of the quick inferential adjustment we do every time we see a bent stick in the water). Often, though, cases in which one cannot take appearances at face value indicate that one is in a worse situation, by knowledge's own lights: someone who's just entered the Hall of Holograms is in a situation which, however fun, is epistemically deficient. Sometimes, then, non-privileged conditions are not just *deviant,* they are *defective,* and a proper understanding of non-privileged conditions involves not merely a justificatory dependence on privileged conditions, but an evaluation in terms of their particular sort of departure from privileged conditions.

One other version of privileging worth mentioning here is idealization-approximation. Consider the ideal gas law, $pv = nrt$. To have any validity as an empirical law of the natural world, this claim must be doing more than making a claim about perfectly spherical, perfectly elastic point bodies (i.e. non-existent entities). And clearly it is. The ideal gas law can function as a law in virtue of the fact that a wide range of actual gases serve to *approximate* the behavior of ideal gases. Roughly, as one gets a natural system more and more similar to the description of an ideal gas, the ideal gas law predictions become more and more accurate; put more formally, there is a continuous monotonic function from similarity to degree of accuracy. Although actual gases differ from ideal gases in all sorts of ways, the predictions that we get by supposing them to be ideal are helpfully approximately accurate.

This case of approximation-idealization, we want to argue, is just a very precise and quantitative version of the general point about defeasible laws, namely, that they function explanatorily in virtue of the fact that to understand them is to understand what sort of difference various deviations from a posited set of standard conditions makes. The gas law (or putative gas law, since of course it may not be ultimately correct) governing both the actual and ideal world, we would argue, is:

   defeasibly $(pv = nrt)$.

There are, then, many different species of privilege and relation-to-privilege that determine compensatory moves. Details aside, what we are looking at in each case is a realm in which one postulates a strategy of explaining all relevant cases in terms of a privileged group. Sometimes this involves no more than showing how a given artifact can be seen as a plausible riff on a paradigmatic theme. Sometimes it requires a detailed justificatory dependence of our conclusions in non-privileged conditions on conclusions drawn in privileged ones. Sometimes, we predict on the basis of the given context's similarity to ideal ones. But in all cases it is the structure of privilege and compensatory adjustment, along with the explanations this generates, that lie at the heart of defeasible generalizations. The fundamental commitment undertaken in asserting a defeasible principle of this sort – in putting it forward as an explanatory principle – is to a particular structuring of a region of possibility space: it is a commitment to classifying and understanding all relevant cases in terms of their relation to ones in which the generalization in question holds.

Of course, whether in the end one is entitled to a given such postulation is its own question. As with any theoretical generalization, a defeasible claim must earn its keep as part of some overall explanatory enterprise. Broadly speaking, the appropriateness of a privileging strategy has one of two sources. Sometimes, a privilege/deviation structure is implicit or internal, as it were, to the concept in question: the meaning of 'chair' is one that anchors certain features – namely, ones that allow the entity to be sat in – as paradigmatic, with deviations judged by the standard of allowing riff. Other times, we come to regard certain conditions as privileged for a kind because of the theoretical benefit one can garner by doing so. Treating perfectly spherical and elastic gas molecules as privileged ideals, for instance, is warranted because doing so gets us well managed compensatory moves, which in turn helps us with prediction: by mapping the world with these ideals at its 'center', we succeed in obtaining a tractable theory across a wide range of worlds. Here, then, 'privileged conditions' are a posit (which, as Quine points out, does not mean unreal).[14]

For another example of the latter, return to fish eggs. There are of course an infinite number of trajectories that fish eggs could take, from developing into fish, to being ennucleated with sheep DNA and becoming a sheep, to breaking down into nutrients for a turtle, to being irradiated and turning into a strange and horrid swamp monster. Nonetheless, developmental biologists elevate one such trajectory as a 'natural' one, namely one that does not call for explanation (at least at this level of theory); and in this sense we circumscribe some developments as expressions of an organism's 'nature' (if a fish egg is a possible salamander, it is a *potential* fish). All of this, though, is reflective of the inductive strategies that have proved successful for the discipline in question – here, the usefulness of elevating a given developmental trajectory, under given conditions, as natural. It is in this way that biologists earn the right to say that what it is to be a fish egg is to be the sort of thing that in standard conditions develops into a fish.

Whichever form they take, though, in proposing these sorts of defeasible generalizations, disciplines posit a structure of privilege and deviation as a strategy useful for some theoretical goal. If it is indeed useful in the way hoped for, the generalization earns its keep.

Given their uncodifiable nature, the epistemology of defeasible generalizations is at base an irreducibly skills-based epistemology. In this respect we are like Dancy. But on our view, the skills are expanded from discernment, gestalt and comparison, to skills of understanding and recognizing what is deviant and normal, what is paradigmatic and emendational, what is conceptually prior or central – in short, the skill of navigating the normative-cum-modal geography of the possibility space relevant to a given discipline.

6 Morality & defeasibility

We want to argue that defeasible generalizations are a promising way to admit the deep contextualism Dancy and others have advanced while retaining what we see as reason and explanation's essential connection to generalization. The exceptions pointed to by particularists can be marks that the explanations in question exhibit the structure of privilege and compensatory moves. We want to argue that many key moral concepts – indeed, the workhorses of moral theory – are the subjects of defeasible moral generalizations. Of course we cannot argue in detail for this claim here, but we can give examples of some directions a morality of defeasible principles would likely move in.

Take the example of pain. We believe it is important to any adequate morality to recognize that defeasibly, pain is bad-making. Here the privileging is meant to mark out a paradigm-riff move. Sometimes, as when the pain contains a phenomenological element of pleasure ('it hurts so good'), we recognize conceptual extension of the plain variation sort – a permitted extension of the category, akin to treating a pick-up soccer game as part of a genus paradigmatically defined by the FIFA game. Other times, non-standard pain – pain which is not bad-making – bears the more complex relation to the paradigm that irony does to non-ironic speech: the good-making pain wears its non-standard meaning 'on its sleeve' as constitutive of its meaning. In athletics, for instance, to give Elijah Millgram's nice example, it is only because pain is paradigmatically something to be avoided that the notion of physical challenge has the meaning, and the status of constitutive good, that it does. It is only *because* pain is normally bad-making, then, that we can understand this sort of good-making instance.

To understand pain's nature, then, is to understand not just that it is sometimes not-bad, but to understand that there is an explanatory asymmetry between cases in which it is bad and cases in which it is not: it is only because pain is paradigmatically bad-making that athletic challenges come to have the meaning they do, and hence provide the kind of rich backdrop against which instances of pain can emerge as not-bad-making, as not always and everywhere to-be-avoided.

A similar analysis, we believe, can make more perspicuous the claim that we are motivated 'under the guise of the good'. As many have urged, an unqualified version of this claim is too strong: it seems possible to love evil and despise the good. Yet loving the good and loving evil are not conceptually on par. More plausible, we believe, is that the good is defeasibly loved. Exceptions can occur, but such cases, on analogy with irony, cannot be understood except *as* perversity. One can understand attraction to evil only parasitically on attraction to good; more specifically, one can understand rational motivation towards evil only as a non-standard reversal of good's normal valence. Pursuit of the good *cannot* be a perversity, though it can be a statistical anomaly; for what gets counted *as* the good is precisely what one is non-perversely attracted to.

Moral privileging can also involve justificatory dependence, with all its attendant complexity. Lying, for instance, is defeasibly wrong-making: it can be right-making or neutral. But justifying that status often makes essential reference to contexts in which it has its classically negative valence. Thus imagine lying while playing the game Diplomacy. Lying is morally neutral in the game because people agree to play a game in which the point is to lie at the crucial moment in a convincing and strategic manner. More specifically, lying here has a neutral valence because of prior agreements, but, crucially, agreements that must be seen as having been made in a context in which the normal moral valence of lying holds. If we are now in a situation in which lying is not wrong-making, then there is nothing prima facie bad about lying when we make agreements about what game to play. Thus, understanding lying's good-making status relies on invoking a notion, consent, that itself cannot be understood without invoking a framework in which the normal case is not to lie. The 'defeasibly-bad-making' nature of lying, thus, leaves a trace: a proper moral understanding of one's situation in Diplomacy includes an awareness of the fact that one is in a non-privileged situation.

In this case, we see a moral-justificatory species of the privilege-compensatory move genus. One can rightly regard some cases of lying as morally unproblematic. Moral understanding crafts coherence upon a mish-mash of cases in which lying has one valence here, another there, by privileging the negative valence cases, and accounting for the range of deviations from the norm in terms of agreements carried out in the privileged conditions.

And sometimes, as in the epistemic case, a moral valence switch indicates, not just deviance but *defect*: the situation is worse by morality's own lights. If it is honorable to tell a falsehood to the Nazi guard, for instance, it's because something has gone awry: there is something badly amiss (namely, the Nazi's evil) from the moral point of view. It is, if you will, a bad-making feature of the situation that lying is now a moral plus (*would* that it weren't honorable here to lie, that there were no people so corrupted that the truth is not owed to them). In these sorts of cases, the connection between lying and the bad leaves a very particular kind of trace. To exhibit moral understanding in the Nazi world – to navigate its moral terrain – requires that one understand one's situation, not just as deviant, but as thereby morally *defective*. Even here, then, when one occupies a world in which most lies are in fact honorable, one must still appreciate that lying has an intimate tie to the bad.

In some cases, the explanatory paradigm involves a moral ideal. Essential to our understanding of a person, we would claim, is that, in certain idealized situations, certain behaviors are owed to them: in conditions of full information, genuine autonomy, and basic trust – the Kingdom of Ends, in short – persons are owed the truth. But it is crucial not to take this special case to be general. The sort of privileging relevant to defeasible generalizations is typically not one of an ideal in this sense; indeed, a great deal of morality functions around a paradigm that is anything *but* ideal. Think of the morality of charity, solidarity, resistance to evil or injustice. We do not doubt that there are crucial defeasible moral generalizations in such areas (defeasibly, one should resist living in ways that are complicit with structural injustice), but these certainly are not to be understood as generalizations holding in morally perfect conditions, lacking as those are in things like poverty, injustice, and evil.

Whether the privileged is also valorized or not, the deeper point is that all situations in which it *is* morally wrong-making to lie are privileged in a deeply conceptual manner: part of what it means to take something to be a *person* is that one understand the creature as belonging to a kind that defeasibly has a claim on our honesty.

As a final illustration, consider the following general norm: defeasibly, not taking people's statements about what they want as expressing their desires is bad-making. (More colloquially, "'No!' means No!'.) There are contexts, such as certain practices of S&M, in which this norm is routinely false: it is not wrong-making to interpret 'Oh, please stop!' as expressing a desire that one continue. Here, too, though, there is a sort of justificatory dependence. It is *because* people have freely agreed to take part in this practice in a context governed by a commitment to the defeasible norm 'take people at their word', that *not* taking them at their word gets to here enjoy positive valence. If a practice of ignoring statements of desire like this were to arise not in any way grounded in open statements of desire to participate, they would remain morally problematic in the usual way. The authority of not taking people at their word in the S&M room, then, is somehow grounded in open statements of desire to participate taken freely in a privileged situation. We have, then, a clear norm – namely, 'take people at their word' – and a clear sense of the justificatory dependence of contexts in which this norm is defeated upon contexts in which it isn't.

Note, again, that it's highly unlikely that we can codify out the content of what folks have consented to, other than some trivial principle such as 'one should take people seriously in a different manner in here than outside'. For there is, we are told, no blanket moral entitlement to ignore people's statements of desire while in the practice of S&M. (Nor are things as simple as 'take them literally when the safe word is used'.) The norms that capture the contours of interpretation are ones that develop, evolve and gain in complexity with the evolution of the practice itself. There is an asymmetric moral dependency between the privileged context in which we take people at their word and the S&M context in which we routinely don't, but the game has its own evolutionary trajectory. Justificatory dependence is quite a different matter from codifiability.

Details aside, the features of an act that are genuinely explanatory of its moral status – as opposed to constituent pieces of a narrative – are, we argue, those that are governed by and caught up in a structure provided by defeasible explanatory generalizations. Though there are cases in which we understand a moral situation by discerning rightness and wrongness in the details that together form a narrative, often we point to features – promise-keeping, lying, inflicting pain – that are explanatory in a way that the various pieces of a storyline are not; and this is because they are features that are the subject of defeasible generalizations. Pointing to the fact that an action is a case of lying is explanatory in a way that pointing to surrounding detail is not (and this even though the moral landscape is rife with exceptions to lying's wrong-making status) because lying is defeasibly wrong-making. It's not that lying always, or must, or even usually has that status, but wrong-making is the valence it has in conditions that are privileged in certain ways, and whatever status it has in deviant circumstances is a function of the relation of those circumstances to the privileged conditions and the compensatory moves called for by that relation. Where lying lacks this valence, as it sometimes or even often does, it is in virtue of the way the context deviates from privileged conditions.

Such a view can maintain a radical position on the valence-switching propensity of moral considerations without flattening the moral field in such a way as to render all morally relevant considerations moral equals. Surprising your partner and the avoidance of pain can both be good-making, may even be the reason something was good in a particular situation, but the similarity ends there. For though surprise can have various moral imports in various contexts, it has none of them defeasibly. In contrast, pain not only can have a negative moral import, it always, and necessarily, has the property of being defeasibly bad-making. In this way, we agree with Dancy that some properties 'come already switched on' with a particular valence, but not understood as some brute metaphysical feature unconnected to the giving of reasons and explanations. Rather, to say that some features have a defeasible valence means that they have that valence in situations that are fundamental in one of the various senses.

Defeasible import, notice, is importantly different from another idea sometimes raised in discussions of defeasibility, namely, *epistemic defaults*. Epistemic defaults are essentially 'start-here' points. A claim, or action, is default reasonable (justified, entitled) in a given context just in case one is entitled to believe or do it unless and until a substantive challenge is presented.

This is a notion of prima facie justification.[15] It has been suggested from time to time that some such epistemic notion of a default might go some way toward softening the particularist position. The idea is that whereas a simple particularism seems to put everything on a par – pretty much anything can be morally good-making, morally bad-making, or neutral against the right contextual background – nonetheless some things come with a 'start-here' moral valence. But epistemic defaults simply won't do for this purpose, precisely because they are contextual in the wrong way.

When we come upon a context in which the known frequency of exceptions to a given connection are common, one is no longer entitled to treat the connection as an epistemic default. But in trying to recover the asymmetry in the moral significance of concepts – for example, in trying to understand the particular depth that the connection between lying and wrong-makingness has and which surprise and good-makingness lacks – we want something that is precisely not contextually variable in *this way*. Whatever the connection between lying and wrong-making is, whatever the deep, theoretically significant explanatory connection that one must grasp in order to so much as take on board the moral concept of lying, it is a connection that persists *always*. Even in situations in which lying is not wrong making – indeed, even in situations like a Nazi take-over in which one doesn't rationally so much as give truth-telling a default status – we want to say that lying is still *defeasibly* wrong-making. One who fails to understand that – that is, one whose grasp of the moral landscape stops at the local reasons and its local defaults – is missing an absolutely crucial feature of the moral landscape. Lying here might be the rational and virtuous moral default, for lying might usually be right-making given the systemic infestation of Nazis; but a morally astute person sees this very fact as deeply morally significant. Lying, one wants to say, calls out for another valence, and its reversal is a crucial feature of the situation.

Such constancy is precisely a feature of defeasibility as we understand it. Although lying is sometimes bad-making, sometimes not, it is always the case that worlds in which lying is bad-making are theoretically privileged. The moral status of lying in any situation whatsoever is measured in relation to the privileged cases. Lying, that is, is necessarily defeasibly bad-making.

Of course, and again, as with any discipline in which one posits theoretical generalizations, defeasible or not, the proof is in the explanatory success. One puts a theory forward, and lets it confront the tribunal of our practice and experience, to see if it is useful to a given explanatory enterprise. In the case of moral theory, we are not dealing (in the first instance, at least) with empirical predictions. Rather, the holistic constraint on the proposal is that it gets right and helps to organize our first-order moral conclusions – whatever those might encompass. Some will think the 'data' of morality to be more analytic, some more synthetic, depending on their position on various other issues in moral philosophy. But whatever one's conception of that which tests a moral explanatory hypothesis, our suggestion is that there is no in-principle obstacle to allowing that hypothesis to work in the way that defeasible generalizations do.

If the view being sketched here is right, then most ethical generalizations are irreducibly porous. They are shot through with exceptions we cannot eliminate. These generalizations can nonetheless count as robustly explanatory and insightful. Adducing them has a power a list of instances does not, for it situates instances within a framework that maintains some as exceptions to others' rule. Attempts to replace such generalizations with statistical or enthymematic surrogates result in a loss, rather than a gain, in explanatory power.

7 Conclusion

Particularists such as Dancy, we believe, give elegant and convincing reasons for believing that exceptions are not the enemy to moral understanding, and that attempts to use generalizations to expunge them are bankrupt. If exceptionless necessary universal generalizations are what one means by a moral principle, we agree that they are suspect entities. (Or, as Dancy says at one point, 'If this is what principles are, we're better off without them.') But once one gives up the widespread assumption that generalizations must be exceptionless if they are to do genuine and fundamental explanatory theoretical work, one can be skeptical of moral 'principles' in this classic sense, without being skeptical of moral explanatory generalizations.

More specifically, ethics can maintain a radical position on the valence-switching capacity of evidential considerations without saying that the hard-won lessons of philosophical reflection are merely useful local inductive tools, or pedagogic crutches to be left behind when enlightenment hits. By reconceiving what theoretical generalizations in morality are like we allow ourselves to accept many of the classic principlist positions: reasons, as explanations, cannot be unmoored from generalizations; concepts, as Sellars so succinctly put it, involve laws and are inconceivable without them; in the absence of an empirically successful theory – even if tentative, implicit and largely inarticulate – one has no good grounds for belief, and in the absence of principles, there is no theory.

Deep moral contextualism is consistent with deep moral theory. Indeed, even if *all* explanatory generalizations in morality turn out to be inelimin-ably exception-laden, morality can still be a terrain governed by theoretical generalizations. We should be anti-principlist, if principle is understood in the classic sense of an exceptionless covering law; but we need not – and should not – be anti-generalist.

Notes

1 Dancy (1993), (2000b), (2004), Little (2000), Murdoch (1970), McNaughton (1988).
2 The pain example is from Milgram (2002), the Diplomacy example a variant from McNaughton (1988), and the sadistic pleasure example from Dancy (1993).

3 See, for instance, the essays in Hooker and Little (2000); for a recent defense of generalism, see McKeever and Ridge (2006).

4 See, for instance, Dancy (2004).

5 Lance and Little (2004), (2006a), (2006b). We used to call ourselves particularists to signal our commitment to the irreducible presence of exceptions, despite our commitment to the importance of explanatory generalizations; 'deep contextualist' now seems a clearer way of registering our position.

6 This article borrows liberally from all of our previous articles; see especially those listed in note 5.

7 McDowell (1979); see also Little (2000: sec. 3); Jackson, Pettit and Smith (2000).

8 The 'broad' is a shift for Little from her (2000), in which she limited exceptions to claimed connections between the natural and the moral. She now believes that the Rawlsian distinction, alluded to above, between concept and conception helpfully disentangles different impulses that theorists may have with respect to thick moral concepts.

9 Our thanks to Dancy for pressing us on this point.

10 Our proposal for the adjectival form of 'Dancy'.

11 There are, of course, other sorts of 'hedged' generalizations, some of them expressed by the same forms of words. So, for example, some generalizations merely serve to isolate a constant force. When we say 'Other things being equal, a mass in motion will continue with the same vector of motion', we are simply expressing that there is a constant inertial force. In moral theory this is the Rossian move, one that is clearly insufficient for anyone who has gone down the road with the radical contextualist. In other cases, a generalization can express a mere epistemic default – a sort of 'start here' position. On this reading, to say, for example, 'provisionally, *P*' is to say that one is entitled to accept *P*, unless and until positive reason is given to deny it. We discuss why this notion cannot do the work of genuinely explanatory defeasible generalizations in Lance and Little (2004). Finally, some generalizations may invoke a simple contextual restriction. Sylvain Bromberger, (1992) argues that certain generalizations simply tell us what goes on in a particular range of circumstances and leaves all else as a black box, telling us nothing at all. Again, such generalizations are severely limited in the theoretical work they can do, since they by definition tell us nothing outside the particular circumscribed range. Our goal here is not to analyze the use(s) of particular bits of natural language, but to isolate a semantic and epistemic function that porous generalizations can play, one that is crucial to the project of moral theory. For this reason, we ignore these different readings in what follows and develop one more suited to the needs of contextualist moral theory.

12 As per Bromberger, see note 11.

13 See Lance and Little (2004).

14 We might put it by saying that some privileging moves are more analytic and others more synthetic. Of course the analytic/synthetic distinction is a dicey business, and we use the idea guardedly. In the end, we think there are reasonable and important versions of this distinction that do not purport to do the sort of work in foundationalist epistemology that Quine criticized. Those interested are directed to chapter 2 of Lance and O'Leary-Hawthorne (1997).

15 Many epistemologists have emphasized the importance of such default entitlements, including Brandom, Michael Williams, and Lance and O'Leary-Hawthorne (1997). The logic of default generalizations is discussed also by many philosophers including Jeff Horty. Dancy's defaults, notice, should also not be confused with epistemic defaults: his are straightforwardly meant to mark a metaphysical status.

5 Usable moral principles[1]

Pekka Väyrynen

1 Introduction

One important strand in moral particularism concerns moral practice. We ought not, particularists maintain, to rely on moral principles in moral thought and judgment because they provide poor guidance for doing the right thing. Another important strand concerns the structure of the moral domain. We ought not, particularists maintain, to see moral theorizing as a project of stating and defending substantive principles concerning the rightness and wrongness of actions, the value of states of affairs, the fairness of societal arrangements, and so on. This is because (depending on the particularist) there are no true moral principles, or we have no good reason to expect there are any, or, even if there are true moral principles, moral facts and distinctions don't depend in any way on there being any. In other work, I defend a generalist account of the structure of the moral domain against the second strand in particularism by defending a novel kind of hedged moral principles that accommodate certain central insights of particularists, but nonetheless support a moderate form of generalism.[2] In this paper, I defend a generalist account of moral guidance against the first strand in particularism and, specifically, its claim of *principle abstinence* (or PA, for short): we ought not to rely on moral principles in moral judgment because they fail to provide adequate moral guidance.[3] My main aim is to show that the kind of hedged principles I defend elsewhere also provide adequate moral guidance, thereby counting as appropriately usable in moral thought. But I also hope that at least the broad outlines of my argument will be found acceptable to generalists more widely.

2 Two arguments for principle abstinence

Ethics aims at action, as the saying goes. Moral theories should enable us to comprehend aspects of ourselves and our world in ways that offer us guidance in our moral lives. Implicit in this thought is a meta-theoretical norm concerning an important and traditional role of moral theories: other things being at least roughly equal, moral theories are better to the extent that they provide adequate moral guidance. If PA is true, then generalist moral theories would seemingly fail to secure this action-guiding role for moral principles, since principles would be poorly suited to enabling us to act rightly or exhibit moral virtue. I'll begin by distinguishing two sorts of argument strategy for PA. I'll argue that one is unsound and the other has yet to be made out in the literature.

The first strategy is to base PA on the theoretical strand in particularism. Jonathan Dancy, for one, offers this sort of argument: 'Particularism claims that generalism is the cause of many bad moral decisions. ... Reasons function in new ways on new occasions, and if we don't recognize this fact and adapt our practice to it, we will make bad decisions' (1993: 64).[4] This is to infer PA from *reasons holism*, the general doctrine about reasons that no necessary connection exists between the property of being a reason and the property of always being the same kind of reason (either positive or negative). The core thought is that applying reasons holism to the moral domain helps to show that there are no (or very few) true general principles that are well suited to enabling us to act rightly or exhibit moral virtue.[5]

We could construct several arguments for PA that instantiate the above strategy. But we needn't bother, because the general strategy is unsound. It is unsound because reasons holism is available to generalists and particularists alike. Certain kinds of (true) substantive moral principles can exist even if reasons holism is true.[6] It remains unsound even if we weaken particularism to the claim that, even if there are true principles, moral facts and distinctions in no way depend on there being any.[7] For this form of particularism leaves open the possibility that there are moral patterns that can be accurately captured by principles or generalizations that also are well suited to enabling us to act rightly and observe moral distinctions, such as that between right and wrong, in the ways of the practically wise. Moral principles may, therefore, be able to function as guides even if, contrary to generalism as I'll understand it, moral facts and distinctions don't depend on the existence of a comprehensive set of true substantive moral principles. (By 'substantive moral principle' I mean a (synthetic) proposition that identifies conditions or properties in virtue of which something has a given moral property such as rightness, and which are thus explanatory of why it is right. A set S of principles is comprehensive in the relevant sense if, for any particular moral fact M, a principle or a set of principles in S is required for M to hold.[8]) As a view in moral metaphysics, generalism implies no particular view of the relation between moral thought and principles. For example, it doesn't imply that the only way people can make moral judgments at all is by basing them on principles.

The second strategy is to base PA on the idea that, even if moral principles play a necessary role in accounting for the nature and basis of moral facts and distinctions, they might have some features other than inaccuracy or context-insensitivity which make them unsuitable, or at least unnecessary, for enabling us to act rightly or exhibit moral virtue. One *prima facie* hurdle for this strategy is that, independently of their role in moral theory, moral principles might be useful practical tools in solving various problems of interpersonal assurance, coordination, and the like.[9] Another is that the most we get from particularists by way of features that allegedly make principles provide poor moral guidance, even if generalism is true, is the claim that principles encourage us to make moral decisions without a sensitive and detailed examination of particular cases.[10] I'll argue in §6 that this particular claim is false because acceptance of moral principles entails a commitment to developing one's moral sensitivity and judgment. But, for all we have seen so far, principles might indeed have features that make them provide poor moral guidance. To assess this possibility, we need to know what constitutes adequate guidance and what it would be for moral principles to provide it.

3 Moral principles and adequate moral guidance

A principle might accurately identify conditions that explain why some such moral property as rightness is instantiated, and so pull its theoretical weight as a standard of right action, without being of much use for agents in their practical thinking. (By 'practical thinking' I mean rational transitions in thought which terminate, if not in action, then at least in a decision to act in a certain way, but which needn't proceed explicitly from premises to conclusions.) Conversely, in order to provide guidance, a generalization needn't identify such conditions with full accuracy or cover all cases. The explanatory and the guiding functions of moral principles are logically distinct. In order for moral principles to function as guides, they need only to provide appropriate guidance to conscientious agents who care about living up to the principles they accept.

Intuitively, moral guidance amounts to offering more than hindsight in the face of moral novelty, uncertainty, and difficulty; it amounts to offering some *strategy* for acting well. More precisely, for a given standard of right action to provide adequate guidance is for it to contribute non-trivially to a reliable overall strategy for doing the right thing for the right reasons that is available to the practical thinking of conscientious, morally committed agents.[11] (I'll abbreviate this idea as 'contributing to a reliable strategy', and 'doing the right thing for the right reasons' as 'acting well', except when greater precision matters.)

We can explicate this idea of what constitutes adequate moral guidance as follows.[12] First, an overall strategy for acting rightly must be reliable to some sufficient degree, because following an unreliable strategy would all too easily direct us to wrong actions. Whatever the sufficient degree of reliability is, the relevant kind of reliability is *conditional reliability*: any strategy for acting well is reliable only to the extent that we operate on an accurate (non-moral) conception of our circumstances.[13] Regarding the scope of reliability, it seems plausible that an overall strategy should exhibit *robust reliability:* it should be reliable across some fairly wide range of possible worlds, and so its reliability should be correspondingly independent of the world the agent happens to inhabit.[14] Robust reliability allows that just what generalizations will figure in a reliable overall strategy may vary across worlds. Someone who adopts a 'shoot first and ask questions later' policy, as part of their overall strategy for acting well in a world in which adhering to the policy just happens reliably to make them perform right actions, isn't deploying a reliable overall strategy unless their acceptance of the policy is sensitive to the fact that such a world is, contingently, the world that they happen to inhabit.[15] If they would just as well have adopted this policy had they lived in a peaceful world where the policy would reliably lead to wrong actions, then theirs isn't a case of moral guidance in the relevant sense. For, given the truth of this counterfactual, the policy 'shoot first and ask questions later' would make no contribution to the reliability of their overall strategy for acting well. The overall package including the selection and deployment of guides isn't robustly reliable in this case. The rationale for the requirement that a guiding generalization must not merely be *part of* a reliable strategy for acting well but must *contribute* to its reliability is that a generalization that fails to play the latter role may be an idle wheel in guidance.

Second, the strategy to whose reliability a guiding generalization must contribute must be a strategy for doing the right thing *for the right reasons*, because even if doing what is right for non-moral reasons (say, to avoid punishment) were a reliable way to act rightly, it wouldn't be a case of *moral* guidance.[16] A generalization provides appropriate guidance to agents who accept it as a guide only to the extent that their acceptance of it leads them to perform right actions if they try to adhere to it.

Third, to assess whether a strategy provides adequate guidance we need only to consider conscientious, morally committed agents. For unreliability in the hands of lazy or careless agents indicates no fault *in the strategy*. But the strategy must be *available* to practical thinking. If the only sort of factors that contribute to its reliability identified features of right actions which not even a conscientious agent can access (or can access only in hindsight), then the strategy would be useless in trying to decide what the right thing to do is. But a guide that is available to one moral agent might be useless (say, too complex or difficult to apply) to another, or it might be available only in some but not all contexts to one and the same agent. So, adequate guidance requires guides for particular types of agents in particular kinds of contexts. A strategy S for acting well is unavailable to a given type of agent A if its use by A requires information or inferences that are unobtainable or infeasible to A. The following *cognitive condition* explains why S cannot be unmanageable to A: S is available to A only if the conditions for using S lie within A's cognitive ken. If moral principles are to provide adequate guidance for normal humans, they must contribute to reliable strategies for acting well which agents with limited cognitive capacities and resources can use.

Fourth, this cognitive condition, and more generally the idea that adequate guidance requires guides for particular types of agents in particular kinds of contexts, might lead us to think that generalist models of moral guidance would fail to apply to most agents, if moral principles could provide accurate standards of right and wrong only by being too complex or difficult to apply for most moral agents. But complexity alone doesn't doom principles to providing poor moral guidance. What adequate guidance requires is that moral principles contribute non-trivially to a reliable and available overall strategy for acting well. A principle may do so either *directly* by figuring in an agent's practical thinking or *indirectly* by recommending modes of deliberation or helping to identify policies, heuristic guides, or simple rules that are sufficiently robustly reliable. For example, some Kantians think of the Categorical Imperative as a back-grounded regulator of maxims of action.

More familiarly, many utilitarians grant that the principle of utility is too difficult for most ordinary agents to apply directly, because the sorts of evidence and calculations which are required in order to determine what maximizes utility tend to be so complex as to violate the cognitive condition introduced above. But utilitarians often argue that the principle of utility provides indirect guidance by selecting for moral precepts which best enable ordinary agents to maximize utility, even as those precepts sometimes misfire by failing to pick out what is right from the utilitarian point of view.[17] Such precepts are, in effect, a series of heuristics that have some false implications concerning what really matters, namely utility. But they may nonetheless be adequate as guides for acting well.

Given this characterization of what adequate moral guidance is, PA in effect says that moral principles fail to contribute non-trivially to a reliable overall strategy for acting well that is available to the practical thinking of conscientious, morally committed agents. If this claim were true, then moral principles seemingly wouldn't provide adequate moral guidance.[18] What I'll call the Guidance Argument against PA and on behalf of generalist moral guidance can be set out as follows:

(G1)   Generalism can provide adequate moral guidance if moral principles can contribute non-trivially to a reliable and available overall strategy for acting well.

(G2)   For any conscientious and morally committed agent *A*, if *A*'s acceptance of true principles shapes *A*'s responsiveness to the right moral reasons, those principles can contribute non-trivially to some reliable strategy for acting well that is available to *A*.

(G3)   For any conscientious and morally committed agent *A*, *A*'s acceptance of (true) moral principles shapes *A*'s responsiveness to (the right) moral reasons.

(C1)   So, for any such agent, there is some reliable and available strategy for acting well such that the principles which the agent accepts can contribute non-trivially to its reliability (where the strategy may be different for different agents). [G2, G3]

(C2)   So, generalism can provide adequate moral guidance. PA is false. [G1, C1]

The Guidance Argument is valid. Since (G1) is true by our hypothesis of what constitutes adequate guidance, I'll take (G1) as given. The action is in defending (G2) and (G3), then. I believe that these premises are defensible by many forms of generalism. My defense of (G2) will appeal to an account of moral principles as a kind of hedged principles that tolerate exceptions. But I begin with (G3).

4 Responsiveness to reasons and acceptance of principles

On any model of moral guidance, acting well involves some kind of responsiveness to the right- and wrong-making features, and hence some kind of responsiveness to moral reasons. I'll argue that acceptance of moral principles shapes conscientious, morally committed agents' responsiveness to moral reasons in ways which make moral principles suited to contribute to a reliable strategy for acting well. To defend (G3), we need to know what it is to be responsive to moral reasons and to accept moral principles.

Responsiveness to moral reasons is but a special case of responsiveness to reasons in general. In rough and generic terms, agents who are responsive to reasons (of a given kind) have a relatively stable tendency to form beliefs and intentions (of the relevant kind) that are more or less determinate functions of such characteristics as the contents of the relevant kind of inputs, such as beliefs, desires, intentions, and experiences and other 'seemings' of various sorts. When not mistaken about their reasons, they form beliefs and intentions on the basis of considerations that in fact are reasons. The natural explanation of what in one's psychological makeup underlies such a tendency is a complex disposition to not merely *conform to* but *be guided by* reason. The disposition in question is a disposition to respond, at least within a certain range of circumstances, with those actions and attitudes for which one has reasons (or, at least, reasons that pass some threshold of deliberative significance), and in a way that at least roughly reflects the relative strengths of those reasons. Being responsive to reasons requires such responses only within a certain range of circumstances, however, because we know that interfering factors may 'mask' the disposition (that is, prevent it from being manifested even under its 'triggering' conditions). Such factors include external manipulation of many forms, as well as various cognitive and temperamental factors, such as certain biases, fatigue, listlessness, and depression, which may contingently interfere with the operation of one's cognitive or practical capacities and abilities.

The disposition to be guided by reason is best understood *de re*, as a disposition to respond on the basis of those considerations that have the property of being a reason, rather than *de dicto*, as a disposition to respond to whatever has the property of being a reason. For example, Olivia, who needs to do well in an exam, may respond to her circumstance simply by taking the necessary means to doing well out of a concern for doing well in the exam rather than a generic concern to follow reasons wherever they lead. In order for Olivia's responses to reflect the strength of some reason R to φ relative to other reasons, she may consider what she thinks of acting on R in view of the other things she is considering, how acting or not acting on R would bear on her other pursuits and to what it would commit her, and monitor her actions in the light of R and of factors and changes relevant to whether φ-ing makes sense in the light of R.[19] Thus Olivia, if reasons-responsive, may well skip a party the night before the exam while quite properly skipping her study and the exam to attend to a family emergency. But if called away on an emergency, she will see the need to notify the professor so as to arrange to take the exam at a later date. Again, interfering factors may mask the disposition. Even if Olivia recognizes her reasons, she may still go to the party if she is weak-willed, or fail to notify the professor if she is distracted or depressed because of the family emergency.

It is important to note that responsiveness to reasons comes in varying degrees of the tightness of fit between recognizing the reasons there are and their relative strengths ('receptivity' to reasons) and translating those reasons into decisions and translating these decisions into behavior ('reactivity' to reasons).[20] For example, an agent may exhibit an intelligible pattern of actual and counterfactual recognition of reasons, but frequently be weak-willed or otherwise unsuccessful in translating their recognition of reasons into decisions or subsequent behavior.

This is important to note, because acceptance of moral principles also comes in varying degrees of strength. Genuinely to accept a set of moral principles is, generically, to have dispositions to respond in certain ways to certain sorts of circumstances and actions in the light of certain features they have, which dispositions underlie one's responses. But what kinds of dispositions, and to what kinds of responses, does one have in virtue of accepting a set of principles?

We can distinguish three types of view on the basis of the three elements of responsiveness to reasons. According to a minimal view, the relevant dispositions consist just in dispositions to form certain moral beliefs. If I accept that lying is *pro tanto* wrong, I will be disposed to form certain beliefs about the morality of actions that I take to constitute lying. These beliefs will be sensitive to my understanding of the context. I will be disposed to regard an act's constituting lying as a weaker reason against doing it when by lying I can protect an innocent person from a murderer, and perhaps to regard an act's constituting lying as no reason at all against doing it when engaged in a game of bluff. The other two views build also certain reactive dispositions into acceptance of moral principles. According to the weaker view, the dispositions that at least morally committed agents have in virtue of accepting a set of moral principles include dispositions to translate one's moral beliefs into decisions to act in accordance with the principles one accepts. If I accept that lying is *pro tanto* wrong, I am disposed to decide not to perform certain actions so far as their constituting lying goes, and not just because lying would get me into trouble. According to the stronger view, the relevant dispositions also include various motivational, affective, and behavioral tendencies. If I accept that lying is *pro tanto* wrong, I am disposed not to lie even when this would be to my advantage, but to act in an honest and sincere fashion, feel guilt if I lie, and resent lying by others.

Each of these views corresponds to a certain conception of what responsiveness to moral reasons requires. Given that principles identify features that make actions right and wrong, they specify the form and nature of conditions that would license one to treat some considerations as moral reasons. Thus the way in which at least conscientious and morally committed agents are responsive to moral reasons is a function of their receptivity and reactivity to those conditions as grounds of moral reasons. If so, then on the minimal view of what it is to accept a moral principle, such acceptance involves having a disposition to recognize moral reasons, at least within a certain range of circumstances. On the two stronger views, it also involves certain reactive dispositions to translate recognition of reasons into decisions or subsequent behavior (again, within a certain range).

A natural way to describe the way in which the acceptance of a set of principles on *any* of these views makes a difference to the dispositions of conscientious and morally committed agents, is to say that it structures the way in which they are responsive to moral reasons by giving a certain shape to certain aspects of their moral conscience. And were such agents to accept true principles, this would presumably shape the relevant aspects of their moral conscience so that they would be responsive to the right moral reasons. Hence, as long as we read 'acceptance of principles' no more weakly than 'responsiveness to reasons', premise (G3) of the Guidance Argument is very plausible.

One complication I should address is that each of the above views of acceptance of moral principles raises questions about the role that moral principles must play in the practical thinking of agents who accept them if they are to function as guides. According to one view, due to Holly Smith, one uses a moral principle as a guide for making a decision on a particular occasion, just in case one decides to perform an act out of a desire to conform to the principle and a belief that the act conforms, which in turn requires that one 'explicitly represent the principle as the content of a propositional attitude' at that occasion (H.M. Smith 1988: 90–92). I find this view objectionable. What, intuitively, should motivate the agent in a case of adequate guidance by moral principles is a concern for the considerations that the principles identify as moral reasons (a concern that has a certain sort of actual and counterfactual shape). In requiring one instead to make one's decisions out of a desire to conform to the principle, Smith makes conformity to the principle seem a kind of fetish.[21] The view also seems too strong. Consider, for analogy, that minimal practical rationality plausibly requires conformity to some principle of instrumental rationality. According to Smith's account, one uses that principle as a guide just in case one engages in a type of instrumental reasoning: one uses it just in case one decides to perform an act out of a desire to conform to the principle and a belief that the act conforms. We cannot, however, require that one use the instrumental principle in this way, since one is capable of so using it only if one *already is* minimally practically rational (cf. Dreier 1997: 93–94). But now it is hard to see why using a moral principle as a guide should require that one decide to perform an act out of a desire to conform to the principle and a belief that the act conforms, when using the instrumental principle as a guide seemingly needn't involve any such cognitive structure.[22]

A weaker view that I find more plausible says that using a principle as a guide on a particular occasion requires only that one have it to some extent available for explicit reasoning, not that one explicitly represent it as the content of a propositional attitude at that time. For moral principles may guide responses to particulars even if known only tacitly by those who so deploy them (O'Neill 1996: 86–87; Garfield 2000: 191). So, one may be using a principle as a guide on a particular occasion even if its guiding role on that occasion is tacit or unreflective. Regarding (G3), this view implies that if acceptance of moral principles shapes our responsiveness to moral reasons, then our actual and counterfactual responses can indicate an understanding of principles even if we cannot fully articulate what underlies our responses.[23] Then using a principle as a guide requires only that we be responsive to the features the principle identifies as reasons for certain actions to be right or wrong, and that the principle be to some extent available for explicit reasoning, not that we also explicitly represent the principle as the content of a propositional attitude.[24] A view of this kind allows that acceptance of moral principles may shape our responsiveness to moral reasons in ways that leave room for us to refine our understanding of these principles. It also helps us not to conflate articulation and under-standing. For our understanding, moral or otherwise, isn't exhausted by what we can explicitly articulate (see e.g. Churchland 1996; Raz 1999; Wright 1999). Our reasoning also often reasonably relies on background assumptions that we leave implicit or take for granted (see e.g. Bach 1984).

A further complication I need to address is that any account of moral guidance (generalist or not) will ultimately need to forge a connection between acceptance of moral principles (or other guides) and motivation, since agents who accept some principles will thereby reliably *act* well only to the extent that their acceptance of those principles is sufficiently moti-vating. The strongest type of view of what it is to accept a moral principle forges such a connection by building motivational dispositions into princi-ple acceptance. But (G3) itself doesn't presuppose such a view of the motivational powers of principle acceptance. Whether such a view is required depends on the motivational demands of morality, which I won't try to descry here. For my purposes, we may work with any interpretation of (G3) on which it is coherent to grant that there are true moral principles but hold that one may be appropriately responsive to the moral reasons which those principles identify without accepting those principles.[25] For then (G3) won't settle the substantive issue whether there are adequate particularist models of moral guidance by conceptual fiat.

5 A model of hedged moral principles

According to premise (G2) of the Guidance Argument, if a conscientious and morally committed agent's acceptance of true principles shapes the agent's responsiveness to the right moral reasons, then those principles can contribute non-trivially to a reliable strategy for acting well that is available to the agent. My defense of (G2) begins with the worry that *any* principle might be such that accepting it *mis*shapes one's responsiveness to moral reasons and so fails to contribute to one's reliability at recognizing (and reacting to) them. No doubt *some* principles are like this, and even conscientious agents might accept principles that misshape their responsiveness to reasons.[26] The worry is whether there might be *no* kind of moral principles whose acceptance can contribute to conscientious and morally committed agents' reliability at detecting the presence of moral reasons.

Particularists often present reasons holism as raising this worry. In §2 I said that holism is available also to generalists because there can be certain kinds of true moral principles even if holism is true. But even if holism leaves room for principles that accurately capture the behavior of moral reasons, its truth would require us to say more about what such principles must be like if they are to contribute to a reliable strategy for acting well. If, as holism holds, there is no necessary connection between the property of being a reason and the property of always being the same kind of reason, then anything that provides a reason for something is, *qua* a reason, a variable reason: in a different context it may be no reason at all, or even an opposite reason. Thus, for any wrong-making feature F considered *qua* a reason, there may be contextual conditions which would be 'unsuitable' for something's being F to be any reason at all for its being wrong (in which case it is morally neutral, unless further conditions obtain that are suitable for its being F to count in favor of its being right). The presence of unsuitable conditions of this kind amounts to the presence of defeaters for F's having any wrong-making force at all, or *undermining defeaters*. An example of an undermining defeater would be that an act's constituting lying doesn't make it at all wrong when playing a game where lying is the point of the contest, or when an honest background agreement to deceive one another is in place.[27] Undermining defeaters are distinct from *overriding defeaters*, whose presence is unsuitable only for something's being F to make it wrong overall. An example of an overriding defeater would be a case where an action is worse for involving a lie but not overall wrong because lying would save an innocent person from Nazi guards at the door. Since an overriding defeater allows that saving the person is nonetheless to some extent wrong in virtue of requiring lying, only capturing the kind of contextual variability of reasons (if any) which is due to undermining defeaters requires holism.

In view of the above, establishing (G2) in a way that accommodates holism seems to require two things. The first is to defend a kind of moral principles that purport to capture the way in which moral reasons behave if holism is true. The second is to show how the acceptance of such principles can contribute to one's reliability at detecting both moral reasons and undermining defeaters. If one is reliable at detecting undermining defeaters, but not because of any contribution from the moral principles one accepts, then the principles wouldn't seem to contribute to one's reliability at recognizing the presence of moral reasons either. For if one is unreliable at detecting undermining defeaters, then one is unreliable at recognizing the presence of moral reasons, and *vice versa*. Thus, if the principles that one accepts didn't contribute to one's reliability at detecting undermining defeaters, then they wouldn't seem to contribute to a reliable a strategy for acting well either.[28]

To build towards the kind of moral principles that achieve these two desiderata, let's note that if holism is true, then cases in which causing pain or breaking a promise isn't at all wrong might seem to make ordinary moral precepts like 'It is wrong to cause pain' and 'One ought to keep one's promises' prone to error. The ways in which many conscientious agents typically rely on such precepts seem, however, to indicate that they regard those precepts as expressing principles that tolerate exceptions and so are structurally more complex than their surface form lets on. For example, many of us judge 'Ravens are black' as true in spite of knowing that there are albino ravens. Just so, many of us would assent to 'It is wrong to cause pain' or 'Pain is bad' in spite of regarding the conditions as unsuitable for pain to have any wrong- or bad-making force at all when causing it is part of a medical procedure that is necessary for saving the patient's life or when it is constitutive of athletic challenge. While the latter case involves consent to pain, we also recognize that consent may not always be an unsuitable condition for pain to be wrong-making. Conditions may well be suitable for pain to be wrong-making when consent is due to manipulation, brainwashing, external conditions that generate adaptive preferences, or the like.[29] We also know of views on punishment, as well as theological views, according to which causing pain may well be right-making when the pain is deserved. Yet, if holism is true, none of this shows that the mere fact that an act would cause pain isn't capable of functioning, in some contexts, as a reason for the act to be wrong.

It seems integral to justification in ethics that when we judge some specific consideration *C* to be (that is, to have the property of being) a reason for an act's being right or wrong, we should be able to explain why *C* is the kind of reason it is.[30] We routinely accept this explanatory demand both in the case of theoretical reasons for beliefs about non-moral matters and in the case of many non-moral practical reasons, such as mundane instrumental reasons for action. To the extent that non-moral and moral reasons have a unified nature *qua* reasons, that demand should be legitimate in the case of moral reasons as well. It seems especially legitimate in the case of variable reasons. If something is a reason of a certain type in certain situations but not others, surely there should be an explanation of why it is a reason when it is and why it isn't a reason when it isn't. Explaining why a variable reason, when a reason at all, is a reason of a certain type involves explaining why certain conditions but not others count as unsuitable conditions for it to be the type of reason in question.

We can meet this explanatory demand in a deep way that serves moral theorists' aspiration to explain what makes actions right and wrong by specifying what I'll call the *normative basis* of a moral reason. By this I mean some evaluative or deontic condition (property, relation, etc.) the presence of which explains why *C* is a reason (when it is) for an action to be right or wrong. What exactly we regard as the basis of any given moral reason will depend on our substantive moral theory. In the case of pain, familiar proposals from normative ethics include the ideas that if causing pain is wrong-making, this is when and because causing pain *produces something intrinsically bad* or *makes the victim worse off*, when and because it *fails to exhibit the kind of concern or respect which the victim merits*, or when and because the fact that the act causes pain is among the reasons why some more general requirement not to cause pain *cannot be reasonably rejected*. These proposals agree that when causing pain is wrong-making, that moral fact has an explanation in terms of a normative basis, and only disagree on what that basis is. Many explanations of right-making features have a similar relational structure: features are right-making when and because acts having them stand in some such relation as *promoting, protecting, honoring*, or *respecting* to a positive evaluative or deontic property. This kind of explanations of moral reasons extend to variable reasons and unsuitable conditions associated with them. For example, one might think that pain isn't wrong-making when it is constitutive of athletic challenge, because under that condition pain doesn't make one worse off, or because causing it to one is compatible with one's exhibiting the kind of concern or respect which persons merit. Each idea appeals to one and the same normative basis in its explanation of why pain is wrong-making, when it is, and why some such fact as that pain is constitutive of athletic challenge is an undermining defeater for the fact that the act causes pain to make any contribution to its wrongness.

This shared structure of reasons and their defeaters seems to be reflected in the way in which many agents' judgments about moral reasons are sensitive, to varying degrees, to changes in the features of situations. The way they treat a principle like 'Causing pain is wrong' reflects a recognition that causing pain isn't wrong-making under certain conditions. But such a recognition doesn't usually lead mature agents to abandon the principle. This suggests that they treat the principle as having a more complex structure than the verbal formulation 'Causing pain is wrong' lets on. If the structure is such as to accommodate reasons holism, and if holism is true, then any apparently simple principles that have such a structure will be less prone to error than they would be if they lacked such a structure.

One way to make moral principles capture this complexity of structure in the behavior of moral reasons, along with the idea that moral reasons have normative bases, is to build a reference to their bases into moral principles. To do this, we need a way of describing normative bases which is suitable for expressing generalizations whose truth tolerates exceptions but remains neutral on the morally substantive question of what these normative bases are. Let *the designated relation* for a property F and a moral property M (such as being right or being wrong) be that relation R, whatever it is, such that x's being F is a reason for x's being M when, and because, x instantiates R. For a given choice of 'F' and 'M', if R is the designated relation for F and M, then what makes conditions suitable for the fact that x is F to contribute to (or, to be a reason for) its being M is that x instantiates R. Intuitively, R is a relation like promoting or respecting something of moral significance which can explain the reasons provided by F. (Sometimes R may be a monadic relational property.) The designated relation for causing pain (F) and wrongness (M) might be something like *failing to exhibit the kind of concern or respect which persons merit*.

Just *which* relation the designated relation is for any given moral reason is a substantive moral question. But the following kind of principle about causing pain is neutral on that question:

(P)   Any act of causing pain is *pro tanto* wrong in virtue of its causing pain, provided that the act instantiates the designated relation for *causing pain* and *being pro tanto wrong*.

(P) is an instance of a kind of principle that is hedged by reference to the designated relation. For any choice of 'F' and 'M', we can speak of 'the designated relation for F and M'. Thus a hedged moral principle of the form (HP) always seems available for consideration (be it true or false):

(HP)   For any x, if x is F, then x is M in virtue of being F, provided that x instantiates the designated relation for F and M.

(HP) gives a general model of hedged moral principles that purport to identify moral reasons. The crucial explanatory gain of the model is that its appeal to the designated relations helps us answer the question *why* the circumstances that count as reasons and unsuitable conditions are morally relevant in the ways they are. The model captures generalism: any moral reason's having a normative basis requires the existence of a true moral principle, because according to this model the normative basis of any given moral reason is the relevant designated relation, (the existence of) which entails a (true) principle of the form (HP). The model also explains holism: a feature that a hedged principle identifies as giving moral reasons of a certain type fails to give a reason of that type if conditions are unsuitable for it to do so. And conditions are unsuitable in this respect when, and because, the relevant designated relation fails to be instantiated. (More precisely, the model explains why holism, if true, is true. It doesn't entail holism: principles of the form (HP) allow for the possibility that the relevant designated relation must be instantiated whenever the relevant F is, so that conditions are never unsuitable.)

Although I hope to have conveyed some intuitive and theoretical merits of this model of moral principles, my aim here isn't to show that it has such merits or argue that it supports generalism. My aim is to show how the acceptance of hedged principles can contribute non-trivially to a reliable strategy for acting well that is relevantly available to the agent, even if holism is true.

6 Hedged principles and adequate moral guidance

Hedged moral principles make good sense of our idea of morally committed persons as ones who take certain moral ideals to be centrally relevant to determining what they should do and why, and so would prefer to be guided by them. Hedged principles also make good sense of the idea that an agent who accepts the principle 'Causing pain is wrong' but causes pain to someone for no good moral reason not only commits a particular wrong but also violates an ideal, such as respect for other people or a concern for their well-being, which the agent endorses. Adhering to the principle on that occasion would symbolize the agent's commitment to upholding the ideal in all instances for which the principle stands. Hedged principles make such sense because the designated relations to which they refer involve moral ideals, in which case accepting such a principle commits one to caring about some moral ideal.

For example, persons who accept 'Causing pain is wrong' may do so out of a concern for justifying their actions to others, or respecting them, or not making them worse off, which would involve accepting (P) on the basis of one or another particular substantive view about what the relevant designated relation is. Even if one accepts 'Causing pain is wrong' out of a direct concern for not causing pain to others, or even comes to accept it in one's moral education as an initially simple precept, one would presumably be a defective moral agent if one accepted the principle even if one thought that there was no basis for regarding the property of causing pain as a wrong-making feature. So its acceptance by a conscientious agent who thinks there is some such basis would seem to indicate a commitment to something like (P).[31]

If the designated relations to which hedged principles refer explain which features are right- and wrong-making and which conditions are unsuitable for them to be so, and if the acceptance of such principles requires some grasp of those relations, then their acceptance shapes one's responsiveness to moral reasons. To illustrate this defense of premise (G2) of the Guidance Argument, we can model the acceptance of hedged principles roughly as involving a commitment to a counterfactual condition.[32] For example, according to a fairly minimal conception of what it is to accept a moral principle, the condition would be something like this: 'I wouldn't take x's being F as a reason for x's being M if x didn't instantiate the designated relation for F and M'.[33] An agent who reliably meets this condition is reliable at detecting the presence of moral reasons and unsuitable conditions. But how exactly can acceptance of hedged principles contribute non-trivially to such reliability?

We can approach this question by asking how best to describe the content of the ability reliably to detect the presence of unsuitable conditions.[34] One way to describe it is to say that it is an ability reliably to apply a list of potentially unsuitable conditions. This view is, however, plausible only to the extent that such a list can be stated in finite and manageable terms. But we cannot simply assume that this is always feasible, and I know of no convincing argument that anything in morality or its action-guiding function requires otherwise. Moreover, grasping such a list would seem to rely at least implicitly on some prior criterion of what makes some condition unsuitable in the first place. Acceptance of hedged principles can make a non-trivial contribution to one's reliability at detecting the presence of unsuitable conditions in part because they supply such a criterion. They imply that unsuitable conditions are those in virtue of which, for the given F and M, something that is F fails to instantiate the designated relation for F and M. (That is, the relevant designated relation provides a condition on which features of situations count as unsuitable for something's being F to contribute to its being M.) What is more, their acceptance can contribute to one's reliability even if we cannot list all potentially unsuitable conditions in finite and manageable terms, since grasping the relevant designated relation doesn't presuppose knowing *just which* specific conditions count as unsuitable. So it seems preferable to describe the content of the ability reliably to detect the presence of unsuitable conditions in terms of grasping the relevant designated relation.

Hedged principles should be able to contribute to a reliable strategy for acting well even if those who accept such principles lack a complete understanding of a full range of correct principles. Just how reliable the acceptance of hedged principles makes one at detecting the presence of moral reasons and unsuitable conditions, and more generally just what role hedged principles play in moral guidance, evidently depends on the degree to which one grasps the relevant designated relation, which may be limited.[35] For we commonly begin with an inchoate sense of our moral ideals and values. I might accept 'Causing pain is wrong' while lacking a full grasp of the normative basis of a concern for not causing pain. I might at first have in mind only some of its implications or identifying characteristics, such as that, whatever it is, it has to do with well-being. Or I might be unsure whether pain is ever deserved or when it is deserved. Still, if my acceptance of a crude rule like 'Causing pain is wrong' involves the thought that pain's being wrong-making has got something to do with its making people worse off, then my judgments about the moral relevance of pain are guided by a pretty good proxy. I will be systematically picking up on the moral relevance of pain, even if I have in mind no particular list of unsuitable conditions. Thus even a partial grasp of the designated relations can instill modes of deliberation and policies for acting well that are reliable (at least within a certain range) but needn't explicitly feature principles of the form (HP) in their content.

We also seem to be able to refine our grasp of our moral ideals and values, and thereby refine our understanding of hedged principles, in light of what moral experience, thought experiments, and reasoning teach us about their implications. If I think that what makes pain wrong-making has got something to do with well-being, reflection on the effects of pain on the lives of those suffering from it, on desert, and so on, might lead me to think, for example, that well-being matters because of its role in enabling and sustaining autonomy and that causing pain is wrong-making when it undermines one's autonomy in ways one hasn't deserved. Or, for a different sort of example, suppose that consenting to pain isn't an unsuitable condition for causing pain to be wrong-making when it is due to adaptive preferences, and that this is because consent fails to be autonomous when due to such preferences. Then if I haven't realized that what sort of attitudes and behavior an appropriate sort of concern and respect for persons requires, depends on whether consent to pain is due to adaptive preferences, I will be less reliable at detecting the presence of moral reasons and unsuitable conditions as regards pain than if I would be if I had come to that realization.

Assuming, however, that practical wisdom and moral knowledge are possible in the first place, moral experience and inquiry can lead us to realizations of this kind. One way this can happen is via witnessing actual cases and reflecting on examples, such as how pain and adaptive preferences affect a person's life. As we know, these may often be particularly vivid and effective ways of testing and refining one's moral views. More generally, examples of unsuitable conditions can function as clues to what makes conditions unsuitable, and so can help to improve one's sense of what the relevant designated relation is or implies. Their consideration may often be epistemically significant.[36]

But the epistemic significance of examples of unsuitable conditions seems often to depend on auxiliary assumptions concerning the kinds of normative relations to which hedged principles refer. For example, we seem unlikely to grasp the relevance of adaptive preferences to whether someone's consent to pain makes causing it permissible, unless we rely on some independent, fairly definite sense of why things like causing pain to someone and their consenting to some treatment themselves matter morally. It also seems possible for us to refine our sense of when causing pain is wrong-making by reflecting more abstractly on such elements of the relevant designated relation as, perhaps, the moral standing of persons or sentient creatures and the roles that pain and consent may play in their lives, and then relying on such reflections and our canons of moral and non-moral reasoning to determine whether some particular conditions are unsuitable to make causing pain wrong-making. In either case, we would rely on our initial grasp of our moral ideals so as to develop a more accurate understanding of how those ideals bear on our choices and thereby gain a better basis for judgments about what would satisfy them. Assuming that moral knowledge is possible, we can proceed in such a way that our judgments about moral reasons and unsuitable conditions draw on an increasingly refined moral understanding which more fully reflects the contents of the relevant hedged principles and reaches beyond the simple verbal formulations which we typically give to our principles.[37]

The foregoing suggests that acceptance of hedged moral principles can contribute to one's reliability at detecting the presence of moral reasons at minimum by providing a starting-point and direction for the sorts of moral inquiry that can improve one's reliability at detecting the presence of moral reasons and unsuitable conditions. Given a more complete grasp of the relevant designated relations, it can so contribute by providing an explicit basis for judgments about what considerations function as moral reasons and when conditions are unsuitable for them to do so. We can also draw out the point that a suitable *set* of hedged principles can contribute to one's reliability at discriminating among the alternatives that its members license in particular cases. Agents whose principles require them to donate to charity can see that they may not contribute by mugging the elderly and donating the proceeds. Even if they have moral reason to do something deceitful in a particular case, they can reliably identify as beneath consideration modes of deception that involve injury or self-abasement. If they ram into a garden gnome to avoid running over a child, they will know to offer compensation to its owner and to take their aesthetic judgment that the gnome was just hideous as no reason to withhold compensation.

The foregoing also suggests a generalist response to the argument that moral principles provide adequate guidance at most in a limited range of cases. The argument claims that the simple rules of ordinary morality, such as 'Knowingly causing human death is wrong' or principles condemning actions but permitting omissions, represent heuristics that are well suited to a certain range of problems, but that we shouldn't treat them as free-standing moral principles because they lead to systematic mistakes when generalized outside that range of problems 'to situations in which their justifications no longer operate' (Sunstein 2005: 531).[38] Earlier we saw that the way in which many ordinary moral agents allow many rules they accept to have defeaters gives us some reason to think that they treat those rules as having a more complicated structure than their surface form lets on. If we tacitly understood such rules as having something like the form (HP), that would entitle us to treat them as freestanding while making us cautious about over-generalizing them. For even if the way in which we apply our rules in earlier stages of moral development reflects the use of error-prone heuristics, a fuller grasp of hedged principles can help us avoid errors because their built-in justifications (that is, the designated relations) constrain their range of application. But, in part because grasping hedged principles doesn't require grasping any exhaustive list of potential defeaters, such principles needn't as a rule be so complex or fine-grained that we are bound to commit more frequent or severe moral errors if we follow them than if we less reflectively follow simple rules.

Pulling the foregoing threads together helps us to see how hedged principles can contribute to reliable and available strategies for acting well because of the ways in which a conscientious, morally committed agent's acceptance of them can shape the agent's responsiveness to moral reasons. Their acceptance can contribute to such strategies either directly or indirectly, depending in part on the degree to which one grasps the designated relations and whether one grasps them as such or via their implications or characterizing features. Either way, the degree to which one is reliable thanks to one's acceptance of hedged principles can be robust in its scope. Acceptance of (P), for example, could contribute to being reliable at detecting the presence of moral reasons, to a degree that is roughly proportional to one's grasp of the relevant designated relation, even if one encountered a world where (P) is regularly defeated, such as a world of exercise nuts or one of massive adaptive preference formation.[39] For if causing pain regularly failed, for whatever contingent reason, to instantiate the relevant designated relation, then (P) would counsel one to presume that causing pain isn't wrong-making. Thus acceptance of (P), together with the appreciation of relevant non-moral information, can instill the kind of sensitivity to morally relevant contingencies which would (at least within a certain range) reliably lead one to true judgments about the reason-giving status of causing pain in such a world were one to inhabit it.[40] Furthermore, hedged principles can contribute to reliable strategies for acting well that are available for normal human agents with limited cognitive capacities and resources. For what suffices to make those strategies available is satisfying such minimal conditions of moral agency as sufficient intelligence and maturity to develop moral ideals and deploy ordinary moral and non-moral reasoning to determine what would promote, sustain, or honor them.

As the last step in defending premise (G2) of the Guidance Argument, the appeal to hedged principles helps generalists to show how the contribution of moral principles to reliable strategies for acting well can be *non-trivial*. The issue of non-triviality remains because generalists grant that grasping an appropriate range of principles is neither necessary nor sufficient for having a reliable strategy for acting well. It isn't necessary because, as we have seen, particularists can coherently allow that there are true moral principles but insist that proper responsiveness to the moral reasons that those principles identify only requires responsiveness to moral reasons that needn't be grounded by acceptance of any principles as guides. It isn't sufficient because principles neither apply themselves nor carry rules for their application in their sleeves. Otherwise we would be off to an infinite regress, as each application rule would need a rule for its own application. So we require a sensitivity to particulars even to judge what moral reasons we have in a given case, let alone to judge what our moral duty is.[41] Moreover, even as the acceptable ways of performing our duty are constrained by other moral principles, principles often allow, and sometimes require, varied implementation in the world of varying cases.[42] So, recognizing whether our principles apply, what they require, and how to implement their requirements, calls for sensitivity to the details of the case at hand and judgment.

The above suggests that any reliable strategy for arriving at correct moral conclusions in new cases requires developing a sensitivity and skill of judgment which enable one reliably to judge particular cases aright. If so, and if any such strategy requires agents to do whatever in their power is necessary for using the strategy, then acceptance of moral principles entails a moral commitment to developing sensitivity and judgment. (These might be either parts of reliable strategies for acting well or skills required for a successful use of such strategies.) It is, therefore, false that generalism encourages us to make moral decisions without a sensitive and detailed examination of particular cases. What raises a problem for generalists here is, rather, that the role of sensitivity to particulars and judgment in guiding action seems to be such that possessing them requires something beyond grasping an appropriate range of moral principles (Blum 1994: 39). For if so, and if grasp of an appropriate range of principles is neither necessary nor sufficient for having a reliable strategy for acting well, then generalists need to explain why sensitivity and good judgment merely *supplement* rather than *supplant* principles, making them superfluous for guiding at least virtuous persons.[43]

Appeal to hedged moral principles helps us solve this problem when we consider it from an appropriate developmental perspective. Whatever it takes to get people off to a start with some grasp of moral principles or some degree of moral sensitivity, any degree of the former requires some degree of the latter. For even on a minimal conception, acceptance of moral principles involves some degree of responsiveness to moral reasons, and we need some degree of moral sensitivity to determine what moral reasons we have in particular cases. But, although none of us is born with a full grasp of a set of moral principles, no more is any of us born with a full-blown moral sensitivity. We must allow that each can be improved over time by education and exercise, that each is nonetheless fallible, that some agents may achieve more development than others, and that even for the best of us such development is constrained by our limited cognitive capacities and resources.

The reason why generalists can deny that sensitivity and judgment supplant principles in guiding action is that grasp of hedged principles can help to improve and refine these skills. What we saw above about the epistemic significance of hedged principles suggests that further reflection on even partially grasped moral ideals that ground the principles that we accept can help bring novel relevant features or combinations of features into salience for us and help us see if they have some novel moral import. For example, reflection on how notions such as autonomy and consent interact can help us see that whether someone's consent to some course of treatment is due to adaptive preferences requires moral attention. Similarly, given even a partial grasp of an ideal like equal respect for persons, reflection on features of persons can help us realize that some of our views on sexual and racial matters, or the ways in which facts about the gender, ethnicity, or religion of the persons affected by our actions influence our decisions, are misguided. For example, someone in charge of personnel decisions who accepts the principle that personnel decisions should be made solely on the basis of professional qualifications might on such reflection come to realize that their decisions have been influenced by mistaken views or bias. Grasp of hedged principles can in this way help us refine our views of which actions count as disrespectful, improperly discriminative, injuring (and so on), and thereby help direct our attention more reliably to the right things.[44]

Since a more refined sensitivity may in turn help us gain a clearer understanding of the moral ideals underlying the principles we accept, improving our grasp of our principles and refining our sensitivities are ongoing processes of moral development which work in tandem and to which my generalist model of moral guidance generates a moral commitment. I suspect there is no level of sensitivity where hedged principles become hindering crutches that we had better discard if we are to improve our reliability at judging particular cases aright. The possibility of novel cases where our old ways of moral attention may not be reliable obtains even in the limiting case of virtuous persons.

7 Some comparisons with particularist guidance

I have defended premise (G2) of the Guidance Argument by arguing that hedged moral principles *can* contribute non-trivially to reliable and available strategies for acting well. But apart from pointing out that their past exercise of sensitivity and judgment may not adequately prepare even virtuous persons for novel circumstances, I have said very little about whether guidance by moral principles is *preferable* to particularist guidance. I would be amiss to neglect this issue, however. For even if moral principles can provide adequate guidance, particularist guidance might (other things being at least roughly equal) be preferable if, for example, particularism provided strategies for acting well that are more reliable or better available to normal humans than the sorts of strategies to which principles can make a nontrivial contribution. This would still position particularists to argue that, all told, we ought not to rely on moral principles in our practical thinking. A full comparison of generalism and particularism on this score is unfortunately beyond the scope of this paper. For example, I cannot hope to address the complex issues whether principled guidance can counteract more effectively than particularist guidance the morally pernicious effects that such widespread biases as 'framing effects' and special pleading for one's own interests often have on our moral judgments.[45] I also lack the space to argue at any sufficient length that guidance by moral principles is preferable to particularist guidance. My aim is the modest one of identifying some important respects in which my generalist model of moral guidance is at least no worse off than extant particularist models.

In the previous section, I sketched an explanation of how a grasp of hedged moral principles can help us improve our reliability at acting well (including detecting moral reasons and unsuitable conditions, refining our moral sensitivity and judgment, and so on). In appealing to the kinds of dispositions and understanding that are involved even in a partial grasp of such principles, the explanation is a *material* one. Any adequate model of moral guidance should supply some material explanation of being reliable at acting well. For when one reliably acts well, something in one's psychological make-up must underlie and explain one's reliability, and understanding what that is would presumably enable at least some of us ordinary folks to know how to improve ourselves.

It is, however, difficult to find serious particularist attempts to give a material account of the capacities that make virtuous persons reliable at acting well. Dancy, for example, describes virtuous persons' capacities merely *formally* as whatever capacities make them consistently successful: 'To have the relevant sensitivities just is to be able to get things right case by case' (1993: 64). He has little to add by way of a material explanation: 'There is nothing that one brings to the new situation other than a contentless ability to discern what matters where it matters, an ability whose presence in us is explained by our having undergone a successful moral education' (1993: 50).[46] Dancy has equally little to say about how to develop such an ability. Sadly, 'for us it is probably too late. As Aristotle held, moral education is the key; for those who are past educating, there is no real remedy' (Dancy 1993: 64). The narrativist, and intentionally metaphorical, moral epistemology that Dancy sketches is equally silent on the material nature of the capacities that enable one to tell the right kind of story of the situation that captures its moral shape, and those capacities don't reduce to the ability to detect moral reasons and defeaters anyway because of general features of narratives (Dancy 1993: 112–14). At least for now, then, describing the content of the ability reliably to detect moral reasons and the presence of unsuitable conditions partly in terms of the kinds of dispositions and understanding involved in the acceptance of hedged principles gives a deeper and more informative material explanation of reliability at detecting moral reasons and of how to improve one's reliability.

We might still wonder, though, whether generalist models of moral guidance can be psychologically realistic in certain significant respects. As I noted in §2, my defense of generalist moral guidance doesn't rely on the implausible claim that the only way that people can make moral judgments in the first place is by basing them on moral principles.[47] But we might nevertheless wonder to what extent generalists can accommodate empirical evidence from cognitive psychology about how people make moral judgments in actual practice. Agents who take themselves regularly to be guided by moral principles might be mistaken, in view of the empirical data that we generally lack reliable access to the actual causes of our judgments in many areas and our explanations of how we reach our judgments often are *post hoc* constructions (Nisbett and Wilson 1977). Further empirical data seem to suggest that moral judgments are typically caused by psychologically immediate unreflective evaluations (often fueled by stereotypes or emotional reactions), and that citing moral principles is usually a *post hoc* attempt to rationalize, and justify to others, judgments made without reliance on principles (Haidt 2001).[48]

These and other data allow that moral judgment is a kind of cognition shaped by a moral sensibility, but many cognitive scientists suggest that a normal human's capacity for moral perception, cognition, and judgment should be understood specifically in terms of 'pattern recognition' skills or in terms of neurally stored 'prototypes', 'schemas', or 'exemplars' of categories like morally significant vs. morally non-significant action and, within the former, morally bad vs. morally good action, and, within the former, such specific categories as killing, stealing, lying, and betraying. For some, the lesson of these models of moral judgment is that neither 'moral experts' nor even the merely morally competent normal humans are really guided by principles.[49] Were this last inference sound, it might justify a preference for particularist guidance.[50]

The inference is dubious, however. Even if our judgments and actions in concrete situations are directly guided by prototypes or exemplars, the latter can themselves be shaped by principles. In the terminology of the Guidance Argument, we can say that even if we understand our sensitivity and capacity to respond to moral reasons in terms of prototypes or exemplars, our sensitivity and responsiveness may themselves be shaped by acceptance of moral principles in the ways I earlier argued they can be.

Consider someone who defends their judgment of an utterance of a falsehood as wrong by saying that the utterance was a lie. If ordinary judgments are driven by prototypes, schemas and exemplars, then the person's judgment is a result of locating the utterance, on the basis of its perceived features, in an abstract multidimensional feature-space stored in the neural network and determining that the utterance has enough of a range of features that the agent associates with a prototypical lie – that is, an abstraction understood as a region in the relevant feature-space which is generated from a range of examples of lies – or with a persona-schema[51] of a liar or a paradigmatic exemplar of a lie. In general, utterances are judged as lies or not on the basis of where they fall in this multidimensional space, and as morally wrong or not on the basis of where they fall relative to the region representing moral wrongness in the multidimensional space representing the category of morally significant actions. Neural networks trained up in this way prime us (as causal antecedents of experience or in some other way) to recognize a movement as aggressive or identify someone as a shifty lawyer or school yard bully on account of their perceived behavior and other contextual clues.[52] The similarity determinations involved in these judgments may be more or less reasoned or articulate, but the bases of such discriminations typically outstrip our capacities for verbal articulation. Any reasoning involved in reaching a judgment is likely to be reasoning by analogy with the relevant prototype, schema, or exemplar in one's neural database.

While the generalist hypothesis that acceptance of moral principles shapes our moral perceptions and responsiveness to moral reasons no doubt requires further empirical investigation, the above kind of picture of moral judgment seems not to undermine that hypothesis. Doubts about the role of principles in shaping, or forming the basis of, moral perception and judgment tend to concern only verbally articulated principles (see Churchland 1996: 106). But, as I argued in §4, principles can guide responses to particulars even if they are only tacitly known, and not explicitly represented as the contents of propositional attitudes, by those who so deploy them. Thus, a verbal articulation of a principle may merely reflect – and perhaps sometimes mark an improvement of – an antecedent grasp of a principle whose typical guiding role is tacit, unreflective, or habitual.[53]

More importantly, principles can guide judgment by shaping the very prototypes, schemas, or exemplars that drive moral judgment (if they do). The role of a prototype, schema, or exemplar is to prime the agent for recognizing various features that are taken to be typical (to various degrees) of members of the category which the prototype, schema, or exemplar represents. It serves this role by making the features in question salient among various cognitive inputs and by making the agent differentially alert to divergences from the constellations of features, by expecting which, the agent approaches new concrete situations. Well constructed moral prototypes that discount misleading or biased similarities can then dispose the agent (at least within a certain range) to respond to morally relevant features and ignore morally irrelevant ones, thereby grounding the capacity to respond to moral reasons. Acceptance of moral principles should then enable us to improve our prototypes by helping us to discount misleading similarities, assign a higher relevance ranking to features that already are parts of our stereotypes, and extend our prototypes to include further relevant features.

One illustration of the point I am making would be someone whose prototype of a wrongful lie is that of uttering a false sentence that the speaker takes to be false. Acceptance of some principle that makes intentions matter to the moral status of actions might well lead one to extend one's prototype of a lie to include uttering a true sentence that the speaker takes to be false (even if the agent in the end classifies such an utterance less readily as a lie than an utterance of a falsehood the speaker takes to be false). It might also lead one to shape one's prototype of a wrongful lie to assign a higher relevance ranking regarding moral wrongness to whether the speaker intended to utter a falsehood than to whether the utterance was in fact true or false.[54]

Another illustration would be someone whose prototype of a wrongful lie doesn't make much of a moral distinction between lying in a game of bluff and lying in the context of a sales transaction. If one accepts a hedged principle concerning the wrongness of lying, reflection on the normative basis of the principle might well shape one's prototype of a wrongful lie by leading one to exclude lies made in a game of bluff, or more generally in contexts where an honest background agreement to deceive one another is in place, from one's stereotype of a wrongful lie. (Further illustrations can be generated from my discussion in §6 of how improving our grasp of the kinds of designated relations to which hedged principles refer can also help us refine our skills of sensitivity and good judgment.)

I have, of course, not shown that the above speculations on behalf of my generalist model of moral guidance are empirically adequate. My point here is that their plausibility doesn't seem to be undermined by descriptive theories according to which moral judgment is driven by prototypes, schemas, or exemplars, and often involves only *ex post facto* verbal expression of moral principles. To that extent, then, my account seems to fit with a realistic psychology of moral judgment. Notice also that in describing what modes of moral cognition are available to normal humans, descriptive theories of moral judgment constrain (to the extent of their accuracy) any model of adequate moral guidance. Hence the ability of generalist models of moral guidance to accommodate those theories and the empirical evidence supporting them strengthens the case that reliable principled strategies for acting well are available for use by normal humans with limited cognitive capacities and resources. Thus I conclude that evidence from cognitive science gives particularism no edge over generalism in making adequate moral guidance available to ordinary moral agents.

I'll finish by considering two problems Holly Smith raises for the ability of moral principles to serve as adequate guides: the *problem of error* and the *problem of doubt*. The problem of error arises when an act that one believes to be right isn't in fact prescribed by the principle one is using as a guide

(H.M. Smith 1988: 94). An example would be a juror who tries to follow a principle requiring adequate compensation for injured plaintiffs but believes, however reasonably but falsely, that granting a plaintiff $100,000 in damages would adequately compensate him when in fact $500,000 is needed. The problem of doubt arises when 'the decision-maker ... lacks the empirical premise necessary to connect the principle to any act, and so cannot come to believe of any act that it is prescribed by the principle' (H.M. Smith 1988: 94). For example, the juror may simply not have enough information to determine what would be an adequate compensation. Likewise, utilitarians might well find themselves in serious doubt about whether to vote for a flat-rate tax or a progressive tax, since they might well be unable to figure out which would maximize overall happiness. For in that case they wouldn't be able to figure out what utilitarianism actually requires them to do (H.M. Smith 1988: 95). My response to these two alleged problems comes in two steps.

The first step is that the problems of error and doubt constitute no problem for the ability of hedged principles as such to function as guides. The problem of error charges in effect that moral principles don't contribute to reliable strategies for acting well because our beliefs about facts that are relevant to the rightness and wrongness of actions are reliably erroneous. But recall from §3 that we can reasonably require only *conditional* reliability from strategies for acting well. If people as a matter of fact often have (reasonable but) false beliefs about what their principles require on a given occasion, this alone shows no fault in a principle that is deployed as a guide. The problem of error threatens generalist moral guidance only to the extent that the conditions for using the relevant strategies for acting well systematically require beliefs that agents with limited cognitive capacities and resources are unlikely to get reliably right. This might be a sound worry about some particular moral principles.[55] But we can reliably find out whether something causes pain to an agent, whether the pain is constitutive of athletic challenge, whether one consents to being caused pain, whether the consent is due to adaptive preferences, and so on. Thus the problem of error seems to pose no serious problem for using the hedged principle (P), introduced in §5, as a guide. And there seems to be no reason to think that (P) is alone among hedged principles in avoiding the problem of error. Similarly, the problem of doubt threatens generalist moral guidance only to the extent that the moral principles one accepts can only contribute to strategies for acting well the use of which requires the sorts of empirical premises of which creatures with limited cognitive capacities and resources are bound to be uncertain to a degree that rules out even partial belief.[56] This might again be a sound worry about some particular principles. But again the empirical premises required for using many hedged principles as guides seem accessible enough even to limited creatures like us.

The second step is that even if the problems of error and doubt did constitute a problem for generalists, they would constitute at least an equally serious problem for particularists. Regarding the problem of error, particularist guidance has no special claim to making agents more reliable at acquiring the true (non-moral) beliefs about their circumstances on which the reliability of moral sensitivity is conditional. For even virtuous persons' cognitive capacities are limited and their sensitivity to the details of their circumstances fallible. So even if there is a problem of error for generalism, there seems to be an equal problem of error for particularism. Similarly, even if there is a problem of doubt for generalism, shouldn't there be equal doubt as to whether one is exercising one's sensitivity on the right things or whether the things that appear salient really should appear salient in one's circumstances? The answer seems to be yes. I conclude that generalists are at least no worse off than particularists regarding the alleged problems of error and doubt.

8 Conclusion

Particularists argue that we ought not to rely on moral principles in moral judgment because principles fail to provide adequate moral guidance. I have argued that this claim of principle abstinence is false. I have done so by defending a generalist model of moral guidance that appeals to a novel kind of hedged moral principles. Such principles can make a non-trivial contribution to reliable strategies for acting well which are available to the practical thinking of normal human agents, even in view of recent evidence from cognitive science concerning how we make moral judgments in actual practice. In particular, accepting and understanding hedged moral principles can make us more reliable at acting well by shaping our responsiveness to the right moral reasons. The conclusion I draw is twofold. First, generalist moral theories can provide adequate moral guidance. Second, they are at least no worse off than particularism regarding the provision of adequate moral guidance. As with sex education, so with moral principles: teaching abstinence isn't the best policy.

Notes

1 This paper derives in large part from my *Ruling Reasons: A Defense of Moral Generalism* (PhD diss., Cornell University, 2002). I am grateful to Terence Irwin for helpful guidance at that stage of the material's gestation. More recently, insightful written comments from Terence Cuneo and especially Sean McKeever helped me to improve the paper in many respects; my warmest thanks to them both.
2 See Väyrynen (2006a) for the argument and (unpublished) for the details of this model of principles.
3 I owe the helpful term 'principle abstinence' to McKeever and Ridge (2005a: 88).
4 Dancy says that a moral principle 'amounts to a reminder of the sort of importance that a property *can* have in suitable circumstances', so that a set of principles can serve as a kind of checklist for morally relevant features (1993: 67). Another writer who bases PA on reasons holism is David McNaughton (1988: 62, 190–93).

5 McNaughton (1988: 190–93), Dancy (1993: 60–62; 2000b: 130–37), and Little (2000: 281) infer particularism from holism.

6 The examples of utilitarian and Kantian principles that presuppose holism presented in McKeever and Ridge (2005b) inspire Dancy (2004: 81) to grant this point. Väyrynen (2006a) defends the point independently.

7 This is the form of particularism that Dancy defends in his most recent writings: 'Moral thought, moral judgement, and the possibility of moral distinctions – none of these depend in any way on the provision of a suitable supply of moral principles. This claim is what I call particularism' (2004: 5). My characterization in the text refers only to moral facts and distinctions, because generalism as I understand it implies no particular psychology of moral thought and judgment, but only that moral judgments depend for their truth on there being true moral principles.

8 Three points of clarification. First, I'll assume that, at least in typical cases, if something provides an explanatory reason why an action is wrong, then it also counts against doing that action in the sense of providing a normative reason not to do it. Second, the language of moral properties, facts, and truths may be construed as minimalistically or, if one prefers, rewritten in terms of moral predicates and sentences. Third, my definitions of generalism and particularism leave logical space for the hybrid view that some moral facts and distinctions depend on moral principles but others don't. But such a fragmented view of the moral domain seems unmotivated until some reason is given to take it seriously, and I'll ignore it henceforth. (A view that adopts principles of *pro tanto* moral reason but eschews principles of overall duty isn't the relevant sort of hybrid view. If moral reasons depend on principles, then so presumably will overall moral duties.)

9 See e.g. Hooker (2000b) and, esp., A.H. Goldman (2002) for discussions of different aspects of this point.

10 See e.g. Dancy (1993: 64) and McNaughton (1988: 190). See also Blum (1994: 39).

11 I owe the term 'reliable strategy for doing the right thing for the right reasons' to McKeever and Ridge (2005a: 86).

12 I provide a fuller presentation of much (but not all) of what follows in the next few paragraphs in Väyrynen (2006b).

13 More prosaically, the idea is that if you feed garbage in, then, no matter how well you process that information, you get garbage out. Compare Alvin Goldman's (1979) discussion of conditionally reliable belief-forming processes.

14 I draw the term 'robust reliability' from Henderson and Horgan (2001), who defend the epistemic significance of robustly reliable belief-forming processes. But see Heller (1995: 505–9) for a weaker robustness requirement.

15 I am indebted to Sean McKeever for this example and part of the point that it illustrates.

16 For another sort of example of non-moral guidance, consider a business executive who says 'I'm making this decision on principle, just to see how it feels' (a cartoon in *The New Yorker*, 10 November 2003, 87).

17 J.S. Mill, for example, argues that ordinary morality progressively captures the 'corollaries from the principle of utility' because these corollaries 'admit of indefinite improvement' and human beings 'have been learning by experience the tendencies of actions' (Mill 2000: 33). See also Sidgwick (1907/1981: 199–216) and Hare (1981).

18 Generalism might then also imply that morally committed agents shouldn't try to adhere to the principles they accept.

19 One may be responsive to a reason R to φ without believing *of* R that it is a reason to φ. One needs only to respond in the light of R, in that one's beliefs and intentions reflect, in some not necessarily explicit fashion, R's (subjectively registered) support for φ-ing. Joseph Raz suggests that the 'reason-guided character'

of even actions that I perform without deliberation 'is manifest in the fact that I monitor them, and will abort them if the situation changes, or is revealed to have changed' (1999: 232). In general, competent agents needn't be articulate about the considerations to which they are responding when they are responding to reasons, even when these considerations are articulable. (On the venerable example of chicken-sexing, see Doyle 2000.) And habitual responses that don't arise from explicit reasoning may nonetheless be responses adopted in the light of one's appreciation of one's circumstances, and in that sense for reasons (MacDonald 1991: 39; Audi 1997: 147). Yet agents on whose thinking reasons impinge in these ways clearly can understand their import to their actions and attitudes and be guided by that understanding.

20 See e.g. the distinction between weak, moderate, and strong reasons-responsiveness in Fischer and Ravizza (1998).

21 I use the term 'fetish' in broadly the same sense as Michael Smith does when he argues that externalist accounts of moral motivation can only explain the reliable connection between making a moral judgment and being motivated to act accordingly, if they portray good people as being motivated to do what they judge to be right, where the content of this motivation is read *de dicto*, but that being so motivated is a fetish which externalism wrongly elevates into moral virtue (see M. Smith 1994: 74–75). One notable difference is that in Holly Smith's account of using a principle as a guide, the content of the fetishistic motivation is to be read *de re*, as the desire that one conform to a particular principle.

22 Holly Smith's rationale for her view is that moral philosophy is concerned with moral principles understood as objects of evaluation which are to be rejected or adopted in view of considerations for or against them, and that this process is most rational when those principles are entertained in propositional form (1988: 90). But even if Smith is right about what it is for *theory selection* in ethics to be rational, it doesn't follow that ordinary moral *reasoning* can be rational only if it involves selecting among moral theories, or that one's moral reasoning, understood as a kind of mental processing, should mirror the structure of the moral theory that justifies and explains the correctness of the outputs of such processing. Surely an agent can be instrumentally rational without selecting among theories of instrumental rationality.

23 Even so committed a generalist as R.M. Hare (1952: 64) stresses the point. A non-moral example is that one can drive without paying conscious attention and yet proceed on the basis of the law that forbids crossing an intersection against a red traffic light. In this respect, moral cognition may be roughly analogous to cognition in domains such as grammar, commonsense physical intuition, expert medical diagnosis, and musical composition. While cognition may differ in many ways between these domains (for example, some, like grammar, may involve generative systems while others don't), what they have in common is that our capacity to offer complex, subtle, and apparently systematic judgments about particular cases requires little conscious access to the mechanisms or principles underlying these judgments (see e.g. Stich 1993).

24 It isn't idiosyncratic to claim that one can use a principle in one's reasoning even without having the concepts required to formulate it. One can well use Leibniz's Law in one's reasoning so long as one has the concept of identity, even if one doesn't have the meta-logical concepts used in formulating the law, let alone explicit beliefs involving those concepts.

25 Here I grant, in effect, the coherence of denying the converse of (G3). I am indebted to Sean McKeever for pressing me to clarify my view on this matter.

26 For example, they might accept as guides principles that have false implications regarding what moral reasons there are, which affect their reliability at recognizing moral reasons even in the circumstances they are likely to encounter.

27 I owe this style of example to Lance and Little (2006b: 306, 314).

28 By the same token, a full defense of (G2) requires showing how acceptance of moral principles can contribute to one's reliability at judging when overriding defeaters are present. Such a case would need as its basis an account of how the right- and wrong-making features which moral principles identify combine to make actions right or wrong overall. Developing such an account is a task large enough to lie beyond the scope of this paper. What I can realistically hope to achieve is to defend (G2) against the particularist claim of principle abstinence. This aim allows me largely to bracket issues about detecting the presence of overriding defeaters, since particularists no less than generalists need an account of how the right- and wrong-making features of particular actions combine to make them right or wrong overall.

29 We may think of these conditions as 'defeaters for defeaters' or 'meta-defeaters': conditions that defeat the status of consent as a defeater for pain's being wrong-making. Thanks to Neil Levy for drawing my attention to adaptive preferences. Lance and Little (2006b: 319 n.1) attribute the athletic challenge example to Elijah Millgram.

30 In the next few pages I traverse rather quickly a territory that I cover with more argument and detail in Väyrynen (2006a, unpublished). Readers with concerns about the account as it is presented here are advised to consult those papers.

31 Familiar moral precepts are simple on their face at least in part because in moral education it is necessary to start by teaching learners *what* to do, primarily in the kinds of circumstances that they are likely to encounter, and leave it for them to find out later *why* (see Hare 1952: 67). The view I am developing explains this handily, since on this view we can come to understand why we ought to do certain things by grasping the relevant designated relations.

32 I say 'roughly' because we may be unable to describe the circumstances relevant to having a disposition, and therefore the dispositions involved in the acceptance of moral principles, simply in terms of counterfactuals. For example, the relevant counterfactuals might be true in virtue of 'finkish' dispositions, or false despite the presence of the relevant genuine dispositions because of the presence of 'antidotes' to them (see Bird 1998). For a defense of moral commitment as a commitment to a counterfactual condition which isn't sensitive to this point, see Stroud (2001).

33 Even if reliably detecting the presence of moral reasons requires reliably satisfying this condition, the present gloss on what it is to accept a moral principle doesn't beg the question against particularism, since it is possible reliably to satisfy the condition without being committed to it. Also notice that one's commitment may mostly operate as a constraint in the background of one's responses, so that one's responses can exhibit a counterfactual sensitivity to the satisfaction of the condition even if they aren't directly prompted by a desire to satisfy it (see Stroud 2001: 384–85).

34 See Väyrynen (unpublished) for a fuller discussion of this issue and the points in this paragraph.

35 No more than general features of reference are needed to secure the possibility that one may accept a principle of the form (HP) while having only a limited understanding of the designated relation to which it refers, or even while being mistaken about some of the relation's aspects. Although it seems clear that the acceptance of a principle requires some minimal threshold of responsiveness to moral reasons, I won't try to determine how unreliable one must be at detecting the presence of moral reasons and defeaters for us to have warrant for denying that one accepts a principle.

36 Terence Irwin makes the congenial point that generalizations that aren't fully spelled out, such as 'One ought to be helpful without being interfering' and those

that include qualifications like 'too much', are 'useful, but do not provide an effective procedure for just anyone, irrespective of their experience of such situations, to identify the actions that conform to them' (Irwin 2000: 128).

37 My account is fairly ecumenical on whether moral understanding can be improved through practical reasoning, rational intuition, or whatnot. This paragraph aims to put a bit more flesh around remarks such as Roger Crisp's claim that 'no rule can on its own, without some independent understanding of the nature of justice or courage, and some capacity to judge what they require in any particular case, satisfactorily guide action' (2000: 29). Scanlon (1998: 201), Irwin (2000: 120–21), and Nussbaum (2000: 238–39) express similar ideas. See also Väyrynen (unpublished).

38 Sunstein grants that simple rules operating as heuristics may provide the best available form of moral guidance despite the errors to which they lead (2005: 534–35, 541). On moral heuristics, see also McKeever and Ridge (2006: ch. 9).

39 Notice that particularism and generalism as such are silent on how frequently the right- and wrong-making features are defeated. Each allows that conditions might regularly be unsuitable in a given world, for the distribution of the relevant particular non-moral facts in a given world is a contingent matter (see Väyrynen 2004: 66–67).

40 The point would seem to hold *whether or not* such circumstances are ones that the agent, situated as the agent actually is, is likely to encounter. In this respect of robust reliability, hedged moral principles would seem to provide better guidance than the kinds of generalities regarding 'presumptive epistemic warrant' which Margaret Little takes moral principles to express. For she writes: 'The judgment that a given principle such as "lying is wrong" will help rather than mislead a moral novice reflects a judgment about the sorts of context she is *likely to encounter*' (2000: 295, emphasis added; cf. 294).

41 On this point, see not only Aristotle (1985: 1094b15–17, 1109b15), but also Kant (1797: Ak. 390). The representative notion of judgment understands it as 'the ability to evaluate a situation, assess evidence, and come to a reasonable decision without following rules' in a psychological sense of 'follow' (Brown 1988: 137–38). Judgment is widely thought to be indispensable also in scientific problem-solving and theory-selection (see e.g. Brown 1988: *passim*), and Aristotle's discussion of 'equity' appears to emphasize the need for judicial judgment in law (1984: 1374a30–b2; 1985: 1137b12–27). Notably, in these parallel cases principles seem to provide a fruitful framework or guidelines for judgment.

42 This twofold point is developed by Onora O'Neill, who gives 'Good teachers should set work that is adjusted to each child's level of ability' as an example of a principle that requires varied rather than uniform implementation, and notes that each principle 'helps to specify ways in which the others might be appropriately met' (O'Neill 1996: 75, 181).

43 Otherwise it might be that acceptance of principles is a useful ladder in teaching children to develop sensitivity and good judgment, but that for purposes of guidance these principles can be replaced by sensitivity and judgment once the latter are developed. See McNaughton (1988: 202). cf. McNaughton (1988: 62, 190) and Dancy (2005).

44 In this respect, my account of the kinds of guiding role that hedged principles can play is similar to Barbara Herman's account of 'rules of moral salience' (though the accounts differ in other respects). Herman understands such rules as defeasible and revisable interpretations of more fundamental moral conceptions (for Herman, the ideals associated with the Kantian Moral Law) which constitute the structure of one's moral sensitivity, thereby enabling one to recognize those elements of one's circumstances or proposed actions that require moral attention. See Herman (1993: 73–93).

45 In all honesty, I would also have little to add to Sean McKeever and Michael Ridge's extended defense of generalist moral guidance against the dangers of framing effects and special pleading (McKeever and Ridge 2006: 202–15).

46 Details of Dancy's view also give grounds for complaint. First, Dancy infers that the ability is contentless from the claim that the virtuous person is 'not conceived of as someone equipped with a full list of moral principles and an ability to correctly subsume the new case under the right one' (1993: 50). This inference is a *non sequitur:* its premise allows that virtuous persons might have a large, but less than full, set of principles (Irwin 2000: 102 n.5), and that their use of those principles might not be subsumptive and might require sensitivity and judgment. Second, in construing this ability as contentless, Dancy takes himself to be following John McDowell's view that the virtuous person's conception of how to live isn't 'codifiable' (McDowell 1998: 57–58, 66–67). But McDowell denies that this ability is contentless: 'What it is for the practical intellect to be as it ought to be, and so equipped to get things right in its proper sphere, is a matter of its having a certain determinate *non-formal* shape' (1998: 184–85, emphasis added).

47 This claim is ably criticized, primarily on the basis of empirical evidence, by Dworkin (1995).

48 It is worth noting that these data are equally problematic (or not) for particularists, since presumably they wouldn't recommend that we form unreflective snap judgments and then construct *post hoc* rationalizations to support them. Also, the claim that Haidt takes his empirical results to support is a descriptive claim that is consistent with the claim that we can and ought to make moral judgments more reflectively on the basis of reasoning or principles (Haidt 2001: 815).

49 See e.g. Johnson (1993) and Churchland (1996); cf. A.I. Goldman (1993). For a dissenting voice concerning the role of principles in certain types of expert cognition, see the discussion of Kirsh and Maglio (1992) in Clark (1996: 118–20).

50 Dancy (1999a) appeals to connectionism and prototype theory to mount a parallel argument for a particularist view of moral learning. I should also note that, with the exception of n. 53 below, the criticisms to follow of this kind of argument were developed independently of similar criticisms which McKeever and Ridge (2006: 215–22) raise against rejections of generalist models of moral guidance that are based on evidence from cognitive science.

51 According to the schema theory, moral experience equips us with moral 'scripts' and 'personae' that enable us to detect morally relevant features (see Greco 2000: 241). For example, we may judge that a person is untrustworthy if we 'see' the person as closely resembling the persona of a shifty lawyer, or as more like a shifty lawyer than Erin Brockovich.

52 It would make no difference to my present aims if we adopted a view of moral judgment as akin to pattern recognition that doesn't rely on classification in terms of prototypes, but on a direct detection that a certain pattern is present, based on features that prompt a recognition of similarity with patterns stored in memory (see e.g. Dworkin 1995: 234).

53 Moreover, as McKeever and Ridge (2006: 221) point out, even if Haidt (2001) is right that we often verbally express principles only *ex post facto* when we want to justify our judgments or actions to ourselves or others, we may thereby, if we are sincere, come to accept principles which then come to shape our perceptions and acquire a guiding role.

54 Whether this shaping would constitute an *improvement* in the moral prototype is, of course, a substantive question, but one that is tangential to my illustrative purpose here.

55 For example, a common objection to consequentialist principles is that the difficulties with acquiring and processing the relevant information about the consequences

of our actions raise just this problem. The equally common reply is that familiar indirection moves solve the problem. Which side is right is a complex question on which I take no stand here.

56 Smith fails to note the possibility of a partial degree of belief concerning the relevant empirical premises. See Lockhart (2000) for discussion of the much neglected issue of moral decision-making under uncertainty.

6 Particularism and the contingent a priori

Sean McKeever and Michael Ridge

How should a particularist understand basic moral facts and our knowledge of them? Since the particularist eschews moral principles, basic moral facts presumably must be facts about particular cases, e.g. that the fact that it would promote pleasure was a reason for her in her actual circumstances. This knowledge must not itself be based on some antecedent moral principle which would apply to other cases. Such basic moral facts are of course contingent. It need not have been the case that her action would promote pleasure at all, much less need it have been the case that the fact that it would promote pleasure is a reason given holism. On the plausible assumption that knowledge of contingent facts is a posteriori, we are led to the conclusion that knowledge of basic moral facts must itself be a posteriori knowledge.

The problem with this approach is that the proposed account leaves no room for non-trivial and distinctively moral knowledge which is itself a priori, and this is implausible. Some naturalists may hold that our moral knowledge is entirely a posteriori, but we take this view to be implausible *when combined with particularism*. For, given particularism, moral properties are not reducible to descriptive properties; otherwise we would have a principle linking the predicates which refer to the relevant descriptive properties to the moral predicate in question. So if our moral knowledge is entirely a posteriori then we must have a posteriori knowledge of the instantiation of *irreducible* moral properties. Moreover, given particularism, this *a posteriori* knowledge cannot be even partly based on the a priori knowledge of a suitable moral principle (generalist versions of reductive naturalism need not embrace this further constraint). However, this combination of views is highly implausible. We certainly do not directly perceive moral properties understood as irreducible features of a situation; that really would be to take the metaphor of moral vision too literally. We do not have a special moral sense which allows us to detect such irreducible moral properties.

The only obvious alternative on a purely a posteriori particularist model is to hold that such irreducible properties figure in the best explanation of our experiences. The epistemology of moral properties on this account becomes much like the epistemology of unobservable entities (and their properties) in science. Following Harman (1977: 3–10), we think this explanatory thesis is problematic. We need not insist on that, though. For there is a more basic point which has often been overlooked in these debates and which is enough for our purposes. That point is that whether moral properties figure in the best explanation of our experiences is not germane to our ability to have moral knowledge. The very idea, that my knowledge that lying is wrong under certain conditions is dependent on the suggestion that wrongness figures in the best explanation of my experiences, is simply alien to ordinary moral practice. Morality should be consistent with science, but fundamental moral knowledge is not itself scientific knowledge. We do not go out into the field and do actual (as opposed to thought) experiments to determine that lying is (in certain kinds of circumstances) wrong-making. This account of moral knowledge gives hostages to fortune in a way that is alien to ordinary moral practice and therefore should be abandoned.

Suppose the particularist agrees that the purely a posteriori account of basic moral knowledge is indefensible, at least when combined with particularism. Indeed, arch-particularist Jonathan Dancy agrees that we should reject a purely a posteriori understanding of our knowledge of basic moral facts, by which he means facts 'about what is a moral reason for what' (Dancy 2004: 141). If particularists reject the idea of a 'moral sense' what alternative epistemology is available to them? Dancy argues that basic moral knowledge is a form of judgment and indeed that our basic moral knowledge is a priori. However, he agrees that as a particularist he must also understand basic moral knowledge as knowledge of contingent facts about particular circumstances. In admirably Leibnizian fashion, Dancy follows his initial assumptions where they lead and concludes that our knowledge of basic moral facts is a priori knowledge of contingent facts. Dancy realizes that the category of contingent a priori will seem, as he puts it, 'alarming' (Dancy 2004: 147) and indeed it is rather alarming. After all, the idea that contingent knowledge simply must be a posteriori in order to be responsive to the relevant contingent facts in the right way is very powerful. As Wesley Salmon puts the challenge, 'But how could we conceivably establish by pure thought that some logically consistent picture of the world is false?' (Salmon 1967: 39). It is no coincidence that so many historical treatments of the a priori have taken it as obvious that whatever we can know a priori must be necessary.

Before turning to the reasons Dancy offers for accepting basic moral knowledge as contingent a priori, we want to emphasize just how steep a hill the particularist must climb. For while Dancy is not alone in defending the contingent a priori, other defenses of the contingent a priori would not be sufficient for the purposes of particularism. Such defenses either fail to establish knowledge of the right kind of contingencies, or else they fail to inspire confidence that we could have enough contingent a priori knowledge to provide a basis for ethics.

Perhaps the most famous recent (putative) example of contingent a priori knowledge has been offered by Kripke who claims that propositions such as, 'The standard meter stick is one meter long' are both knowable a priori and contingent (Kripke 1972). Such a claim is supposed to be knowable a priori because someone who fully understands the term 'meter' understands that its reference is fixed by a particular object in the actual world – the standard meter stick. Yet there are other possible worlds in which that very object is not one meter long, so what is known is contingent. Whether such examples are genuine instances of contingent a priori knowledge is controversial,[1] but it is not a controversy which we need here to decide. The truth (in the actual world) of 'The standard meter stick is one meter long', while contingent, simply derives from the semantics for 'meter.' We simply assume for the sake of argument that Kripke and his followers are right about the semantics here.[2]

Clearly this kind of case, even if it is rightly counted as contingent a priori knowledge, cannot serve as a basis for particularism's epistemology of basic moral knowledge. For, emphatically, particularists do not wish to claim that the truth of our basic moral knowledge (in the actual world) is derivable simply from the semantics for moral terms. Moreover, even if we turned out to be wrong about this, there is the worry that any semantics for moral terms which was analogous to the familiar semantics offered for terms such as 'meter' would bring in its wake moral principles. For example, if the standard of rightness were simply fixed by reference to the reactions of a particular and actual virtuous person – call him Fred – then,

Whatever Fred approves of is right.

would be a kind of valid moral principle. Of course the principle would be contingent. In other possible worlds, Fred might react very differently, and thus approve of things that are not right. The difficulties with such an understanding of moral language are familiar. Just as obviously, though, this picture of moral facts is not at all the kind of picture that particularists have been trying to paint.[3] What particularists need is a very different kind of contingent a priori knowledge.

Following Evans (1985), we can distinguish between deeply contingent truths and superficially contingent truths. Deeply contingent truths are such that there is no semantic guarantee of their truth in the actual world. What particularists need, then, is a priori knowledge of deeply contingent truths. Such truths will not be knowable simply in virtue of understanding the semantics of the relevant terms because those semantics leave open whether there is any world at which the sentence is true. The elements of basic moral knowledge that Dancy would count as contingent a priori are facts about what is a reason for what in particular circumstances. For example, we may know that the fact that Sue consoling Jill would bring pleasure to Jill is a reason for Sue to console Jill. Assuming that we have such knowledge, what is known is deeply contingent because the fact that Sue consoling Jill would bring Jill pleasure is itself deeply contingent.

Recently, John Hawthorne (2002) has urged that the obstacles to a priori knowledge of deeply contingent truths are not insurmountable. Hawthorne asks us to reflect not only upon a prioricity and contingency, but also on the concept of knowledge. He notes that, 'We feel a defeasible propensity to ascribe knowledge when presented with various reliable methods of belief formation. We then feel reluctant to ascribe knowledge insofar as various kinds of mistakes are made to look saliently similar to the case at hand' (Hawthorne 2002: 268). To see more clearly what Hawthorne has in mind, consider one of his tentative examples. Swampscientist has an 'innate storehouse that correctly represents the basic principles of interaction between physical bodies' (252). Although he does not represent such principles as expressing necessities or have (or believe himself to have) any experiences to confirm the principles, the swampscientist can use his storehouse of principles to generate beliefs about the behavior of physical objects. Interestingly, Hawthorne suggests that our intuitions about whether such beliefs count as knowledge are driven largely by whether we see salient similarities between the beliefs of the swampscientist and a range of ways things could go wrong. If we think of the swampscientist as doing something analogous to consulting a watch, we are more inclined to count his beliefs as knowledge. Though watches are often faulty, we discount this possibility and readily ascribe knowledge to someone who consults an accurate watch. If we think of the swampscientist along with other more typical scientists, there is little urge to ascribe knowledge. In this context we do not ascribe knowledge to scientists whose beliefs are not based on sufficient evidence or who have failed to consider relevant alternative theories.

We shall not pass judgment on Hawthorne's examples. For even if one takes a favorable view of them they are unlikely to be of service to the particularist. Hawthorne's examples all have two features that are conspicuously absent in the case of particularism. First, the objects of knowledge in Hawthorne's examples are all knowable a posteriori, without any basis in contingent a priori knowledge. Second, the putative knowers in Hawthorne's examples all employ some inferential method. In the case of those versions of particularism which understand basic moral knowledge as always contingent a priori, though, neither of these features is present. In the first instance, though such particularists can allow a posteriori knowledge of basic moral facts (as in the case of reliance on testimony), such knowledge is parasitic upon someone having contingent a priori knowledge. In the second instance, Dancy himself emphasizes that contingent a priori moral knowledge is not reached via inference.[4] These two features are relevant because it is in virtue of them that we can even make sense of salient resemblances to other cases of knowledge. It is by comparing the method of the swampscientist to the method of either the person consulting a watch or the method of the successful working scientist (both themselves a posteriori methods!), that we pump our intuitions about whether the swampscientist has knowledge. By contrast if we have no sense that there is any method by which someone reaches a piece of putative contingent a priori knowledge, and if there is no independent way to achieve the same knowledge, then it is hard to see clear and salient resemblances between such putative knowledge and other cases of knowledge. If anything such putative knowledge would look more like a purely arbitrary judgment. On the other hand, to the extent that there is a method to particularist judgment, it seems to be a posteriori – or at least to contain an a posteriori element. For it is only upon learning that Sue consoling Jill would bring welcome comfort to Jill that we judge that this fact provides a reason. If the judgment that Sue's action will provide welcome comfort provides part of the basis for drawing a conclusion about our reasons, then we have some discernable method, but just as obviously the resulting knowledge is a posteriori. Consequently, Dancy would not yet have identified any contingent a priori moral knowledge.

Our purpose in discussing Kripke and Hawthorne has not been to evaluate Dancy's defense of the contingent a priori, for he does not rely upon their arguments. Nevertheless, what emerges from our discussion of these other defenses of the contingent a priori is a sense of just how radical Dancy's suggestion must be. For what Dancy must really be proposing is that deeply contingent a priori knowledge that is not the result of any discernable method nevertheless forms the basis for a whole branch of human knowledge. That is far more alarming than the suggestion that there may be some penumbral cases of contingent a priori knowledge. But before abandoning the contingent a priori we should consider Dancy's own defense.

Dancy offers two reasons for supposing that widespread alarm at the contingent a priori is misplaced. First, he draws a distinction between positive and negative dependence, a distinction also defended by Marcus Giaquinto (1998). Dancy appeals to this distinction to argue that a belief that would be abandoned if experience becomes awkward for it need not therefore be thought of as a posteriori, for such a belief is in Dancy's sense only negatively dependent on experience. However, Dancy suggests, a belief is a posteriori only if it is positively dependent on experience. Dancy then maintains that with the contingent a priori we have mere negative dependence on experience but no positive dependence. So, the argument concludes, the tendency to assume that all contingent knowledge must be a posteriori rests on a failure to distinguish positive from negative dependence on experience.

Dancy's defense of the contingent a priori is highly elliptical. Recall that for Dancy basic moral knowledge is knowledge of the form, 'Fact F is a reason for A to φ'. Clearly, our knowledge of such propositions does depend on experience, in that our knowledge that F is indeed a fact in the first place is dependent on experience, the experience which provides our evidence that F. Dancy's idea seems to be that this is mere negative dependence on experience, which does not entail that our knowledge that F is a reason for A to φ is a posteriori. It would follow that the knowledge is a posteriori in Dancy's (and Giaquinto's) sense only if certain experiences served as *grounds* for the belief. How, though, do we determine when a given experience serves as grounds for a belief? For presumably if we know that F is a reason for A to φ then we know that F, where F is some contingent fact which we know through ordinary a posteriori methods. For example, F might be the fact that A's φ-ing would promote pleasure. Why do the a posteriori grounds for F itself not also constitute grounds for the judgment that F is a reason for A to φ? Presumably, F is a presupposition of the proposition that F is a reason for A to φ. After all, we can accept Giaquinto's distinction without denying that the grounds for a presupposition, so to speak, 'leak through' as grounds for the propositions for which they are presuppositions. We can think of presuppositions as epistemic 'enablers' of our reasons to believe the proposition which makes the relevant presuppositions, or we can instead think of presuppositions as part of the grounds for belief in those propositions. Dancy's discussion simply emphasizes the legitimacy of the distinction between enablers and grounds, and does not really provide any reason for classifying presuppositions as mere enablers rather than grounds. So perhaps we should return to Giaquinto's original discussion.

Giaquinto is interested in the epistemology of 'the obvious' – non-inferential knowledge which we typically acquire in a kind of 'Aha!' experience in which everything suddenly seems clear and distinct. His leading example is of the slave boy in *The Meno*, who suddenly learns certain geometrical facts by being exposed to certain experiences (drawings of squares and the like). For two reasons this paradigm is not helpful for Dancy. First geometrical knowledge is knowledge of necessary truths and second basic moral knowledge is not always obvious or acquired in an 'Aha!' experience. Put these disanalogies to one side, though. The question is why, according to Giaquinto, the experiences which prompt the slave boy to draw his geometrical conclusions do not provide grounds for those conclusions, in which case his knowledge would be a posteriori. Giaquinto's plausible answer is that the boy's knowledge does not depend on the veridicality of his experiences or even upon his taking them as veridical.

> ... [T]hose experiences do not serve as reasons or grounds for the belief, because the believing does not depend on the believer's taking the experiences to be veridical. (Giaquinto 1998: 199)

If Socrates' drawings were not perfect squares (and they almost certainly were not) then the boy's experiences of them as perfect squares would not be veridical, but this would not undermine the status of his geometrical conclusions as knowledge. It is a complex question in epistemology, and indeed psychology, just how exposure to such drawings might rationally prompt someone to grasp and accept some new geometrical truth. However,

Giaquinto's basic idea that the status of one's geometrical conclusions as knowledge does not depend upon the veridicality of the original experiences is extremely plausible, and this does seem to vindicate the 'taken as veridical' criterion. So let us suppose with Giaquinto that this is the (or at least a) way to distinguish positive from negative dependence.

Now return to the moral case in which I have basic moral knowledge in Dancy's sense. Suppose I know that the fact that her action would promote pleasure is a reason for her to do it. For me to know this I presumably must also know that her action would promote pleasure, but Dancy will insist that this is an enabler and not a ground for my belief that this fact is a reason for her to do it. However, Giaquinto's criterion does not support this conclusion. My knowledge that her action would promote pleasure is a posteriori and depends on some experience, call it E, perhaps my having seen her perform similar actions in the past and having also seen these actions as producing pleasure. The crucial point is that in this case my believing that the fact that her action would promote pleasure is a reason for her to do it does indeed depend on my taking E to be veridical. If I thought the relevant experiences were not veridical then I would not have so much as thought that it was a fact that her action would promote pleasure, much less would I have thought that this putative fact is a reason for anything. The case stands in sharp contrast to Giaquinto's case of the slave boy, where the boy's believing as he did really did not depend on his taking the experiences to be veridical. The slave boy could have agreed with Socrates that there are no perfect squares in the world of appearances but still learned his geometry lesson from Socrates' drawings.

At this point Dancy might argue that Giaquinto's criterion provides only a necessary condition on an experience's counting as grounds for a given belief and that there may well be other such necessary conditions. Indeed, there may well be, but Dancy has not yet told us what they are or why we should think that they will rule out presuppositions, so at the very least we need a further argument here.

In addition to invoking the distinction between positive and negative dependence, Dancy also offers a 'companions in guilt' argument:

> However, there are companions in guilt, and once we realize this, most of our worries will subside. There are unmysterious examples of a priori knowledge that not only require antecedent a posteriori knowledge ... but is also acquired using no method at all, so far as one can tell. Consider our ability to assess similarities. We have four things, *A*, *B*, *C*, and *D*; we can ask whether the first two are more similar to each other than are the second two. Let us say that *A* is a house designed by Frank Lloyd Wright, *B* is a house designed by Le Corbusier, *C* is an apartment block by Frank Lloyd Wright, and *D* is an apartment block by Le Corbusier. Is *A* more similar to *B* than *C* is to *D*? Are the two houses designed by these architects more similar to each other than are the two

apartment blocks? In order to answer this question we need a posteriori knowledge of the independent nature of the four buildings; but that knowledge is not in itself enough. Nor would it be enough to have listed the points of similarity and dissimilarity on either side of the two comparisons. The difficulty is that some similarities are more telling than others. No list of points of similarity will suffice for a judgement about which of these points is most telling in the present comparison. The matter is reserved for judgement, perfectly properly, and that judgement is one for which there is no method; but such judgements can yield knowledge. So here we have a more or less perfect analogy, and one which, I would claim, takes the mystery out of the situation. If this sort of knowledge can be thought of as a priori, so can knowledge of basic moral facts. (Dancy 2004: 148)

We doubt we are alone in thinking that that this example hardly inspires confidence. It is not clear that we have here a case of a priori knowledge. Why not classify it as a slightly odd case of a posteriori knowledge? Without good reason to count this as a case of a priori knowledge, this is a rather thin reed on which to base one's case for a thesis as ambitious as the thesis that there can be a priori knowledge of contingent facts, much less that all basic moral knowledge is contingent a priori. Dancy's main reason for thinking that our knowledge that the two houses are more similar than the two apartment blocks is a priori is that which dimensions of similarity are most salient in a given context of comparison is itself a priori. Is this true, though? By way of analogy, when comparing two keys' similarity, shape rather than color typically will be most salient since we presumably will be interested in opening doors. However, knowing that this is the relevant dimension of similarity seems to be a posteriori knowledge of the purposes for which we are making the comparison. Third, though, even if knowledge of which dimensions of similarity are most salient is a priori, this will not entail that our knowledge that (e.g.) the two houses are more similar than the two apartment blocks is a priori. At most, it shows that our knowledge that the one pair is more similar than the other is grounded in part on an a priori premise. We have already seen, though, that this is not sufficient for our conclusion to be a priori. So long as my knowledge is also based on some a posteriori premise or form of reasoning which is not a priori valid, the knowledge in question remains a posteriori in spite of being based *in part* on an a priori premise. By way of analogy, the inference, 'Joe is a bachelor, all bachelors are unmarried, so Joe is unmarried' invokes a premise which is a priori true and deploys an a priori valid form of reasoning but the conclusion clearly is not a priori in virtue of the first premise's status as a posteriori. So the inference from 'which dimensions of similarity are most salient is a priori' to 'our knowledge of which pair is more similar is also a priori' is simply a non sequitur. Dancy's conclusion would follow only if the other grounds for our belief about which pair is more similar were also a priori, and Dancy does nothing to argue for this further premise. Indeed, Dancy explicitly allows that our knowledge of the natures of the different buildings involved is a posteriori and this must be correct; we can know the height and shape of a particular building only a posteriori. So it is hard to see how Dancy could think that the resulting knowledge is a priori unless he thinks that our knowledge of such facts does not provide grounds for our conclusions of relative similarity. However, this is itself highly implausible and, moreover, we have good independent reasons to resist it if our reductio of the contingent a priori is sound.

Notes

1 For a plausible dissenting view, arguing with some plausibility that what is knowable a priori is not a claim about a particular object but rather a claim about the length of whatever object is used to fix the length of a term such as 'meter', see Bonjour (1998: 12–13).
2 Sometimes this point is put in terms of Gareth Evans' distinction between 'superficially contingent' and 'deeply contingent' truths. See Evans (1985: 178–213).
3 As Dancy puts it, 'But nobody could suppose that knowledge of a basic moral fact is gained purely by examining one's concepts, nor by thinking about the meanings of words' (Dancy 2004: 148).
4 See Dancy (2004: 101–8). As Dancy rightly notes we have no generally agreed upon account of what movements of thought deserve to be called inferences. The critical point we make here, however, is able to sidestep this partly terminological issue. For on Dancy's view, there is no method at all, inferential or otherwise, by which we move from our knowledge of the descriptive fact, that Sue consoling Jill would bring welcome comfort, to a piece of moral knowledge, that the fact that Sue consoling Jill would bring welcome comfort is a reason to console. As Dancy puts it in speaking of basic moral knowledge, 'In fact, there doesn't seem to be a *method* of acquiring that sort of knowledge at all' (2004: 148, emphasis in original).

7 Are basic moral facts both contingent and a priori?

Jonathan Dancy

This short paper is a response to Michael Ridge and Sean McKeever's 'Particularism and the Contingent A Priori'.

I

I start by looking again at one of the claims of mine that Ridge and McKeever leave unchallenged. Is it true that basic moral facts, that is, facts about what is a moral reason for what in a particular case, are clearly contingent? Holism maintains that a feature that is a reason in one case need be no reason in another, and will not be if some necessary enabler, present in the first case, is missing in the second. Whether this feature is here a reason, therefore, seems to be properly contingent; that same feature might not be a reason in other circumstances.

One might suggest, however, that this train of thought is a mistake. Whether the relevant feature is a reason *in these circumstances* is not a contingent matter, so long as we cast the notion of 'relevant circumstances' wide enough. And one might go on to say that knowledge that this feature is a reason in these more widely conceived circumstances is a priori. By contrast, simple knowledge that this feature is a reason in this instance, conceived narrowly, is empirical (if available at all), and what is known is contingent. This would restore the standard pattern, under which the truths we know a priori are universal and necessary, while those we know a posteriori are primarily particular, and contingent. (I don't mean to suggest that we cannot know any universal truths empirically, of course.)[1]

The worry that I have about this resolution is that it bids fair to turn far too many contingent truths into necessary ones. It is a necessary truth that Mark, given his actual height, is taller than Jonathan, given his actual height. But the necessity of that truth is compatible with its being a stubbornly contingent truth that Mark is taller than Jonathan. The necessary truth is a consequence of the contingent one, and, I would say, known only by knowing the contingent one.

The analogous claim for the moral case might seem to make difficulties. If, as holists maintain, whether this feature is here a reason depends in all sorts of ways on how things are elsewhere – on whether required enablers are present and threatening disablers absent – some would say that one cannot know that this feature is here a reason without checking on all those other things first. If so, the supposedly contingent truth that this is here a reason is a consequence of the necessary one – or at least the necessary one could not be known by knowing the contingent one, since we need to check on the enablers and disablers *first*. Luckily, however, this train of thought is an instance of a classic mistake in epistemology. If knowledge is possible at all, it *must* be possible to know that *p* without checking on all the facts which, if they were the case, would render it false that *p*. I must be able to know that there is a zebra before me without checking to make sure, for example, that it is not a cleverly disguised mule. Since this must be so in general, it is no objection to moral knowledge that it is another instance.

Nonetheless we might be disconcerted by the thought that it is a necessary truth that this feature is, in the circumstances widely conceived, a reason. If R is a reason in situation A (widely conceived), then in all A-worlds, R is a reason. A truth about all worlds is a necessary truth. A necessary truth cannot hold just because a contingent truth does. So that R is a reason in A must be a necessary truth.

Consider the following formulation SUP:

SUP: Nec[(R is a reason in W & DW) ⊃ ∀*w*(D*w* ⊃ R is a reason in *w*)]

(In this formulation, W is a world, *w* is a variable ranging over worlds, and D is an entire world-description.) The first thing that I want to say about this is that a truth about all worlds need not be a necessary truth, and will not be if the truth-maker for that truth is a contingent truth.[2] Various points are relevant here. The first is that we only know the right-hand side of SUP by knowing the left-hand side. The second is that the right-hand side is the case because the left-hand side is the case. The third is that if the right-hand side is a necessary truth, we would have to say the same of all resultant truths. The fourth is that the Nec operator does not detach.

It is normal to understand the supervenience of the moral on the non-moral in the following sort of way. Take a state of affairs that has certain non-moral properties and certain moral ones. We know, from this, that any state of affairs with exactly the same non-moral properties will have the same moral ones. How are we to map necessity and contingency on this? We might start by supposing that a contingent particular reason guarantees that all cases have the same reason. But this would seem to mean that the contingent particular case makes itself necessary, and that is impossible. All that we really know is that however things are here – and this may be an entirely contingent matter – they will be the same in all relevantly similar situations. Those of a logical frame of mind may be tempted to try to extract a necessity operator out of this, in the following way (where N*x* ranges over natural properties, M*x* over moral ones, and G is the grounding relation):

$\text{Nec}(\exists x(\text{N}x \ \& \ \text{M}x \ \& \ \text{G}(\text{M}x, \text{N}x) \supset \forall x(\text{N}x \supset \text{M}x))$

$\exists x(\text{N}x \ \& \ \text{M}x \ \& \ \text{G}(\text{M}x, \text{N}x))$

$\text{Nec}(\forall x(\text{N}x \supset \text{M}x)$

But this is a plain modal fallacy. There is a substantial question how to derive the conclusion of this argument from the premises if not by means of this fallacy. My own suspicion is that it cannot be done.

My conclusion, after all this, is that we should stick to the view that propositions about basic moral reasons are contingent, but I recognize that the matter remains contentious. (It would of course be a lot easier for me, holding that we know them a priori, to allow that they are necessary, as Moore, for instance, held them to be.)

II

Are we sure that a posteriori knowledge of the facts that are the reasons does not render knowledge of the facts that those facts are reasons also a posteriori? In revisiting this issue, I acknowledge that I would have done better to have said what I meant by a priori and a posteriori. There are two competing understandings of the a posteriori:

1   a posteriori knowledge is knowledge that cannot be gained without some appeal to experience.
2   a posteriori knowledge is knowledge that can be gained by empirical means alone.

Take some supposed relation between two facts, that p and that q, namely pRq. If we can only know that p, or that q, by appeal to experience, the same will be true of our knowledge that pRq. In the first sense of 'a posteriori', then, all knowledge that requires some appeal to experience somewhere along the way will count as a posteriori. In this sense, all basic moral knowledge (in the sense that I gave to that term) is a posteriori.

In my book I was wary of this argument, because I wanted to respect Giaquinto's distinction between positive and negative dependence. That distinction causes us to ask what is meant by the phrase 'without some appeal' in 1 above. Giaquinto's idea was that not all appeals are the same. Some appeals appeal to experience as a ground; others do not. It seemed to me that a fact, say the fact that she is in trouble, can act as ground for the fact that we have some reason to help, or ought to help, but it cannot act as a ground for the fact that it itself grounds the fact that we ought to help (and hence cannot do so for the fact that it itself is a reason to help). Ridge and McKeever challenge this view, and I discuss it in the next section. But for present purposes we might finesse this issue and admit that if our belief that p and our belief that q are both positively dependent on experience, then so will be our belief that pRq.

However this may be, things look rather different if we work with the second conception of the a posteriori. If we can know that p and that q by empirical means alone (whatever that means), it does not follow that we can know that pRq by empirical means alone. It would all depend on the relation R. If, for instance, R is the relation of entailment, p is 'this is a square' and q is 'this is not a triangle', it would seem that even if our knowledge that p and that q is a posteriori, our knowledge that pRq may not be.

This is how I take things to be in the moral case. I need to alter the terms a bit, because, in knowing what is a reason for what, I am not knowing a relation between two facts, but rather a relation in which a fact stands to acting in one way rather than another. Pretty well every such fact is only knowable a posteriori (in either sense). But, in the second sense of 'a posteriori', it does not follow that our knowledge of the reason given by such a fact is also a posteriori. (In the first sense, however, this does follow.)

My original question was whether our knowledge of what is a reason for what is a priori or empirical. If I had announced that such knowledge is respectably empirical because it is a posteriori in the first sense, this would really have avoided the interesting issue. That issue is the question whether moral knowledge is *entirely* empirical – as empirical through and through as the knowledge that she is in trouble. To insist that it cannot be gained without some (or some relevant) appeal to experience would simply not address this issue. And of course I had in mind the nature of the thought involved when someone, having already established the relevant matter of fact – say, that she would rather we didn't do it – then turns to ask whether that is a reason for us not to do it. The answer to *this* question is what interests me – that, and the nature of the process involved in reaching the answer, and of the knowledge that we acquire when we reach that answer. And one does nothing to show that the process, or the knowledge, is itself a posteriori by showing that the matter of fact which it takes as a given, and about whose normative status (as a reason, say) we are inquiring, is a posteriori.

III

Ridge and McKeever, in pursuing the relation between knowledge of the reason-giving facts and knowledge that those facts give us reasons, consider various suggestions about how the two sorts of facts might be related. Their aim is to show that the facts themselves constitute *grounds* for the judgment that those facts provide reasons. This expression needs to be treated carefully; all it means is that just as the wrongness of an action is grounded in its nonchalant cruelty, so this feature's providing a reason is grounded in the presence of this feature. ('Grounds' here are not grounds for judging, epistemic grounds. What they ground is the normative fact.) If the relevant facts do constitute grounds for the normative fact, it would follow, on the first understanding of the a posteriori, that if our knowledge of the facts is a posteriori, so is our basic moral knowledge. Of course this would not follow on the second understanding of the a posteriori, the one that I was using. But there is more to be said here than just that.

We can all agree that the fact that p can be the ground for the fact that one has some reason to φ. The question we are dealing with is whether the fact that p can be the ground for the meta-fact that the fact that p is a reason for us to φ. Whether it is the case that p is clearly relevant to whether the fact that p is a reason to φ. But what form does that relevance take? Well, what 'forms' of relevance do we know? Ridge and McKeever mention three candidates: being a ground, being an enabling condition that is not a ground, and being a presupposition. Which if any of these should we choose? My own view is that it is none of the above. The relation between the fact that p and the meta-fact that the fact that p is a reason to φ is revealed by looking at two other sorts of meta-fact. First, and supposing for present purposes that causation is a relation between facts, consider the causal meta-fact that the fact that the bridge was poorly built was the cause of its collapse, that is, of the fact that it collapsed. Here the causal relation relates one fact to another fact. The causal meta-fact entails each of those two facts, since it cannot be true unless they are. Causal statements are doubly factive. This relation of entailment is a form of relevance, but it is none of the three mentioned above. Now consider an instance of the grounding relation, where what is grounded is the fact that one ought to help. That she is in trouble and needs help is the ground for the fact that we ought to help. Here again we have two facts related to each other; the statement of grounding expresses a normative meta-fact. What is the form of relevance that the two facts have to the normative meta-fact? It is the same in each case, namely that the normative meta-fact entails each of the two others (one of which is normative and the other is not).

Can we say more than this? Can we say, for instance, as I would like to do, that nothing can be a ground for itself, nor for anything that necessarily includes itself? This looks like an incautious overgeneralisation. If I have a cold, and I am one of the people in the room, this might be thought of as reason to believe that everyone in the room, including me, has a cold. It is, as it were, the beginning of a case to that effect. This is not a perfect analogy, however, because a reason to believe that p is not the same as a ground for the fact that p. But we could ask whether the fact that I have a reason to φ is a ground for the normative fact (and it is normative facts that can be grounded) that everyone in the room has a reason to φ. And if the answer to this question is yes, we would have a case where some fact is a ground for a fact that includes that fact. Since we are quickly entering murky waters, I leave this issue unresolved, and base my position here solely on the previous paragraph.

Can we show that the three suggestions aired by Ridge and McKeever are not correct accounts of the relation between the fact that p and the fact that the fact that p is a reason to φ? I have claimed that the correct account is that the meta-fact entails the other two. But what then is the ground for the meta-fact that the fact that p is a reason to φ? My answer to this is that this fact has no ground. There is nothing that, in the relevant sense, makes it the case. The fact that there is reason to φ has a ground, but the statement of that ground *as* a ground does not also have a ground, and does not need one.

I would also say that the fact that p is not an enabling condition for the meta-fact that the fact that p is a reason to φ. What enables that fact to be a reason cannot be that it is a fact. An enabling condition, to put it crudely, turns something that is a fact but not yet a reason into a fact that is a reason. It is hard to see how this could be done by the fact itself. More generally, we should not confuse the relation of being a necessary condition for x with that of enabling x.

There remains presupposition. As I learnt to use this notion, the idea was that one statement presupposes another if, where that other is not the case, the first one has no truth value. So the statement 'you have not yet stopped beating your wife' presupposes that you have been beating your wife, and if you have not in fact been doing so, it is neither true nor false. But this is not a promising relation for our purposes. My suggestion has been that the relation between the meta-fact and the contributing fact (that is, the fact which the meta-fact cites as the reason) is one of entailment. But if that is right, the statement that the fact that p is a reason to φ will be false if it is not the case that p. I see no reason to suppose that we are dealing here with truth-value gaps.

IV

Consider now the example that I gave in my book, in which we are trying to determine whether A is more similar to B than C is to D. I maintained here that of course we need a posteriori knowledge of the nature of each of these four things, but that this failed to reveal the nature of the process of thought by which we move from that knowledge to something not entailed by it, namely the answer to our question about comparative similarity. It seemed to me that the kind of assessment of the significance of different aspects of similarity that is required if we are to answer that question cannot itself be gained by empirical means, because it is not by appeal to experience that we determine which similarities are the most telling in the present comparison. I still believe this to be the case. And I would say the same about a number of other questions of a second-order style, for instance the question whether a fact is relevant to some enquiry. I may only be able to know the fact itself a posteriori, but this does not show that my knowledge of relevance is a posteriori. Further work would need to be done.

Ridge and McKeever end by saying that 'it is hard to see how Dancy could think that the resulting knowledge is a priori unless he thinks that our knowledge of such facts do not provide grounds for our conclusions of relative similarity'. Of course I do think that the facts about A, B, C and D do provide grounds for those judgements. But in the second sense of 'a posteriori', which is the right one to use in these contexts, that my knowledge of those facts is a posteriori does nothing to show that my resulting knowledge of comparative similarities is itself a posteriori.

There is one final suggestion that they make along the way and that needs to be addressed. This is that the question which dimensions of similarity are most salient in a given context is not, as I suggest, a priori. 'By way of analogy, when comparing two keys' similarity, shape rather than color will typically be most salient since we presumably will be interested in opening doors. However, knowing that this is the relevant dimension of similarity seems to be a posteriori knowledge of the purposes for which we are making the comparison.' In response to this, I would say that even if there are some occasions when the purposes of the comparison dictate which of various dimensions of similarity is the one at issue, there are other occasions that are not like this. Further, my suggestion was that the matter for judgment was which similarities are most telling, assuming that there are various relevant respects in which the various objects can be assessed for similarity, but that it might be that a small difference in one respect was more telling than a large difference in some other respect.

In the architectural example that I gave, there are many things that need to be considered in order to determine whether the two architects' houses are more similar to each other than are their apartment blocks. Since the matter was meant to be merely architectural, some dimensions of similarity may already be excluded. But many remain relevant, and I suggested, and still suggest, that once we know, for each dimension of similarity, whether the houses are more similar to each other than the apartment blocks are (with respect to that dimension alone), we still have to decide which respects are the more telling for the purposes of the overall comparison. I still do not see how this decision, or judgment, can be thought of as a posteriori.

Notes

1 I am grateful to Malcolm Budd for pressing me on this.
2 One might also say that the right-hand side of SUP is necessary, but only shallowly necessary, appealing here to Evans' distinction between deep and shallow necessity, referred to by Ridge and McKeever.

8 Contextual semantics and particularist normativity

Terry Horgan and Matjaž Potrč

Contextual semantics, a general approach to truth and ontology, asserts that truth is semantically correct affirmability under contextually variable semantic standards, that truth is frequently an indirect form of correspondence between thought/language and the world, and that many Quinean commitments are not genuine ontological commitments. Here we will briefly sketch this position (which is developed at greater length elsewhere[1]), and we will argue that contextualist semantics fits very naturally with the view that the pertinent semantic standards are particularist rather than being systematizable as exceptionless general principles.

Contextual semantics

Contextual semantics construes truth as semantically correct affirmability, under contextually variable semantic standards, and falsity as semantically correct deniability. Truth is not monolithic over a range of situations, because semantic standards for correct affirmability sometimes vary from one occasion to another by virtue of situational factors that influence the operative settings of contextually variable semantic parameters. A statement that is true under one setting of such parameters may well be false under another. For instance, the statement that a given sidewalk is *flat* may well be true under typical standards governing 'flat' as applied to sidewalks, but false in a context where more rigorous standards are operative. Similarly, a statement like 'Finland is a member of Schengen treaty' may well be true under typical standards governing talk of posits like nations and multi-nation organizations, but false in a context on ontological inquiry in which the question at hand is whether the right ontology includes entities answering to such posits.[2]

What do a thought and a sentence correspond to in the case when a thought is true and when a natural-language sentence expressing it is true as well? One item that serves generically as a correspondence-relatum is *the world itself*. This idea is familiar, and is frequently invoked: truth is often described as *correspondence to the world*. There are importantly different species of correspondence to the world. Nevertheless, there is real unity among these differing species: correspondence to the world is a unified genus. The idea of truth as correspondence to the world fits nicely with a familiar conception of truth *conditions*: namely the idea that a thought's or sentence's truth conditions are constituted by a range (probably a somewhat vague range) of *possible worlds* – or, better, by a range of 'centered' possible worlds with a designated location as the location of the thinker/utterer of the thought/sentence. A centered possible world is a *potential* way the world is. It can be usefully thought of as a *maximal self-involving property*, instantiable by the entire cosmos. Thus, a thought or sentence corresponds to the world just in case the world instantiates one of the maximal self-involving properties that collectively constitute the thought's/sentence's truth conditions. Notice that this approach says nothing at all about whether or how the sub-propositional constituents of a thought or sentence should be linked to specific *items* in the world, in order for the world to instantiate one of the truth-constituting maximal properties that constitute the thought's/sentence's truth conditions. That is, it says nothing at all about whether or how singular or quantificational constituents should be linked to *objects* in the world, or about how predicative constituents should be linked to *properties* or *relations* that are instantiated by objects in the world.

One species of correspondence is very familiar: it is the form of correspondence that tends to be equated with the entire genus. We call it *direct* correspondence. A logically atomic thought/statement directly corresponds to the world just in case (1) there are objects $o_1, \ldots, o_n$ in the correct ontology that are respectively denoted by the respective singular constituents of the thought/statement, (2) there is a monadic or polyadic relation R in the correct ontology that is expressed by the predicative constituent of the thought/statement, and (3) R is jointly instantiated by $o_1, \ldots, o_n$ (in that order). When the logically atomic thought/statement directly corresponds to the world, the *truth-maker* – as we here use this philosophical term of art – is the specific state of affairs in the world consisting of the objects $o_1, \ldots, o_n$ jointly instantiating (in that order) the relation R.

When truth is direct correspondence, the relation between truth and ontology is stark and straightforward. A thought/statement is ontologically committed (in Quine's famous phrase) to objects answering to its singular constituents and its quantificational constituents, and to monadic and polyadic relations answering to its various predicative constituents. Truth, as direct correspondence, is a matter of (1) there being such objects and relations in the right ontology, and (2) the objects instantiating the relations in the ways required by the given thought/statement. But another species of correspondence between thought/language and the world is not a matter of singular, quantificational, and predicative constituents picking out objects, properties or relations that are part of the correct ontology – and thus also is not a matter of the instantiation of such properties or relations by such objects. We call this species *indirect* correspondence. In the case of a logically atomic thought/statement, the idea is that correspondence between this thought/statement and the world does not consist in there being objects $o_1, \ldots o_n$ respectively denoted by the thought/statement's constituents and a (monadic or polyadic) relation R expressed by the thought/statement's predicative constituent, such that $o_1, \ldots, o_n$ jointly instantiate (in that order) R. The correct ontology need not include any such objects or any such relation, and hence also need not include any such state of affairs. Instead, correspondence is a less direct relation between thought/language and the world.

Indirect correspondence involves two factors, working in tandem. On one hand there are contextually operative standards for semantic correctness. On the other hand there is the actual distribution of genuine properties by genuine objects in the world, and thus the actual distribution of states of affairs. Indirect correspondence, for a given thought/statement, is *semantic correctness under contextually operative semantic standards.*[3] Normally, whether or not a thought/statement has this status does indeed depend on how things are in the world. That is, it depends on which centered possible world is actual – i.e. which self-involving maximal property possibly instantiated by the world is actually instantiated by the world. Thus, the semantic correctness of a thought/statement depends on which objects in the world instantiate which properties and relations.

So, being semantically correct under contextually operative semantic standards is indeed a form of correspondence to the world, under the generic rubric of correspondence. But it is distinct from direct correspondence. The specific *kind* of indirect correspondence that counts as truth, in a given context of thought/discourse, is semantic correctness under the specific semantic-correctness standards at work in that context. Is indirect correspondence, in the case of a logically atomic thought/statement, a relation between the thought/statement and some particular state of affairs that is the thought's/statement's 'truth-maker'? No. Although normally there will be various states of affairs – in some cases, rather extensive ranges of states of affairs – that contribute fairly significantly to the semantic correctness of the thought/statement, none of these states of affairs (and no combination of them) will count in isolation as a (or the) truth-maker for the thought/statement. For, none of these states of affairs will involve objects, properties, or relations that are picked out by the singular, quantificational, and predicative constituents of the thought/statement.[4] In a sense, the thought/statement is made true by the world as a corporate body, rather than by any specific state of affairs.

According to the indirect correspondence construal of truth, the contextually operative semantic standards conspire with the world to render the thought/statement correctly affirmable, but the thought/statement does not incur ontological commitment to its posits. Consider the statement

(B) The Bled particularism conference lasted six days.

Statement (B) happens to be true. But, on the plausible supposition that the correct ontology does not include such items as philosophy conferences or days (whereof more below), this statement's truth is not a matter of direct correspondence to a state of affairs involving mind-independently real items falling under categories like 'philosophy conference' and 'day'. Rather, (B) is true in virtue of the fact that the actual world (i.e. the self-involving maximal property actually instantiated by the world) is among the range of possible ways the world might be, that collectively constitute, under the contextually operative semantic standards governing the constituents of (B), its truth conditions.

As an illustration of the contextual variability of semantic parameters, consider a monologue comprising the following question-and-answer sequence:

(S) Are there philosophy conferences? Of course! Are there *really* philosophy conferences? No!

In such a monologue, the speaker initially employs philosophy-conference talk in conformity with semantic parameters that normally govern such talk, so that the claim 'There are philosophy conferences' is unproblematically true (i.e. semantically correct, under the operative parameters). Then the speaker shifts into a mode of discourse aimed at serious ontological inquiry; and if in fact the speaker is right to think that the correct ontology does not include entities that fall under the category 'philosophy conference', then under this (somewhat rarefied) setting of the contextual parameters for this rubric, the statement 'There are no philosophy conferences' is indeed true.

In general, if a statement S is semantically correct under certain frequently operative semantic standards, but S is not semantically correct under maximally strict semantic standards, then S is not equivalent in meaning to – or approximately equivalent in meaning to – a statement that is correctly affirmable under maximally strict semantic standards. Do contextual variations in the operative semantic standards governing semantically correct affirmability, from one context to another, constitute the deployment (in thought) of different *concepts* and the deployment (in language) of different *meanings*? Under contextual semantics, the general answer to this question is no: such trans-contextual variations generally do not constitute the use of non-identical concepts or non-identical word-meanings. It is more accurate to view matters of concept identity and meaning identity in the following way. (1) Generic semantic standards have certain contextually variable parameters (often implicit). (2) Specific, contextually operative, semantic standards involve particular values of those parameters; these parameter values determine what David Lewis (1983b) called the 'score in the language game'. (3) The generic semantic standards hold trans-contextually, whereas the specific parameter values differ from one context to another. (4) Concept identity and meaning identity remain constant trans-contextually, because of the constancy of generic semantic standards. (5) Contextual variability in parameter values constitutes a more subtle, more fine-grained, kind of semantic variation than does non-identity of concepts or meanings.

One motivation for contextual semantics concerns what we call *metaphysically lightweight posits* – of which the Bled particularism conference furnishes one example. We use the phrase 'metaphysically lightweight posit' in a deliberately vague way. Under this rubric we include 'socially constructed' institutional entities like corporations, universities, nations, and multinational organizations (e.g. the Schengen treaty). We also include various non-concrete cultural artifacts, like Mahler's first symphony (as distinct from concrete performances of it) and Fodor's book *Language of Thought* (as distinct from concrete tokens of it). One is inclined to think that the world itself does not contain entities answering to posits like universities, symphonies, or the Schengen treaty. One is also inclined to think that everyday beliefs about such items are somehow true even so.

It is not plausible that institutional entities like corporations and universities are denizens of the world itself, *over and above* entities like persons, buildings, land masses, items of office equipment, and the like.[5] Yet, when one considers whether it might be possible to 'reduce' a putative entity like a university to these other kinds of entities – say, by identifying each university with some set of them (or some 'mereological sum' of them), or by systematically paraphrasing statements that posit universities into statements that do not – there is no plausible reductive account remotely in sight. For, the project of systematically paraphrasing university-talk into statements that eschew all talk of universities looks hopeless; and the trouble with attempts to *identify* a university with some set (or sum) of buildings, persons, computers, etc. is that there are always numerous equally eligible candidate-sets (or candidate-sums), and there is no reason to identify the university with any one of these over against any of the others. Likewise, *mutatis mutandis*, for other kinds of institutional entities like corporations and nations, and for non-concrete cultural artifacts like Mahler's first symphony and Fodor's *Language of Thought*.

The case of metaphysically lightweight posits is appropriate for motivating contextual semantics. Each of the following three claims is prima facie very plausible: (i) paraphrases of claims containing lightweight posits are normally not available, (ii) the right ontology does not include entities answering to lightweight posits, yet (iii) people still do make true assertions employing such posits. Contextual semantics provides a way to accommodate all three of these claims simultaneously – namely by 'going soft on truth' and claiming that for such claims as typically employed, truth is indirect correspondence.

Another motivation for contextual semantics – and for the contention that vast portions of human language and thought are governed by indirect-correspondence semantic standards – comes from considering the nature of vagueness. Vagueness essentially involves what Mark Sainsbury (1990) calls *boundarylessness* – namely status transitions among successive items in a sorites sequence, but *no fact of the matter* about such transitions. Such boundarylessness essentially involves three mutually unsatisfiable but simultaneously operative status-principles, which can be briefly summarized this way: (i) sufficiently small differences don't make a difference; (ii) sufficiently large differences do make a difference; and (iii) sufficiently many iterations of sufficiently small differences result in a sufficiently large difference.

Consider, for instance a sorites sequence of statements B(1), B(2), ..., $B(10^7)$ with respect to mutually incompatible semantic statuses such as *true*, *false*, and *neither true nor false* – where 'B(n)' abbreviates 'a man with n hairs on his head is bald'. In the case of language and thought (as opposed to ontology), the simultaneous operation of the three principles (i)–(iii) is intelligible, despite their mutual unsatisfiability. For, such simultaneous operation in language and thought can be understood in terms of two mutually obeyable prohibitions on *affirmatory practice* – namely (1) what we call the *Individualistic Status-Attribution Prohibition*, which prohibits attributing a specific status (e.g. truth) to an item in a sorites sequence and a different, incompatible status (e.g. being neither true nor false) to its immediate neighbor, and (2) what we call the *Collectivistic Status-Attribution Prohibition*, which prohibits affirming any determinate overall assignment of statuses to the items in a sorites sequence. Affirmatory practice that obeys these two prohibitions, while also attributing truth to *some* of the statements in a sorites sequence and attributing falsity to some others, thereby simultaneously *respects* each of the three principles (i)–(iii) as well as possible, given their mutual unsatisfiability – and well enough. Being thus respected is a way that principles (i)–(iii) are simultaneously *operative* in language and thought, despite being mutually unsatisfiable.

But with regard to the question whether there is, or can be, ontological vagueness – i.e. vague *objects* and/or *properties* as denizens of the correct ontology – there is simply no intelligible analogue of mutually obeyable practice prohibitions whose obedience constitutes the simultaneous applicability of mutually unsatisfiable status principles. Rather, the only way that the world-in-itself could exhibit boundarylessness would be by simultaneously *satisfying* the status-principles (i)–(iii) – which is impossible. For instance, it is impossible for there to be a sequence of objects such that (i) initial items in the sequence are heaps, (ii) whenever an item in the sequence is a heap then so is its successor, and (iii) eventually in the sequence there are non-heaps. Thus, heaphood cannot be a genuine property, a property that belongs to the correct ontology. Similarly, it is impossible for there to be a sequence of closely spaced grains of sand such that (i) initial grains are on Mt Triglav, (ii) whenever a grain in the sequence is on Mt Triglav then so is its immediate successor, and (iii) eventually in the sequence there are grains not on Mt Triglav. Thus, Mt Triglav cannot be a genuine object, an object that belongs to the correct ontology. Likewise, mutatis mutandis, for putative ontological vagueness in general.

Attending carefully to the nature of vagueness, one thus finds oneself forced to the radical-looking conclusion that ontological vagueness is impossible, and hence that the correct ontology cannot contain any vague objects, properties, or relations. Needless to say, this conclusion flies directly in the face of the idea that truth is always – or at least often – direct correspondence involving ontological commitment to the posits of language and thought. For, virtually all the putative objects, properties, and relations posited in common-sense thought/discourse – and very many of those posited in scientific theorizing as well – are vague. Thus, the impossibility of ontological vagueness means that none of these posits are included in the right ontology. But since human thought and discourse predominantly deals with vague posits, the paradigm of which are so called middle-sized dry goods, truth as indirect correspondence has to be a ubiquitous phenomenon. Otherwise, almost nothing that people ever think or say would be true!

Challenges for contextual semantics

Two kinds of challenges are apt to be posed for contextual semantics, perhaps in an attitude of skepticism about whether these challenges can be met. The first demand is for *vertical systematizability*.[6] It starts by granting (at least for the sake of the argument) the claim that truth is often indirect correspondence. But then it claims that this approach to truth will only have a chance if it complies with the following requirement:

Give a general, systematic, exceptionless, truth theory for statements that are governed by indirect-correspondence semantic standards – a theory that entails, for each such statement S, a cognitively surveyable formulation of S's truth conditions, formulated in a way that quantifies over only ontologically 'kosher' entities. Articulate these general principles *in an austere vocabulary that eschews any mention of items other than those posited by an austere ontology.* For, unless and until you can deliver such *austere* formulations of the relevant general principles, you will not have really eliminated ontological commitment to the various putative objects and properties that are eschewed by austere ontologies.

The vertical systematizability demand allows for the distinction between truth as direct correspondence and truth as indirect correspondence. But it requires there to be a truth theory, itself governed by direct correspondence standards and thus ontologically committed to its posits, that provides for each statement S a cognitively surveyable formulation of S's truth conditions – where the only posits cited in the truth conditions are items to which the truth theory is ontologically committed. For the case of metaphysically lightweight posits, in effect this amounts to the requirement of systematic *analyses* (via the truth theory) that will provide a paraphrase of each statement S employing ontologically dubious posits in terms of an associated statement S* (namely the statement of S's truth conditions) employing only ontologically kosher posits. Take the already given statement:

(B) The Bled particularism conference lasted six days.

Assuming that the correct ontology does not include items that fall under the rubric 'philosophy conference' or the rubric 'day', the vertical system-atizability demand requires of contextual semantics that it deliver a tract-able, cognitively surveyable, formulation of (B)'s truth conditions that does not posit such items as philosophy conferences or days. More generally, the demand is for a truth theory that systematically generates cognitively sur-veyable, ontologically perspicuous, truth conditions for *every* statement that is governed by indirect-correspondence semantic standards and is not ontologically committed to its posits.

A second challenge apt to be posed to contextual semantics is the *hor-izontal systematizability* demand. If indeed there are contextually variable semantic standards, as is claimed by contextual semantics, then the task is to formulate general, exceptionless, cognitively surveyable, rules governing the dynamics of such contextual variation. Such rules need not necessarily be formulated in an ontologically austere vocabulary whose only posits are items in the correct ontology. Rather, the rules might well be governed by indirect-correspondence standards themselves, and thus might well employ posits that are not items in the correct ontology. In the final analysis, though, the vertical systematizability demand is apt to be applied to such horizontal rules too: there should be a truth theory (perhaps in a second-order metalanguage) that systematically generates truth conditions for *these rules* – truth conditions that are cognitively surveyable and employ only ontologically kosher posits.

Why suppose that there are general principles that horizontally system-atize intra-context semantic normativity of any given kind, and yet more general horizontal principles by which specific normativity is determined within any given context and is altered across any given change in context? Likewise, why suppose that there are general principles that vertically sys-tematize all indirect-correspondence semantic normativity in a way that would systematically generate cognitively surveyable, ontologically austere, truth conditions? Why think that there *must* be fully exceptionless general principles at work, horizontally and vertically?

One line of reasoning that is apt to come to mind appeals to the thought that without such principles, semantic normativity would be too complex and unsystematic and idiosyncratic to be learnable and masterable by humans. We call this the *learnability argument*. The reasoning is that semantic standards for indirect correspondence must be vertically and horizontally systematizable, because otherwise they could not be internalized and mastered by humans. We think there is strong reason to believe that the learnability argument is seriously mistaken. Its premise is false: learnable/masterable semantic normativity need not conform to exceptionless general principles. And its conclusion is false too: the kinds of semantic normativity normally at work in human thought and discourse just do not conform to such principles; rather, the operative kinds of normativity are more subtle, more complex, and more nuanced than that.

Addressing challenges for contextual semantics

Our own view (cf. Horgan 2002, Potrč and Strahovnik 2004b) is that (i) the kinds of demands we have mentioned probably cannot be met, but (ii) they very probably *do not need* to be met. We doubt very much that semantic normativity conforms to fully general principles at all – let alone to fully general principles that could be stated in an ontologically austere vocabulary. We also doubt very much that semantic normativity needs to conform to such principles in order to be learnable and masterable by humans.

One powerful-looking line of argument for the claim that semantic normativity does not in fact conform to exceptionless general principles can be extracted from van Inwagen's (1990) investigation of the Special Composition Question (the SCQ: under what conditions do several entities compose another entity?). If there are exceptionless general semantic principles that are conformed to by the kind of semantic normativity normally at work in common-sense thought and discourse, then these principles presumably ought to generate some kind of exceptionless general answer to the SCQ – an exceptionless general answer that nicely systematizes people's various common-sense judgments about whether or not, in various specific cases, a bunch of things jointly compose a whole thing. But the apparent lesson of van Inwagen's careful investigation of the SCQ is that *common-sense judgments about composition do not conform to any such general principle.* (That is why one gets driven to an austere ontology, insofar as one seeks a systematic general answer to the SCQ.) Rather, common-sense judgments about object composition are something of an unsystematic hodgepodge – which presumably means that the semantic-normative standards these common-sense judgments reflect are also an unsystematic hodgepodge – which presumably means, in turn, that as far as object-composition judgments/statements in ordinary contexts is concerned, *semantic normativity does not conform to exceptionless general principles.*

The point can be generalized. For thought and discourse in general, there is just no obvious reason why the semantic normativity that governs it, in ordinary contexts, needs to be fully systematizable via exceptionless general principles. On the contrary, we think there is a heavy burden of proof upon those who would insist that it must conform to such principles; and we would argue that that burden cannot be discharged.

Let us come back to the earlier mentioned challenges. We doubt that either the vertical systematizability demand or the horizontal system-atizability demand can be met: we doubt that semantic normativity con-forms to exceptionless general principles of the kind envisioned. We also contend, however, that the lack of such principles would not prevent humans from being able to internalize and master semantic normativity that involves contextually variable semantic parameters and indirect-correspondence semantic standards. The learnability argument, we maintain, is mistaken. Our reasons for these claims involve what is known as the *relevance problem* in cognitive science, also sometimes called the 'frame problem' (in a broad sense of this expression). Here we will briefly summarize these reasons, which are articulated at greater length elsewhere.[7]

There has been a persistent pattern of failure in computational cognitive science to generate plausible models of what Jerry Fodor (1983) calls 'cen-tral' cognitive processes – processes like (i) the rational generation of new beliefs on the basis of prior background information plus newly acquired sensory information, and (ii) rational planning. As Fodor has persuasively argued for quite a long time – e.g. in the late parts of Fodor (1983) and more recently in Fodor (2001) – and as was argued at some length (in ela-boration of Fodor's argument) by Horgan and Tienson (1996), there is good reason to believe that the problems with attempts to computationally model such central cognitive processes are *in-principle* problems. These problems involve the fact that the relevant kind of information processing normally needs to be highly holistic in nature, potentially drawing upon virtually any item of information the cognitive system might possess, and sometimes (e.g. in making comparative-simplicity assessments of particular hypotheses) drawing upon highly holistic features of large bodies of information (e.g. large bodies of information relative to which the given hypotheses are effectively being assessed for relative simplicity). These two aspects of the holism of central cognitive processes are what Fodor (1983) calls the *iso-tropic* and *Quineian* features, respectively. It bears emphasis that they are also aspects of the holism of *reasons* – specifically, non-demonstrative reasons in support of specific beliefs and/or specific plans of action.[8]

Horgan and Tienson (1996) argue that the problem plaguing attempts to produce computational models of central cognitive processes lies with the assumption that the relevant sort of holistically information-sensitive pro-cessing is *computation* over representations – that is, the assumption that such processing conforms to *exceptionless rules* of symbol-manipulation, rules expressible as a computer program. (So does Fodor, in effect – as becomes quite explicit in Fodor 2001.) Horgan and Tienson also describe a non-classical framework for cognitive science, drawing upon certain ideas from connectionism and from the mathematics that goes naturally with it – namely dynamical systems theory. They call it *dynamical cognition*. (This framework retains the idea of a 'language of thought', although with syntax conceived somewhat differently than within the computational paradigm.)

Under the dynamical cognition framework, cognitively competent cognitive-state transitions will be only *partially* systematizable, via certain inherently exception-ridden generalizations with built-in ceteris paribus clauses – generalizations that Horgan and Tienson call *soft laws*. Such soft laws are not – and cannot be refined into – exceptionless algorithmic rules. Nor can they be refined into general rules that are exceptionless apart from cognition-external factors (e.g. having a stroke or being hit by a bus). Rather, within the domain of cognition itself, competent and content-appropriate cognitive-state transitions will be too subtle and too complex to conform to exceptionless general rules – especially insofar as cognition accommodates holistic aspects of background information: i.e. central cognitive processes are too subtle to be a matter of *computation* (i.e. rule-governed symbol manipulation) over mental representations.

But if indeed relevance-accommodating human *cognition* (e.g. belief updating) is too complex to conform to exceptionless general rules, then presumably so too are the *normative* standards for *appropriateness* of cognitive-state transitions. In particular, *epistemic* normativity presumably will fail to conform to exceptionless general rules – since such rules, if they did exist, could presumably generate exceptionless, programmable, rules for forming and updating beliefs. Likewise, *semantic* normativity governing indirect correspondence presumably will fail to conform to exceptionless general rules too – since *contextually appropriate* settings of contextually variable semantic parameters often will depend heavily on isotropic and Quinean aspects of holistic background information (whereof more below).

So we repudiate the vertical systematizability demand and the horizontal systematizability demand. We maintain (i) that these demands very probably cannot be met, but (ii) they very probably *do not need* to be met. The semantic normativity that governs indirect correspondence is normally particularistic in nature, rather than conforming to exceptionless general rules (either vertical or horizontal).

We turn now to further articulation of the particularist conception of semantic normativity, as a prelude to providing direct replies to the vertical-systematizability demand and the horizontal-systematizability demand. Statements governed by indirect-correspondence standards, we claim, just need not – and very probably *do* not – have short, sweet, cognitively surveyable, truth conditions formulable in an ontologically austere vocabulary that quantifies over only 'kosher' entities. (In effect, such formulations of truth conditions would constitute reductive paraphrases of just the kind that are unlikely to be forthcoming.) Still less do statements governed by indirect-correspondence standard conform to highly general, exceptionless, semantic principles that constitute a truth theory of the kind envisioned – a truth theory that entails, as instantiations, a reductive formulation of truth conditions for each object-language statement governed by indirect-correspondence semantic standards. The contextually operative semantic standards governing indirect correspondence simply need not – and very probably do not – conform to a reductive truth-theory of the kind demanded. Humans can, and do, master the semantic standards despite the non-existence of such a truth theory.

Well then, what is actually required by way of cognitive competence, in order for humans to learn and master indirect-correspondence semantic standards? Basically, this: humans should be reasonably good at tracking and judging context-specific semantic correctness, modulo available evidence. And humans are indeed quite good at doing so, modulo available evidence. In the first instance, they are quite good at forming judgments about when various claims are epistemically *warranted* (under contextually operative semantic standards), given the available evidence. And thus, to the extent that the available evidence is not misleading, they thereby are quite good at forming judgments about when various claims are *true* (i.e. semantically correct, under contextually operative standards).

This is a subtle cognitive *skill* – too subtle to conform to programmable general rules of the kind envisioned in computational cognitive science, because the underlying semantic normativity is itself too subtle to conform to the kind of truth theory envisioned by the vertical-systematizability demand. We will call this skill *particularistic projection* – the idea being that someone who has mastered the relevant semantic normativity is able to project appropriately from previous contextually-appropriate indirect-correspondence uses of concepts and terms to new such uses, even though there are no exceptionless general principles guiding such projection. The dynamical cognition framework for cognitive science, as described by Horgan and Tienson (1996), provides the general outlines of a positive, non-computational, scientific approach to human cognition that has promise for explaining how such a particularistic skill might be within the capacity of humans.

Holistic aspects of relevance figure importantly in the semantic normativity that governs context-specific semantic correctness. For example, point-and-purpose factors that lie behind specific uses of concepts and language, in specific circumstances, figure importantly in determining the contextually appropriate settings of semantic parameters. Furthermore, the determination of such settings normally will depend on how such factors link up, in holistic Quineian/isotropic ways, to a ramified body of relevant background information. In order to illustrate this point, it is useful to envision someone who is somewhat deficient in the capacity for particularist projection, who we will call a *category klutz*[9] – someone who is susceptible to what Gilbert Ryle famously called 'category mistakes'. Such a person does not fully master what normal humans easily do – e.g. the typical contextual parameters governing semantically correct use of such notions as 'philosophy conference'. The categorization klutz might say, for instance: 'Where is this philosophy conference you were telling me about? All I see is people talking, and interacting in meeting rooms and restaurants, discussing philosophy. I don't see, over and above these people, rooms, restaurants, etc., some further thing – some item that is the thing you are referring to with the expression "the 2005 Bled philosophy conference." There is no conference here'.

Varieties of the category-klutz construct can be used to illustrate a whole range of linguistic/conceptual practices that normal humans skillfully master over a variety of cases, in the course of exercising their holistically relevance-sensitive capacity for particularistic projection. We will return to this theme below.

Taking into account lessons to be learned from the relevance problem in computational cognitive science, and what we said about practices of skillfully mastering discursive/conceptual engagements that are holistically dependent on the rich structured cognitive background in ways so puzzling for the category klutz, it is very unlikely that semantic normative standards would conform to the vertical-systematizability demand. They seem rather to be particularistic.

We turn now to the horizontal-systematizability demand. Various point-and-purpose factors are normally behind contextually appropriate semantic standards, and behind contextually appropriate *variation* of such standards. Such factors are often linked to a highly ramified structure of relevant background information–for instance, information about a ramified body of interconnected social practices and social institutional structures. Because of the richness of this background, and because of its isotropic/Quinean holistic relevance to context-specific uses of language and concepts, it is most unlikely that the dynamics of contextual determination and trans-contextual variation in semantic parameters conforms to any set of exceptionless general normative principles: i.e. it is most unlikely that the demand for horizontal systematizability can be met – or needs to be met in order for humans to master the normativity that governs such contextual dynamics.

It is also plausible, however, that there are certain *soft* general principles that govern contextual dynamics – the synchronic score in the language game, and diachronic changes of score. Such generalizations would contain ineliminable *ceteris paribus* clauses, and hence would partially – but not completely – systematize normative appropriateness of scores and score-changes. They would have normative authority, rather than being mere statistical summaries of bodies of particular normative fact – and hence would provide some degree of generalist rationale for specific score-settings and score-changes. Nonetheless, they would leave lots of 'slack' to be taken up by cognitively competent semantic judgment that does not conform to algorithmic rules – for instance, judgment about whether or not *cetera* are *paria* in a specific circumstance (so that soft general principle applies), and judgment about how exactly to best apply a soft principle in a specific circumstance.

A position claiming that a given form of normativity conforms to such soft generalizations, but not to exceptionless ones, can be called *softly-generalist particularism*. Although particularistic judgment plays a critical

and ineliminable role, so too do (soft) general principles that carry normative authority. *Extreme* particularism about some form of normativity, by
contrast, would claim that it conforms to no normatively authoritative
generalizations at all, not even soft ones. Softly-generalist particularism
about normativity is well worthy of the label 'particularism', we maintain,
because of both (1) its emphasis on the failure of such normativity to be
fully systematizable by exceptionless, authoritative, generalizations (such
systematizability being the hallmark of traditional generalist aspirations in
normative theorizing), and (2) its emphasis on the ineliminable need for
particularist judgment, for instance in determining whether or not a soft
generalization applies in a given circumstance and (if so) in determining
how best to apply it.[10]

As an example of a normatively authoritative soft horizontal generalization about the dynamics of score, consider Lewis's *rule of accommodation
for presupposition*, which he formulates as follows:

> If at time *t* something is said that requires presupposition *P* to be
> acceptable, and if *P* is not presupposed just before *t*, then – *ceteris
> paribus* and within certain limits – presupposition *P* comes into exis-
> tence at *t*. (Lewis 1983b: 234)

This rule is overtly soft, by virtue of its *ceteris paribus* clause. It is normatively authoritative, since it provides a *rationale* for the kind of accommodation it prescribes. Yet, accommodation in accordance with the rule
clearly requires particularistic skill – even though humans are so good at
exercising such skill that often they do not even notice the implicit contextual parameters (in this case, presuppositions) at work, or the dynamic
changes in such parameters that occur in the course of a well run conversation, or their own accommodations to such changes. In the case of the
rule of accommodation for presupposition, for instance, particularistic skill
is needed to ascertain whether or not a given proposition *P* really is a
required presupposition in order for what was just said to be acceptable; in
light of the Quinean and isotropic aspects of the holism of relevance, there
is no reason to expect there to be rules for how to do *that*. In addition,
particularistic skill is also required to ascertain whether or not allowing *P* to
become hereafter a presupposition in the conversation would fall *within
appropriate limits* for accommodation – again, something that often will
involve Quinean and isotropic aspects of the holism of relevance.

To thematize such particularistic skill in action, it is useful to resort again
to our hypothetical friend the category klutz – who we will call Karl. Suppose, for instance, that Karl and his friend have just checked into the conference hotel in Bled, and as they were checking in they overheard the clerk
inform a guest that the hotel does not allow children. A few minutes later
Karl's conversation partner says this, as the conversation partner peers from
the hotel window out onto Lake Bled and the surrounding mountains: 'It is

so beautiful and peaceful here. Another thing I like about it is that there are no children here.' To this Karl replies: 'What do you mean? Of course there are children here. I saw some children playing in the park yesterday.' Karl has failed to accommodate properly, vis-à-vis a contextual presupposition-parameter governing the operative scope of the term 'here'; he has failed to realize that this parameter shifted, midway through his conversation partner's remarks, from referring to Bled and surroundings to referring to the interior of the hotel. Klutzy, yes – but this mistake helps one see how subtle and complex are the cognitive aspects of accommodation, even though humans are so good at it that typically they do not even notice they are doing it.

The skill of particularist projection, already at work in fairly mundane cases like ascertaining the contextually appropriate presuppositions governing the use of indexicals like 'here', also is operative with respect to the myriad of ways that various kinds of thought and discourse can correspond indirectly to the world. On this matter, the following remarks of Jonathan Dancy seem eminently applicable:

> To know the meaning of the term is to know the *sorts* of semantic contribution that a term can make to a larger context, and to have a general understanding of what *sorts* of context are those in which it will make this or that *sort* of contribution. There is nothing here that could be captured in a rule. Rules, in the sense with which we are here concerned, must be articulable in principle, even if our competent speaker is incapable of articulating them in practice. But if the meaning of the term consists in an open-ended *range* of available *sorts of* contribution in this way, it is essentially inarticulable. Competence with it will therefore have to consist in a kind of skill. ... To know the meaning of the term is, then, already to be a competent judge of how to project it. (Dancy 2004: 196)

Projection consists in applying to *this* situation a competence that stems from mastering a wider holistic net of possible contributions. Just consider grasping the meaning of the following statement:

(C) The Coalition of the Willing invaded Iraq.

In order to grasp the meaning of (C), one first has to possess an implicit mastery of the typical semantical workings of metaphysically lightweight posits such as coalition of states. This is a complex accommodation skill in itself, involving as it does the Quinean and isotropic holistic relevance of an enormous and highly ramified background of interconnected concepts and the various purposes for which they are typically employed – war, nation, international alliance, form of government, oppression, etc. The accommodation usually happens effortlessly. But suppose that Karl the category klutz, hearing (C), says: 'I understand that soldiers drove tanks. And there were military personnel around together with their leaders, following orders from still higher leaders in distant locations. But where the heck is this coalition? I did not see coalition dropping bombs. People, not coalition, fly airplanes. What is the "Coalition"?' The case of (C) offers an interacting range of concepts, such as government, nation, and political conflict. You do not master one without mastering many of these social constructs, and you do not correctly apply one without deploying particularistic projection in a way that suitably reflects the Quinean and isotropic relevance of others within the whole conceptually interconnected network.

Plausibly, such particularistic projection operates in human cognition via psychological processes that are too subtle and complex to conform to exceptionless, general, programmable rules – and perhaps operate in accordance with the non-computational framework that Horgan and Tienson (1996) call dynamical cognition. And plausibly, the need for such non-computational, non-algorithmic, *psychological* processes reflects the fact that *normative* semantic standards governing indirect correspondence are themselves too subtle and complex – largely because of the Quinean and isotropic aspects of the holism of reasons – to conform to exceptionless general normative principles (either vertical or horizontal). It does seem likely, though, that indirect-correspondence standards nonetheless do conform to certain soft horizontal generalizations with normative authority, such as Lewis's rule of accommodation for presupposition. Softly-generalist particularism is still full-fledged particularism, both because of its repudiation of exceptionless normative generalizations and because of its emphasis on the skill of particularistic projection.

Notes

1 See Barnard and Horgan (2006), Horgan (1991, 1998, 2001, 2002), Horgan and Potrč (2000, 2002, forthcoming a, forthcoming b), Horgan and Timmons (2002), Potrč (2003).
2 Contrary to neo-pragmatism, truth is not radically epistemic; for, semantically correct affirmability is distinct from warranted assertibility, and even from 'ideal' warranted assertibility and from 'superassertibility'.
3 Direct correspondence fits under this generic characterization too, with the semantic standards conspiring with the world in an especially straightforward way to determine correctness.
4 In principle, mixed cases are possible in which some, but not all, of the singular, quantificational, and predicative constituents of a thought or statement are being employed in an ontologically committing way under the contextually operative semantic standards. But even in such cases, truth will not be a matter of direct correspondence to a worldly truth-maker for the given thought/statement.
5 This common sense opinion was well captured by Ryle (1949) in his discussion of what he called category mistakes. We develop this theme below, with a twist.
6 See Reicher (2002), and Horgan's reply to Reicher in Horgan (2002).
7 See Barnard and Horgan (2006), Horgan (2002), Horgan and Potrč (forthcoming a, forthcoming b), Potrč and Strahovnik (2004), Horgan and Tienson (1996).

8 Particularists in moral theory typically emphasize two other putative aspects of the holism of reasons, namely so-called 'silencing' and 'reversal'. But, regardless whether these features are genuine, and (if they are) regardless how important they are, one general lesson of our discussion in this chapter will be that the isotropic and Quinean aspects of holism are *extremely* important in motivating at least some forms of normative particularism – notably, particularism about epistemic normativity and about semantic normativity.

9 Thanks to Mark Timmons for suggesting this phrase.

10 In earlier writings we have sometimes used the expression 'quasi-particularism' for what we are now calling softly-generalist particularism. See, for instance, Barnard and Horgan (2006), Horgan and Potrč (forthcoming a), Potrč (2000). But it now appears to us that 'quasi-particularism' is overly concessive to those who would apply the label 'particularism' only to an extreme version of the position.

9 When the plot thickens
Dancy on thick concepts[1]

Nenad Miščević

This paper discusses the issue of thick moral concepts and properties. Agreeing with Dancy's stress on the central importance of these, and on the view that they essentially involve response(s) of observers, it reminds the reader that in his earlier paper (Dancy 1986) Dancy forcefully argues against response-dispositional accounts of moral concepts and properties. The first part of the present paper further argues that an anti-dispositional view is incompatible with the first two points concerning thick concepts. If the argument is right, Dancy is implicitly committed to a kind of response-dependentism.

The second part proposes a response-dependentist alternative. First, response-dependence is not built into the ordinary thick moral concept itself, since ordinary moral phenomenology is not response-dependentist. A response-dependent account is a theoretical, philosophical account, and not a part of moral commonsense. Second, thick moral concepts are defined by an implicitly held commonsense *theory*, which can be either true or false, in spite of being constitutive for the concept. Third, the semantics of these concepts is very close to the semantics of serious pejoratives, and a single theory can account for both.

1 Introduction

Thick concepts combining a descriptive and an evaluative dimension play important roles in various domains of evaluation. When evaluating a policy in prudential terms we sometimes describe it as wasteful, stating that it wastes resources and implying that it is therefore less then adequate. Decisions are sometimes criticized as rash, people as being greedy. On the epistemic side, a proposal might be praised as thoughtful, and an idea as deep. On the aesthetic side, thick concepts are the building blocks of art criticism; think of ones like ELEGANT, KITSCH, or TOUCHING (I will adopt the convention of writing concept terms in capitals). Thick concept-words are often likened to serious pejoratives ('Kraut', 'faggot'), another topic of quite intense research, although some authors deny similarity. However, most of the work done on thick concepts has been dedicated to moral ones, depicting virtues and vices, like COURAGE(OUS), CRUEL(TY), LEWD,

NOBLE. Some ten years ago Dancy (1995) argued for the crucial importance of thick concepts and properties, and offered an analysis of them. Three important points emerge: first, they are of paramount importance in ethics, second, they essentially involve response(s) of observers, and third, the response(s) can be interpreted in a way that nicely fits the pattern of context-dependent resultance; thick concepts are well suited for a particularist grounding of moral theory. However, in his earlier work (1986) Dancy forcefully argues against response-dispositional accounts of moral concepts and properties. I want to argue that an anti-dispositional view is incompatible with the first two points concerning thick concepts. If they are paramount and ubiquitous in moral thought and reality, and if they are essentially tied to our responses, then anti-dispositionalism is false. I suggest that the particularist should embrace the three points concerning thick concepts, and reject anti-dispositionalism.

Let me announce the plot of the paper. Section 2 sets the scene by briefly presenting Dancy's views on thick concepts and in particular his application of particularism to this topic. Section 3 summarizes his line on secondary qualities and values, and in Section 4 the plot thickens: it presents the criticism, and attempts to establish an incompatibility between Dancy's treatment of thickness and his treatment of response-dependence. In short, for Dancy, thick concepts and corresponding properties involve our merited response in an essential way. I am arguing that this essential involvement amounts to response-dependence under a different name. The suggestion is then to accept response-dependence. Section 5 offers a very sketchy constructive proposal on the structure of thick concepts: ordinary thick ethical concepts do not explicitly appeal to attitudes, but involve links to moral concepts like GOOD or BAD. It is only at the level of theoretical account, not at the level of ordinary moral thought, that response-dependence makes its appearance.

2 Thick concepts

How should we think of moral properties? Dancy wants them to be part of the fabric of the world, but distinct from merely natural properties. Natural properties are 'shapeless' in relation to the moral ones. But how then can we pass from a merely natural description of an action to an abstract moral judgment approving of it or condemning it? We need morally shaped intermediaries that would guide our final judgment. The ideal candidates would be concepts that are descriptively rich, but already morally shaped, since they would bridge the natural/moral gap in an elegant and persuasive fashion. This is a task tailor-made for thick moral concepts like 'courageous', in distinction to abstract, thin ones like 'good' and 'right'.

> Overall, then, there are three layers: the non-ethical at the bottom, the thick ethical in the middle, and the thin ethical at the top. (Dancy 2004: 84)

We should now consider thick moral concepts. Everyone's favorite seems to be the concept LEWD, introduced into philosophical discussion many years ago by Gibbard (1992). The original story of thick concepts, as told by B. Williams (1985), was that they carry the moral-evaluative attitude on their sleeves, plus that the attitude is fixed within a very narrow range: courage is admirable, period. Change the attitude, and the concept is gone. This does not fit well with strong forms of particularism which predict changes of valence of properties people often take to be most determinately good or bad, e.g. cruelty. Thus even properties captured by thick concepts should have a flexible valence: what is lewd in one context might lack the negative moral features of lewdness in another. Dancy's work on thick concepts is geared among other things, to amending this alleged shortcoming. Let me summarize his extremely rich and involved discussion in two steps (I am concentrating upon sections VIII and IX of Dancy 1995).

Step one, the general characterization. In the case of thick concepts the description and the evaluation are 'truly intertwined', so that Dancy ultimately refuses to distinguish them as elements of a thick concept. So called evaluation encompasses a range of merited attitudes. The so-called descriptive element includes features, numbered by Dancy as 'features 1, 2, 3 ...'. I suppose that in the case of LEWD these features have to do with overt sexual display and mockery of normal proprieties. The descriptive characterization should be minimal, and simply place the concept in a right domain (in the case at hand I assume, since Dancy gives no example, it would be the domain of sexuality and sexual display). Next, the descriptive element includes *having the features 1, 2, 3 ... in the right way.* And it is the 'right way' that carries the burden: the 'right way' is the sort of way that *merits* a certain sort of complex response – the sort of response that can only be captured by saying that it is a response merited by the lewdness. Since it is the merited attitude that picks the features-cum-ways, the similarity between different lewd actions will elude a purely natural characterization, so that outsiders will not be able to light on the purely descriptive element of the thick concept. I must admit that I am a bit puzzled about 'ways of having a property'; is there a special way in which the book has the property of being thick or a particular way in which a summer day has the property of being warm? And in what way are these ways right or wrong?[2] But I let this pass (and will suggest bellow that Dancy might have in mind the influence of context on an action having properties 1, 2, 3 ...).

In general case, we have actions with features that merit approval (direction from action to approval), and then merited approval making it the case that the action satisfies a thick concept G (direction from approval to action).

Therefore A is G

←

ACTION A has f. 1, 2, 3- in the right way   approval

→

merits approval

Similarly, in the case of LEWD, it is a response from the set of relevant responses, that makes it the case that some action φ satisfies LEWD:

Therefore φ is LEWD

←

ACTION φ has f. 1, 2, 3-   response R
in the right way

→

Therefore φ merits response R

This concludes the summary and reconstruction of Dancy's proposal. It might come as a surprise, after so much talk about response, that Dancy is a staunch critic of the response-dependentist view of moral concepts and properties. To this problem we now turn.

3 Dancy against response-dependence

This subsection presents, briefly and without much discussion, Dancy's criticism of theories of moral concepts and properties that are focused upon human response. These theories in general address the issue how to place the moral reality, and our understanding of it in relation to natural reality. Dancy introduces his account of them by distinguishing two senses of a phenomenon's being 'subjective' or 'anthropocentric' (1986: 169). In the first sense, which is not relevant to our present purposes, to be anthropocentric is to be such as not to be cognitively accessible to beings who did not share in characteristic human concerns. In the second sense, which will be relevant to our discusison, to be anthropocentric is to be 'constituted by the possibility or availability of a characteristic human response'.[3] Following Dancy's talk of 'response', I will talk about response-dependentist or response-dispositionalist theories, or simply about response-dependentism (initially using these expressions as synonyms in order to point to the underlying unity of the terminology used by different authors quoted).

In order to have a handy formulation of response-dependentism I propose the following working characterization.[4] Start from the standard idea of disposition:

The property F is a dispositional property just in case there is an identity of the form
The property F = the disposition to produce R in S under C, where R is the manifestation of the disposition, S is the locus of the manifestation, and C is the condition of manifestation.

Now, for response-dispositionality: consider dispositions of subjects – loci of disposition to give response R that essentially involve some mental process, all this under specified circumstances C. The twin concepts of the relevant dispositions in subjects (to issue R) and in the object (to prompt R) are then response-dependent concepts. To put it as a principle, it is necessary for F being a response-dependent property that the following Basic Equation holds:

x is F iff x tends to elicit such-and-such response from such-and-such persons under specified circumstances.

And of course, the Equation is to be read from right to left: x is F *in virtue of* eliciting a certain response (call this, with C. Wright, 'the right order of determination').[5] Second, a property is a response-dependent one in a wide sense if it is either response-dependent or a combination of properties with at least one non-redundant narrowly response-dependent component.

Applied to moral properties, and primarily to values, the thought is that value is constitutively dependent on evaluators' responses or dispositions to respond. Here is a proposal:

X has value *V* iff evaluators would, under appropriate conditions, respond to *X* with reaction *R*. (Brower 1993: 222)

One important task is then to specify conditions and reactions. David Lewis, for example, proposes the following schema:

x is a value iff we would be disposed to value *x* under conditions of the fullest imaginative acquaintance with *x*. (Lewis 1989: 113)[6]

Let me now pass to the role of the concept of response-dependence. It helps to situate secondary qualities, like colors and smells, as well as other interesting properties, like emotional and moral ones in the naturalist picture of the world. The response-dependentist proposal usually distinguishes between the manifest image and the scientific image. In the manifest image the surface is colored, and the dog is frightful, but the image does not necessarily reveal the exact nature of color or frightfulness. (This modest sense of 'manifest' is rather ordinary. 'It was manifest to everybody that Helen was worried' entails that Helen's worry was manifest; but very little about worries can be known by some of their manifestations.) The dispositionalist suggests that our responses are the paint with which the manifest image is painted.

What about concepts of such qualities? Here is one line of thought. We, the theoreticians should introduce a response-dependent concept (or re-interpret an existing concept as response-dependent) only if we cannot identify a suitable categorial basis, or think there are principled reasons that prevent the thinker from referring to them. The attribution thus has a certain deflationary taste. And the attribution is often theoretical, rather than commonsensical: many central response-dependent concepts only *refer* to dispositional properties, but do not present their referents *as* being dispositional.[7]

A further distinction is needed at this juncture. Some response-dispositional concepts, for instance, *sexy* wear their response-dispositional character on their sleeve: they might come to appear such even to a naive thinker on sufficient reflection. For such a concept the test involves an appeal to counterfactual situations: given the thinker's cognitive, perceptual and emotional apparatus, how would she react to changed circumstances? Would she call a person sexy if he had completely different categorical properties, but her dispositions to react were suitably adapted to the new properties, so that her primary response remained the same? If yes, the concept and the corresponding property are response-dependent. Other concepts and properties, such as the naive concept *red*, do not contain an appeal to a subject's response, but stand for a property that in fact involves such a response. (Notoriously, a naive thinker sees colors as simple properties of material bodies.) In these cases, we should put metaphysics first and count the concept as response-dependent if it stands for a mind-involving quality. We have to be generous in this way, since, as we noted, many central response-dependent concepts (for instance, 'red') *refer* to dispositional properties, without presenting their referents *as* being dispositional.

Let me now place response-dependence in a wider context. Many items, properties or concepts involve responses or reference to responses. They are response-involving. This prompts an important distinction. First, there is the distinction in degree of involvement: if involving the response (some way or another) is *necessary* for the item to be instantiated, then the item is *response-dependent*, otherwise it is *merely* response-involving. (Similarly, D'Arms and Jacobson (2006) propose 'response-evoking' as a genus, of which 'response-dependent' is a species.) This first distinction will be crucial for us in the sequel.

Let me proceed by distinguishing further ways in which an item can be response-involving. The second distinction concerns items that are characterized as response-involving: is it concept only, or the property as well (in which case the correct concept will presumably also be response-involving)? Some authors stress concepts (C. Wright), others stress properties (M. Johnston). Third, there is the distinction between the function of involvement: is it merely epistemic (and then presumably constitutive of correct concepts), or is it also metaphysical? For instance, Jackson and Pettit (2002), and Pettit in a series of papers (listed in Jackson and Pettit 2002) stress the epistemic role of response-dependence. Redness (at least in one sense) just is a determinate, fully objective disjunctive property; the involvement in response is what makes us (*re-*) *cognize* it as redness. The first and the second pair of distinctions are closely related (and may be at the bottom identical), but this is not crucial for the present discussion.

Fourth, there is the distinction between descriptively and normatively specified responses, important for all normative response-involving properties.

On the descriptive side we have mere causing (the property in question just produces the response, and/or the relevant concept is of causing the response). On the normative side there is something like *meriting*. An emotional property, like being frightening can be taken descriptively: a dog is frightening if it would normally frighten the average passer-by. It can be taken normatively: a dog is frightening if it is dangerous, if the fear is justified, merited, rational and the like.

We now pass to Dancy's objections to the idea that value properties and moral properties in general are response-dependent. The first and, by Dancy's own lights (1986: 172), most important objection concerns moral phenomenology. Interestingly, it derives partly from Wiggins, who is himself a response-dependentist, and whose target is non-cognitivism, not response-dependentist views of moral reality. Dancy distinguishes a simple variant from the complex one, and chooses to address the simple one in more detail (and we shall comply with his choice in what follows). It starts from two premises, and moves to a preliminary conclusion:

> First, 'we take moral value to be part of the fabric of the world; taking our experience at face value, we judge it to be experience of the moral properties of actions and agents in the world'.
>
> Second, 'if we are to work with the presumption that the world is the way our experience represents it to us as being, we should take it in the absence of contrary considerations that actions and agents do have the sorts of moral properties we experience in them'. Therefore, (we should assume that)
>
> Third, very probably, the world is such that it contains moral properties as part of its fabric.[8]

Dancy does not elaborate the critical point of the argument. I assume that it is the following:

> Fourth, response-dependentist theories do not count moral properties as part of the fabric of the world. Therefore,
>
> Fifth, response-dependentist theories predict a wrong phenomenology of our moral experience, or, alternatively, are not able to account for the phenomenology it actually presents.

The complex form of Dancy's argument concerns moral choice. The critical fact is that 'in moral choice we struggle to find, not any answer that we can bring ourselves to accept, nor any answer that we can accept in consistency with previous answers, but the right answer. We present our search to ourselves as one governed by a criterion which does not lie in ourselves' (Dancy 1986: 172). The rest is then parallel to the simple form: if we are to understand moral choice, we have to assume that there is an objective moral criterion independent from us. Response-dependentist theories do not admit such a criterion, therefore they predict a wrong phenomenology of our moral choices, or, alternatively, are not able to account for the phenomenology it actually presents.[9]

Dancy's second objection concerns the motivational force of moral judgments. Remember that for a response-dependentist, X has value V iff evaluators would, under appropriate conditions, respond to X by some specified response. Dancy now considers the response and the conditions. Here is then the objection in its general form of a destructive dilemma:

> First, the response-dependentist account stipulates that a determinate moral property is a disposition to cause a certain moral response in specified circumstances. Relevant circumstances are either the normal ones or the idealized ones.
>
> Second, normal situations are precisely not very good ones for discerning the moral properties of the choices we face. (We have to deal with distractions, contrary influences, prejudices, lack of time and similar problems.)
>
> Third, our actual moral experience never occurs in ideal circumstances, so they are unsuitable for defining the property actual experience represents. The conclusion follows.
>
> Our actual moral experience cannot represent moral properties conceived as dispositions to cause R in ideal situations, which we never experience.[10]

Dancy does not give examples. Let me adapt a classical example due to R. Hare (1963). Peter owes me a large sum, which he cannot pay back in the foreseeable future. I need money, and I am overcome by anger at Peter, and I judge that he should be put in prison for not repaying. This is an overreaction, which cannot determine what the right conduct would be. If I were in ideal circumstances, I would not get so angry at Peter, and would have a more appropriate reaction. Unfortunately, this does not help in the actual circumstances.

Since his opponent in the paper is McDowell, Dancy assumes motivational internalism as their common ground, so that a part of the proper response to a perceived moral property is concern, i.e. a motivational state. With this assumption in mind Dancy again raises the question of distractions: 'If, for instance, I am drunk or overcome by greed, or even surrounded by and distracted by ordinary concerns, why should I care about the disposition an action may have to cause certain responses in me in situations in which I do not at present find myself?' (Dancy 1986: 180). To return to our example, I am not motivated to pardon Peter, which would be a morally correct attitude. So, the second premise of the above argument becomes that

> a moral property, conceived as a disposition to elicit a certain response in ideal circumstances, is not for that reason internally related to the will of a perceiver who is not himself in those circumstances. (Dancy 1986: 180)

Notice that Dancy takes 'normal' to include states of drunkenness or being overcome by greed. We shall return to this rather Falstaffian assumption later. The argument then proceeds in the same way as the general version: response-dependence cannot secure the identification of the motivating moral property either in our normal situation, or by appeal to some ideal situation made from the actual normal one, so response-dependentism fails. Central moral properties are not response-dependent, and perhaps even no moral properties are.

My main question is going to be whether the dependence of concept and property on response introduces response-dependence in the standard philosophical sense. So, for purposes of discussion, I could stop the retelling of Dancy's story right now. However, I want to mention briefly, in fairness to Dancy, his most original particularistic step, namely step two. He is unfortunately quite brief about it (and he does not present it in a paper as a move proper to particularism, but prefers to connect it with general consideration of thickness). Here is an attempt at reconstruction, and this is our step two.

Start with the natural basis. Two token actions, a1 and a2, considered in themselves, can have the same natural properties, but still be distinguishable on the level of the thick, since the applicability of a thick concept is not fully determined on natural grounds. Approval or disapproval involve more than natural properties. Dancy is very laconic on this point. I propose that we understand him in the following way. First, we have his claim about underdetermination of the thick (and of *merited* attitude) by the natural. Second, we have his claim that merited attitudes of approval are bestowed upon action, not in virtue of its having features 1, 2, 3 . . ., but in virtue of having them in the right way, where *right* is itself evaluative. If we put the two claims together, we should conclude that the natural base are features 1, 2, 3 . . ., whereas the non-natural supplement is the right way of having them. But even a lewd action might be morally acceptable, say in the context of a carnival. So, we have the following layers *a-f* underlying moral judgments involving thick concepts:

a) the natural basis, feature 1, 2, 3 . . .
b) the right and wrong ways of having them (ways that merit a response)
c) the thick property involving *a* and *b* and right relations between them,
d) exemplified in a concrete situation;

the exemplification yields
e) reasons for judgment, which in their turn justify
f) moral judgment involving thick concept (e.g. a1 is lewd and bad, a1 is lewd and none the worse for that, a2 is not lewd).

Let me reiterate that Dancy himself does not say in section IX, where the layers of the natural and the thick are introduced, that it is the layer *b* that goes beyond natural properties. He stresses its evaluative role in section

VIII, and does not come back to it later. Still, I think that this is the best reconstruction of the whole picture available.

The following question naturally arises at this juncture. What is the nature of layer *b*, the ways of having the property, that distinguishes between the status of two actions, our a1 and a2? Dancy is not explicit about it. The general particularistic line would suggest some role for respective contexts in which actions take place. Here is a possibility, introduced by example. Let a1 be a case of overt sexual display in a canteen of a factory, aimed at exciting and amusing the audience of opposite sex. Assume it merits a slightly negative attitude, which then promotes (or demotes) it to the status of being lewd. Let a2 be the exact natural replica of a1, only placed in the canteen for guards of a concentration camp. The camp inmate performing sexually overt acts is aiming at exciting and amusing the guards in order to prolong his or her life a few more days. Most people I know would think that a2 does not merit any negative attitude, but rather understanding and compassion. So, a2 is probably not lewd.

However, we have an additional degree of freedom on particularist construal, captured by *d* and *e*: not only does the overt sexual display change its moral status, being lewd in the canteen of a factory and not lewd, but rather tragic in a concentration camp, but LEWD itself can change its valence: an action can be lewd and therefore appropriate, say at a carnival.

The upshot is that context provides one way in which a narrow set of properties that would most often result in lewdness is prevented from making the action lewd. In the usual context the token action is lewd. Its way of being sexually overt is morally awkward in this context, which then grounds lewdness. In the perverted context of a concentration camp its twin token action has the same property in a way that is not objectionable; so, the action is not lewd. This gives us the intermediate thick level, from which our correct judgments flow. In a personal communication Dancy has also reminded me that one could also interpret the example differently, claiming that even in the concentration camp the dance *is* lewd, 'but none the worse for that'. And he has noted that he considers this second degree of freedom more central than the first one. I reiterate that the context is just one possible factor influencing the rightness of some way of having the relevant natural property, and the particularist might think of other possibilities. This concludes my reconstruction of Dancy's ideas.

4 Criticism: incompatibility

Let me pass to my negative argument. I want to argue that Dancy's treatment of thick concepts is incompatible with his rejection of response-dispositionalism, given his other assumptions. Let me put my cards on the table, and present the bare bones of the argument straight-forwardly. Thick concepts are central to ethics, Dancy claims. But, thick concepts appeal to appropriate attitudes which are our moral response(s) to properties of actions and ways of having these properties. Of course, the relevant attitude-responses are inseparable from the concept. This makes thick concepts into a kind of *response-dependent* concepts and doesn't fit well with his rejection of response-dependence. But, in truth, Dancy has argued primarily against response-dependence of properties, not concepts. Still, he can't avoid response-dependence of moral properties, it seems, since he insists that moral thought and talk are to be construed realistically. But then he must agree that there are properties (and ways of having them) tracked by (or referred to) by thick concepts. Call them 'thick properties (and ways)'. These are central moral properties. Plausibly, the structure of thick properties mirrors the structure of thick concepts. In particular, the relevant attitude-responses are inseparable from the property. But then, thick properties (and ways) are response-dependent, therefore the central moral properties (and ways) are response-dependent. Let me now briefly elaborate on each step.

1 Thick concepts are central to ethics.

This is not problematic. Dancy repeatedly claims (most recently 2004: 84) that the thick layer is the crucial layer connecting the natural, morally shapeless facts to thin moral judgments.

2 Thick concepts appeal to appropriate response(s), so that the relevant attitude-responses are inseparable from the concept.

Dancy is firm about the inseparability of (appeal to) response from the thick concept. This is the main point of his criticism of Gibbard, and an overarching constraint on the right account, that dictates flexibility of response and excludes unique narrow characterizations of responses. More interestingly, he is also quite explicit about the relation between 'meriting a response' and 'eliciting a merited response'. He admits that it is tempting to identify the two, and, more importantly, defends the temptation. He almost endorses the identification, and then challenges his opponent, McDowell, to produce the same identification in the case of color.

> It is tempting therefore to think of the moral property of meriting a response as identical with the disposition to elicit a merited response. This fits the metaphysical nature of the situation, and it does not distort the phenomenology. The experience of value is the experience of a situation as calling for a certain response, and we can see this as a disposition in the case to extract a merited response from us. But now the question is whether similar remarks can be made about colour. McDowell needs to make such remarks if the analogy between colour and value is to do what he wants it to, and I doubt whether this can be made to work. (Dancy 1993: 161)

Rejecting premise 1. is not a live option for Dancy. Neither is rejecting 2. and claiming that the attitude is clearly separable from the thick concept. This would place Dancy in the same camp with Blackburn, which he would very much wish to avoid. He might try to tinker with claims having to do with realism, (see steps 4–7 later in this subsection). He would not reject realism in general. He might try downplaying reference for concepts. Concepts do not stand for robust properties, he might propose. But claiming that they don't refer at all would saddle him with thick fictionalism: thick concepts only purport to refer, in fact they stand for fictions. Not very promising given their role in giving and supporting reasons, and given the factual nature of reasons. A full-blown fact (Leonidas' action at Thermopylae being *courageous*) can hardly consist of Leonidas, action *and* a fictional entity, the non-property of being courageous, as a guest-star. A better move would be to try to deflate properties, following the example of S. Schiffer who talks of 'pleonastic properties', (2003) mere shadows of our thoughts. But then, Dancy would have to deflate facts accordingly. If 'being courageous' is pleonastic, so is the corresponding fact about Leonidas. But then factual reasons (he praises Leonidas *for his being courageous*) are pleonastic, mere shadows of psychological reasons. This would be the end of the world for dedicated reason-factualists.

Let me now focus upon the inseparability of attitude, i.e. of the merited response. Concepts that essentially involve appeal to a response, normal, merited or appropriate, and that apply to some item in virtue of its relation to a response, are response-involving concepts. Now we have encountered a distinction in degree of involvement: if involving the response (some way or another) is *necessary* for the item to be instantiated and makes it into the item that it is, then the item is *response-dependent*, otherwise it is *merely* response-involving. The first question is then whether the relation to the response is really necessary for the concept to be what it is. The next question is whether the relevant item falls under the concept *because* it is linked to the response in the right way.

Now, to start with the later question, Dancy is clear that by his lights, an action is, say lewd, *because* it merits a particular (kind of) attitude as response. But then, LEWD depends on availability of this attitude(-type), which makes it dependent on response(-type). In short, the *order of determination* proposed by Dancy is the correct one for response-dependence: the action is lewd to a large extent *because* it merits a response from the relevant range. We may agree that being response-involving is wider that being response-dependent, which is a stronger notion, still the specific difference defining the latter seems to be precisely a dependence, captured by the 'because' proposed by Dancy.

Secondly, the inseparability of response from the concept seems to involve the idea that response is *constitutive* of the concept. So, by both criteria, thick concepts seem to be not merely response-involving but response-dependent. Some commentators have simply assumed that Dancy is a response dispositionalist. D'Arms and Jacobson (2006) take Dancy's paper on thick concepts (1995) to stand broadly within the dispositionalist program:

> The alternative form of perceptivism about value, which has been dubbed sensibility theory, seeks to capture the intuitively compelling aspects of dispositionalism while accommodating this disanalogy between value and color. The most difficult of these positions to characterize directly, this approach is exemplified by the work of John McDowell, David Wiggins, and David McNaughton; it is also embraced in some respects by Bernard Williams (1985, 1996) and Jonathan Dancy (1995), although each rejects other parts of the program (D'Arms and Jacobson 2006).

However, response-dispositionalism or dependentism seems to lead to inconsistency in a few unproblematic steps: on the one hand Dancy is critical of response-dependence, on the other hand he gives a central role to the thick concepts. Add to this the fact that he is a staunch moral realist, very eager to have moral reality correspond to correct moral thought, and you end up with response-dependent moral properties as well. So, the conjecture that thick concepts and corresponding properties are response-dependent would present a real problem for Dancy.

All the defenders of Dancy in the discussion and afterwards have therefore concentrated upon the step from premise 2. to the conjecture that moral items are response-dependent. They all propose the same line: thick properties essentially involve our responses-attitudes but they are not therefore response-dependent. The involvement is of a different kind. This was proposed by Little at the Bled conference.[11]

Let me distinguish two lines. The one would simply suggest that 'mere meriting' does not make in item response-dependent because it is a normative, and not descriptive property. This line is a non-starter. There is a wide ranging consensus in the literature about non-reductive normative candidates for response-dependency: precisely the properties that both merit some response (or concepts that involve meriting a response), which makes them response-dependent, and are irreducibly normative, since the meriting cannot be reduced to a descriptive concept and/or property. (See Blackburn 1992; D'Arms and Jacobson 2006.) I know of no instance in the literature where *meriting* would count *against* being response-dependent. The line introduces a new, and unusual concept of response-dependence, in fact the restriction of the usual concept to its descriptive sub-species, and the restriction of the class of response-dependent properties to its non-normative sub-class. (If Dancy had originally had such a new concept in mind, he would have surely said so.)

The second line, actually proposed by Little, is to resist the temptation mentioned in discussing our premise 2., 'to identify the moral property of meriting a response as identical with the disposition to elicit a merited response'. Remember that Dancy himself thinks that the identification 'fits the metaphysical nature of the situation, and it does not distort the phenomenology'. Now, Little's ingenious proposal is that our particularist should *divorce meriting from eliciting*. Not every merited attitude gets actually elicited, unfortunately. According to her proposal (and I note in passing that at the conference it has elicited Dancy's merited approval), our particularist should enter the following divorce claim:

> The normative property of meriting a response (or attitude) is completely different and independent from actually having a disposition to elicit the response. The latter is causal-descriptive, the former is purely normative. Response-dependence has to do with the causal process of eliciting, the thickness of moral concepts with the normative status of meriting. Once we particularists divorce the two, we can go on rejecting the first, and endorsing the use of the second. There is no incompatibility between the centrality of thick, attitude-involving moral properties and the rejection of response-dependence. The two can go hand in hand, once the normative is clearly distinguished from the causal.

However, there are two replies. First, the notion of being a *response*, involves an important causal aspect, no matter whether the response is actual or only merited. A response is something directed to, and presumably, in human case, occasioned by its object. Mere coincidence is insufficient for the state or event being a response: it's not enough that I just happen to feel disgust when food is presented, if the disgust is not a response to the food. Second, as a consequence the idea of X meriting a response implicitly involves the claim that were the situation the way X merits, it would receive the response. And indeed, the response would be elicited by X. Third, on standard possible-world semantics for normative claims, the marriage of eliciting and meriting cannot be dissolved. The simple account is that an action merits disapproval iff it is disapproved of in the nearest (almost) ideal world, i.e. the world in which bad actions happen, but get disapproved of (in all metaphysically meritocratic worlds, so to speak). The more complicated one translates meriting into obligation: so an action merits disapproval if relevant persons are obligated to disapprove of it. And an agent obligated to do F iff she does F in all ideal worlds. So, to merit disapproval is to be such as to elicit disapproval in morally favorable circumstances.

Let us write down the two conditions (we are interested in them being necessary, so I will use the 'only if' formulation) and give them names:

(D)   X has P only if X merits the response R.
(RD)   X has P* only if it elicits a merited response R.

The two look very similar. Moreover, the analogous characterizations would be taken to be almost synonymous in related areas. Take the property of being fearful in the weakly normative sense. There you have

(d)   X is fearful only if X requires and justifies fear as a response.
(rd)   X is fearful only if it elicits justified fear as a response.

My intuition tells me that one would count fearfulness as response-dependent both on (d) and on (rd). To return to (D) and (RD), note that the two not only look the same, but that we have Dancy's own admission about how plausible it would be to identify them.

Well, the particularist could say, you still don't have the causal link. The attitude and the action just occur together in the right worlds. The response-dependentist can offer two answers. The more modest one is to agree. Yes, we just need counterfactual dependence for response-dependence, and the semantics gives us the counterfactual dependence needed: if A had not behaved lewdly, B would not have disapproved of him. The less modest is to argue that the attitude must be taken *a propos* the action; therefore, there must be a causal link, as we have learned from causal theories of perception and causal considerations about knowledge. The scenario is analogous to the food example. Imagine a world in which an unfortunate moralist hallucinates a lewd act A and has the thought 'This is very bad!' As the Gettier luck would have it, there is a lewd act B just happening in front of the hallucinating moralist. Well, the moralist does not have the thought *a propos* B, but only *a propos* A, so he did not disapprove of B, just of A. No causal link, no disapproval.

Finally, is the appeal to non-actual worlds damaging? No, since all standard response-dependentist proposals for understanding moral concepts and properties are couched in what *would* happen under the right circumstances. (Remember Lewis's 'x is a value iff we would be disposed to value x' and Brower's 'X has value V iff evaluators would, under appropriate conditions, respond to X with reaction R' quoted in section 3.) Moreover, in specifying the circumstances, virtually *every* response-dependentist notes that bad circumstances featuring moral blindness just don't count, so they do in fact look at circumstances where the action does elicit a response it *merits* (and then reductionists try to reduce 'meriting', whereas anti-reductionists leave it unreduced). So, the attention to the merited attitude-response has been, implicitly and often explicitly, part and parcel of the response-dependentist account of value (the idealization involved in specifying the relevant situation will be discussed in a moment). This suggests the strong claim, which I find plausible, that (D) and (RD) are just verbal variants of each other.

The defender can also argue in the following way. There is no conflict between a purely normative view and Dancy's contention (in the first objection) that 'the world is such that it contains moral properties as part of its fabric'. Consider the quote from Dancy from n. 9: 'In moral choice we struggle to find, not any answer that we can bring ourselves to accept, nor any answer that we can accept in consistency with previous answers, but the right answer.' This point, if correct, can be used against a causal-descriptive view; but clearly not against a purely normative view.

Answer: Note that Dancy is arguing against McDowell's version of response-dependence, which includes the anti-reductionist proviso to the effect that the object elicits a *merited* response. If Dancy's objection is inefficient against a purely normative view, than it is similarly inefficient against McDowell's version, against which it was originally raised. There is no reason for moral phenomenology to be different in the two cases. If the objection can hurt McDowell's variant, than it hurts Dancy's variant as well.

He seems to think that the only variant that Dancy argues against is the reductionist causal-descriptive view, and not McDowell's anti-reductionist line, combining causation and meriting. But then he should explain why McDowell is *the only opponent explicitly mentioned in Dancy's paper*, and I don't see how this can be consistently done.

This is not all. In fact, the critic (myself, in the present case) does not need such a strong suggestion. (D) and (RD) might have slightly different senses, (D) being more explicitly normative, (RD) more explicitly causal. Still, they seem to be necessarily co-extensive. Suppose, X had P* in virtue of eliciting merited R in the right situations, those where everything gets what it merits. But then, P merits R. Inversely, suppose X has P in virtue of meriting R as a response. Then, in the right situations (the meritocratic ones, where everything gets what it merits), X elicits R as a merited response.

We can even go beyond co-extensiveness. It is very probable that the candidate properties P and P* that X has in virtue of satisfying either (D) or (RD) are in fact one and the same property. What could possibly be a ground of difference? What makes X elicit a merited response is what makes it merit such a response, and vice versa. So, even if (D) and (RD) do not have strictly identical senses, they are coextensive, and might have the same referent. Since we are ultimately interested in properties, this is enough to make thick concepts response-dependent.

However, the critic needs even less. Even if the defender of Dancy dug in her heels and claimed that the properties under consideration somehow must be distinct, it does not show that they are *relevantly* distinct. Remember that the motivation of response-dependentist accounts is to point out commonalities between a wide range of properties (colors, tastes, emotional properties, moral properties) that are essentially dependent on our subjectivity. For this classificatory and explanatory purpose, the difference between (D)-property and (RD)-property is just irrelevant. Both make having the property contingent on the presence of response, either elicited actually in usual situations, or elicited in normatively right situations. And this is a very firm ground to classify them together, if your interest is in the contribution of our subjectivity: the contribution is of the same kind in both cases.

Of course I agree that Little has very perceptively put her finger on an important distinction *within* the family of response-dependent properties. Although disposition to elicit the relevant response must be present in all cases belonging to the family, moral properties would be embedded in a different network of relations than, say, colors. This does not show that thick concepts and properties are not response-dependent, only that they belong to a different branch of the same family. The divorce claim does not help our particularist. This brings us to the first intermediate conclusion.

3 Thick concepts are response-dependent concepts.

Dancy is right that the temptation to equate eliciting a merited response, and meriting a response to be elicited in the right situation is great, and probably justified. And D'Arms is similarly right that Dancy is committed to response-dispositionalism (or -dependentism). We now pass to metaphysics.

What about the referents of thick concepts? For this we need a new assumption from Dancy.

4 Moral thought and talk are to be construed realistically.

Dancy is very keen on *practical and moral reality*. First, he is generally a tough realist about the moral domain. Second, he is a factualist about practical reasons: a reason is not a psychological state, but an objective normative fact, out there in the world. His *Practical Reality* (2000a) is to a large extent dedicated to the defense of this claim, basically from its indispensability for justifying practical and, in particular, moral reasoning and rational(-istic) accounts of actions. Dancy is thus a metaphysically serious realist about morality (his realism is not just the claim that moral rules are intersubjectively valid, nor any such ersatzist claim).

Serious realism is then relevant for determining the referents of thick concepts.

5 There are properties (and ways of having them) tracked by (or referred to) by thick concepts. Call them 'thick properties (and ways)'.

A metaphysically serious moral and practical realist is committed to the reality of what moral thought and talk is about. Thick concepts are predicates used in moral thoughts. They are sometimes satisfied by some items in reality, say actions. The serious moral realist must assume that crucial predicates also stand for something had by those items (e.g. actions) satisfying them. The usual formulation is that they stand for properties. Properties might be universals, or they might be tropes; the argument is indifferent between the two. (Even the Lewisian characterization of properties as privileged classes, called 'natural' by him, is compatible with the argument.)

Thick concepts are an important moral kind. Therefore, on the realist assumption, they pick up a kind in reality referred to. So, there is a kind of properties satisfying thick moral concepts. These are precisely thick properties.

6 Thick properties (and ways) are central moral properties.

We need an additional assumption connected with serious realism. The assumption claims that concepts central for the theory of a given domain normally stand for properties central to the very same domain. If MASS and FORCE are central to mechanics, then mass and force are central for mechanical processes and things participating in them. Applied to ethics, if thick concepts are central to moral thought, then thick properties should be central moral properties.

7 The structure of thick properties mirrors the structure of thick concepts. In particular, the relevant attitude-responses are inseparable from the property.

Concepts that combine some attitude(s) and descriptive property can pick up various properties. One possibility is that they pick up a non-moral descriptive property, the way Gibbard thinks of thick concepts. Another, more sophisticated one is that they pick up a descriptive property (role-filler), which is in fact moral property. This is 'response-dependence without tears' defended by Jackson and Pettit (2002). In all these cases, the descriptive part and the responsive-attitudinal part of the (definition of) the concept can be pried apart from each other.

Rejecting 7 has unpalatable consequences. On one reading, it trivializes the talk of inseparability in the concept: although the descriptive and the attitudinal component of the referent (say, of courage) can be accessed separately, we merely cannot put their characterization into our present thick concept (e.g. COURAGE). One is reminded of the folk-concept WATER, that does not contain the concept HYDROGEN, but nothing very exciting about chemical reality follows from this. Alternatively it makes the inseparability talk false, since the reference to separate real components can be taken as characterization-refinement of the concept as well.

Dancy is himself adamant about the non-separability of the descriptive from the attitudinal. The two are not even elements of the concept; they are so intertwined that they melt together. But then, there is no fixed property independent from the attitude referred to by a thick concept, or such that it can be picked up by the concept. In other words, whatever is picked up by a thick concept, is itself such that it 'melts together' an attitude and a descriptive basis. The referents of thick concepts are themselves thick in this demanding sense. Thus, the structure (or lack of one) of thick properties mirrors the structure (or lack of it) of thick concepts. If thick concepts are response-dependent and thick properties mirror their structure, then thick properties are themselves response-dependent. Being lewd is such as to merit a certain attitude; the merited attitude is not separable from lewdness 'in the thing'.

Before concluding, let me briefly return to the kinds of response-involvement. We have stressed the distinction in degree of such involvement: if involving the response (some way or another) is *necessary* for the item to be instantiated, then the item is *response-dependent*; otherwise it is *merely* response-involving. We have noted that what makes an item response-dependent is its constitutive dependence on response. We have noted the distinction between mere response-dependency of a concept and the response-dependency of the property as well (the correct concept will presumably also be response-involving). We have mentioned the related distinction between the function of involvement, between the merely epistemic one, and the metaphysical one. Finally, there is the distinction between descriptively and normatively specified response, important for all normative response-involving properties. On the descriptive side we have mere causing (the property in question just produces the response, and/or the relevant concept is of causing the response). On the normative side there is something like *meriting*. An emotional property, like being fearful, can be taken descriptively: a dog is fearful if it would normally frighten the average passer-by. It can be taken normatively: a dog is fearful if it is dangerous, if the fear is justified, merited, rational and the like. The most important point in the present context is that the normative/descriptive and merely involving/dependent are *mutually orthogonal*: a property can be metaphysically response-dependent, either in virtue of its normally causing an X-related response, or of meriting an X-related response. This brings us to the conclusion:

8 Thick properties (and ways) are response-dependent.

Therefore, the following holds:

9 The central moral properties (and ways) are response-dependent.

The conclusion seems clearly incompatible with Dancy's strictures against response-dispositional accounts. We have already considered various defenses, concentrated mostly on the step from essential involvement of response to response-dependence, and found them wanting. However, accepting response-dependence is no tragedy for the particularist: there is no intrinsic conflict between particularism and response-dependence. We leave it at that, and turn directly to thick moral concepts.

5 The structure of thick concepts

What should a response-dependentist alternative look like? I will limit myself to a few sketchy remarks. First, note that Dancy is not very explicit about the nature of concepts themselves, and the conceptual structure of thick concepts. One candidate structure is the inferential(ist) one. It has been developed for pejoratives, by authors like Dummett and Brandom, and can be applied, *mutatis mutandis*, to thick concepts. The inferential paradigm features some descriptive concept *D*, its corresponding thick concept Θ, and the evaluative concept *E*. In the case of our thick concept example, LEWD, the descriptive concept is something like INVOLVES OVERT DISPLAY OF SEXUALITY, and the evaluative concept is OBJECTIONABLE or WRONG. A given act *a* satisfies *D*, and this licenses inference that it satisfies Θ as well:

$$\frac{Da}{\Theta a}$$

Now, if *a* satisfies the thick concept, say it is lewd, then one may conclude that it is also morally objectionable:

$$\frac{\Theta a}{Ea}$$

The purely inferential account does not explain what licenses the inference. A more informative assumption is that thick moral concepts are defined by an implicitly held commonsense *theory*. One can see the semantics of these concepts as being very close to the semantics of serious pejoratives in spite of recent denials of the similarity. Eklund (2004) claims that the important difference consists in the locus of evaluation: with thick concepts evaluation is part of the sense, with pejoratives, it is merely part of the tone. However, there is no shortage of claims that evaluation is not part of the sense of thick concepts (Brower 1988), and, on the other hand that it is part of the sense (or conventional implicature) of pejoratives (Brandom 1994; Williamson 2003). Therefore, it is better to assume that the situation is similar in both cases, and try to offer a unified account which then can be tested both on thick concepts and pejoratives. A theory-based account presumably could do the job.

Let me mention two problems common to inferential and theory-based accounts. What about concepts like our LEWD, which are disowned by many thinkers (the way in which offensive pejoratives like 'Nigger' or 'Kike' are disowned by decent speakers)?

In what sense does the LEWD disowner possess the concept she disowns? There are two mutually related senses of 'possessing a concept' and rejecting necessity for the less demanding of them. On the stronger sense, taking inferential commitments (or believing the truth) in relation to 'Fs are Gs' is both necessary and sufficient for possessing a concept. In this sense, our

LEWD-disowner does not possess the concept LEWD (nor does a non-racist strongly possess the concept NIGGER, nor does an atheist strongly possess the concept BLASPHEMY). These are not their concepts, as Oscar Wilde would put it. Most concepts are acquired by endorsing the corresponding inferential commitment (accepting the corresponding belief). Exceptionally, one acquires F-concept *meta-conceptually*, by learning that *others* accept 'Fs are Gs'. Then, one has F-concept in a weak sense. A non-racist, knowledgeable about racist discourse, possesses racist pejoratives in such a weak sense. To put it in Brandom's terminology, the non-racist does not endorse a deontic commitment of racist pejoratives. What she does is then open for further analysis: she might simulate the commitments, or engage in pretended endorsement and the like. Such ersatz endorsement is sufficient for concept possession in the weak sense.

The second problem is more serious. The mini-theories the inadequate thick concepts (and pejoratives) embody, as well as inferences they license, are incorrect: the theories are false (e.g. there is nothing morally bad about explicit sexuality) and the inferences are unsound (e.g. inference from 'explicitly sexual' to 'morally wrong', or from 'being a black' to 'being brutish'). How is this possible? How can propositions (or inferences) constitutive for a concept be false or unsound? Eklund has discussed descriptive components of thick concepts in a similar vein; I am here more interested in the normative-descriptive link. Well, such concepts involve materially false (incorrect) components (inference rules or propositions). And the consequence is that *propositions and inferences analyzing these concepts are neither necessarily true, nor correct, nor a priori knowable.* The result is a bit shocking, and many would prefer to replace it with a less radical conclusion. I will not defend it here, and will limit myself to noting that it seems to be entailed by the natural understanding of what is constitutive for a given concept.[12]

I now pass to the evaluative element proper, and the issue of response-dependence. I have been agreeing with Dancy that ordinary moral *phenomenology* is not response-dependentist. Accordingly, ordinary moral concepts do not directly point to human response. The response-dependent account is a theoretical, philosophical account of moral commonsense, and not an explicit part of it. Therefore, we should admit that response-dependence is *not built into the ordinary thick moral concept itself.* So, the evaluative component of LEWD should not be put directly in terms of approval, merited or not. It is rather to be characterized in terms of being (morally) objectionable, or even plainly morally wrong, in some way to be determined. A Rossian might put it in terms of being *prima facie* objectionable: an action is lewd only if it is *prima facie* objectionable. A particularist of the brand of Lance and Little (see the paper in the present volume) might put it in terms of a default valence, that lewd action has *ceteris paribus.* And finally, a particularist of a more Dancyan stripe might claim that there is no recognizable evaluative element, an 'atom' that can be added to descriptive atoms to form a thick 'molecule': rather, an action that is properly characterized as lewd will be morally objectionable in the context in which no special defeaters to being thus objectionable are present.

A virtue of this more objectifying account is that it preserves the objectivist phenomenology. Another virtue is that it is readily generalized. The two combine. Consider thick concepts in other domains, for instance the epistemic ones like INGENIOUS, ORIGINAL, HASTY (said of a generalization) or the pairs of contraries like SOPHISTICATED vs. PRIMITIVE (or even IDIOTIC) and DEEP vs. SUPERFICIAL. They involve praise or blame, but in an objectifying way: a discovery is deep if it is remarkable and of high quality because it has certain descriptive features, like revealing crucial but non-manifest features of reality. Similarly, prudential thick concepts like THOUGHTFUL, (IM)PRUDENT, (UN)WISE, RASH, GREEDY, WASTEFUL involve blame and praise, but also suggest that there is something objectively valuable or objectively wrong about the trait and its bearer.[13] The phenomenology is unitary and objectivist across the board. Response-dependence comes into the picture later, when one builds a theory about the deep nature of the qualities in question, and of the metaphysically correct concepts of them. The final verdict on this issue need not be unitary. It can turn out that some of the properties are more objective, and some less. For instance, epistemic rationality might be more amenable to objectivist treatment than morality: being ingenious or original might be more of an objective matter than being kind or cruel, although all four seem on a par as far as phenomenology is concerned, since their goodness or badness seems phenomenally to be an objective property. So the phenomenal unity does not dictate the verdict about the underlying natures.

There are other reasons for objectifying, like simplicity and its concomitants. 'You should not burn the cat alive because it is cruel, and therefore bad' is simpler than 'because it is cruel and merits disapproval'. Indeed, as Gibbard (forthcoming) has pointed out, the objectifying stance is more primitive and children take this stance way before they can think in terms of relativizing properties to subjective attitudes. Further, as the prohibition about burning the cat alive shows, the commonsense offers an explanatory role to thick properties that are better captured by straightforward objective reading: the wrongness of the act makes it the case that it is forbidden.

A defender of Dancy might reply that when it comes to concepts she prefers speaking of an attitude, e.g. approval, to introducing an objective conceptual component (or mark) like GOOD or OBJECTIONABLE, as we did here, in order to avoid a well known complication. The complication is illustrated by T.M. Scanlon who argues in his paper on thick concepts (2003) against Williams that the thick concept typically involves a thin 'mark' (e.g. that 'MORALLY WRONG' is analytic of 'CRUEL'). How can then the thick concept be epistemically prior? One would then have to draw the consequence of the negative answer that it is the thin group that is prior, or that none is. (Similarly, one would then argue about properties, that thick properties are secondary to thin ones, which are among their basic constituents). The answer is that the thin mark is implicit. Moral learning starts from thick concepts and from implicit judgment involved in the deployment of such concepts and only then proceeds towards the explicit, thin concepts. So, there is no danger, and we should not needlessly complicate the account, introducing response-dependence into the naive concept, rather than in the theoretical explanation and account of the property itself that the concept refers to.

6 Conclusion

In the first and longer part of the paper, we have been examining three tenets of Dancy's meta-ethics, have found them incompatible, and have proposed a response-dependentist (or response-dispositional) solution. The first tenet is the central importance of thick concepts and properties. The second is that such concepts essentially involve response(s) of observers, which Dancy interprets in a way that fits the pattern of context-dependent resultance: thick concepts are well suited for the particularist grounding of moral theory. However, and this is the third tenet, elsewhere Dancy forcefully argues against a response-dispositional account of moral concepts and properties. We have argued that an anti-dispositional view is incompatible with the first two points concerning thick concepts. If thick concepts and properties are paramount and ubiquitous in moral thought and reality, and if they are essentially tied to human responses, then anti-dispositionalism is false. Dancy himself avoids obvious contradiction by characterizing thick items (concepts) differently from the usual characterization of response-dependent items. Actions that satisfy thick concepts do so in virtue of *meriting* a determinate response. The non-reductionist response-dependentist usually puts it slightly differently: such actions satisfy a given moral concept in virtue of *eliciting a merited response.* I have argued at length that this tenuous difference in formulation is too weak to support a relevant difference *in rebus.* If the argument is right, Dancy is implicitly committed to a kind of response-dispositionalism, as some commentators have already noted.

Finally, I have argued that the situation is not dramatic: the particularist should embrace thick concepts and properties, and reject anti-dispositionalism. However, this would bring back the analogy with color and other secondary qualities. Since there are *ceteris paribus* laws governing such properties, the analogy suggests that moral properties might also be best accounted for by a *ceteris paribus* or hedged account, a compromise between traditional generalism and the particularism of Dancy's variety.

Our central negative argument, about the incompatibility of thickness, as understood by Dancy, and his rejection of response-dependentism, can be put in a more constructive way. A lot of moral thought and discourse implicitly relies on our response, emotional, specifically moral, and the like. Morality is largely response-involving. There is no wonder that this involvement of response points to a stronger possibility, serious response-dependence. Response-dependentists develop this line, claiming that the deep response-dependence of moral properties and concepts accounts for so much response-involvement at the surface. This is the royal road from thickness to response-dependence.

Notes

1 Thanks go to Jonathan Dancy for his help and support, to George Rey, Maggie Little and Mark Lance for encouragement and help, and to Friderik Klampfer, Danilo Šuster and Vojko Strahovnik.

2 Some interesting criticisms and an interesting alternative can be found in M. Eklund's recent paper (2004).

3 Here is Dancy's formulation:
Moral concepts, then, are subjective, and this claim is one, but only one, sense of the idea that moral properties are anthropocentric. They are anthropocentric because the concepts of those properties could not be grasped by beings who did not share in characteristic human concerns.

There is however another sense we could give to the idea that moral properties are anthropocentric, which has already emerged in discussion of the two accounts of what it is for a property to be a real property of objects. We might say that moral properties are anthropocentric because they are constituted by the possibility or availability of a characteristic human response. And this would give anyone who, though tempted by moral realism, was also convinced by the disentangling argument that moral concepts are subjective, a strong incentive to stick to the weaker conception of real properties. For such a person ends up in the apparently comfortable position of maintaining that moral properties are anthropocentric in both senses, but still real properties of objects (Dancy 1986: 169).

4 I am following Mark Johnston and replacing his concept-talk with property-talk. Mark Johnston defines response-dependent concepts in two steps. First, and most importantly comes response-dispositionality. Start from the standard idea of disposition:
The concept F is a dispositional concept just in case there is an identity of the form.
The concept F = the concept of the disposition to produce R in S under C, where R is the manifestation of the disposition, S is the locus of the manifestation and C is the condition of manifestation (Johnston 1993: 103).

5 This is inspired by Blackburn's nicely general formulation from his (1993: 260).

6 Lewis's further proposal is the following: 'I say that to be valued by us means to be that which we desire to desire' (Lewis 1989: 116).

7 I argue for this point at length in Miščević (1998).

8 Here is Dancy's own formulation:
I take there to be two forms of the argument, one simple and one more complex. The simple form can be found in Mackie's view that we take moral value to be part of the fabric of the world; taking our experience at face value, we judge it to be experience of the moral properties of actions and agents in the world. And if we are to work with the presumption that the world is the way our experience represents it to us as being, we should take it in the absence of contrary considerations that actions and agents do have the sorts of moral properties we

experience in them. This is an argument about the nature of moral experience, which moves from that nature to the probable nature of the world. . . . It is the simple form of the argument that will concern us for the remainder of this paper, for only the simple form is concerned with our experience of the moral properties of actions we perform or see performed in front of us (Dancy 1986: 172–73). The argument is echoed by other writers in more recent papers. Here is Terence Cuneo:

> . . . if it is necessary [sic] the case that moral qualities are identical with dispositions, then that fact would figure in our experience of moral qualities. Our experience of apprehending . . . moral quality is not that of apprehending a disposition.
>
> (Cuneo 2001: 574)

He illustrates his point, pointing to the disanalogy of moral properties, say being good with being nauseating, that wears its response-dependent nature on its sleeve.
9 And here is his original formulation of the complex argument:
This starts from Wiggins' suggestion that non-cognitivism distorts the phenomenology of moral choice. In moral choice we struggle to find, not any answer that we can bring ourselves to accept, nor any answer that we can accept in consistency with previous answers, but the right answer . . . The criterion for choice then is the desirability of the action, rather than the criterion for desirability being our choice (desire). The complex form is more to do with the phenomenology of moral *choice* than that of moral experience, and this means that the sense in which it combines with the simple to make a single case is not perfectly clear (Dancy 1986: 172–73).
10 Here is the crucial quote:

> . . . we cannot suppose that a determinate moral property is a disposition to cause a certain moral response in normal circumstances. Normal situations are precisely not very good ones for discerning the moral properties of the choices we face. We have to deal with distractions, contrary influences, prejudices, lack of time and similar problems. More promising, it seems, is to conceive of the moral property of rightness, for example, as a disposition to cause a certain response (approval) in *ideal* circumstances. (I allow this notion of ideal circumstances to package together what are really two requirements, that the perceiver be 'ideal' and that the situation be 'ideal' too.)
>
> Our question now is whether it is possible for our moral experience, which never occurs in ideal circumstances, to represent to us moral properties conceived now as dispositions to cause certain responses in us in ideal situations, which we never experience. In such a case, though our experience may be indistinguishable from the experience which the relevant disposition is a disposition to elicit, it is not that experience itself. And this means that our first model turns out to be inapplicable. . . .
>
> This argument, and the distinction which it uses between the normal and ideal, is what undermines McDowell's main independent argument in favor of the weaker conception of moral realism, referred to at the end of section I. The crucial consideration is that a moral property, conceived as a disposition to elicit a certain response in ideal circumstances, is not for that reason internally related to the will of a perceiver who is not himself in those circumstances. If, for instance, I am drunk or overcome by greed, or even surrounded by and distracted by ordinary concerns, why should I care about the disposition an action may have to cause certain responses in

me in situations in which I do not at present find myself? (Dancy 1986: 178–79).

11 And by the anonymous referee (of the first version of the paper), who has been warning me that not any old involvement amounts to dependence.
12 For an extensive discussion of the issue of false concept-analyzing propositions see Miščević (2005a, 2005b, and forthcoming).
13 I leave aside for the moment aesthetic ones like ELEGANT or KITSCH.

10 Holism about value[1]

David McNaughton and Piers Rawling

In *Principia Ethica* (1903; the page references below are to the 1966 paperback edition), G.E. Moore famously claims that there are 'organic wholes', the intrinsic values of which differ 'from the sum[s] of the values of [their] parts' (p. 36). This is his 'principle of organic unities' (p. 184), and is the form of holism about value with which we begin, but from which we will depart.

Moore on value

In chapter three of *Principia Ethica*, Moore argues against Hedonism – the view that pleasure is the sole good. He sees its prevalence as owing to commission of the 'naturalistic fallacy'; but we set discussion of this aside here to focus on his direct arguments against the view. His first complaint is that if we consider pleasure in isolation from everything else – including consciousness of it – we see that 'the pleasure would be comparatively valueless without the consciousness' (p. 89). This is an application of Moore's 'method of absolute isolation' (p. 188) – 'the only method that can be safely used, when we wish to discover what degree of value a thing has in itself' (p. 91). So the Hedonist would do better to claim, as Moore (pp. 90–96) sees Sidgwick as doing, that it is consciousness of pleasure that is the sole good.

On Moore's account, Sidgwick argues that all wholes of value have consciousness of pleasure as a component, and that the other components of these wholes have no value – as determined by applying the method of isolation. However, Sidgwick does not apply this method to the consciousness of pleasure – he 'does not ask the question: If consciousness of pleasure existed absolutely by itself, would a sober judgment be able to attribute much value to it?' (p. 93). Rather, in each case, Sidgwick subtracts the value of the other components – which is zero – from the value of the whole, and concludes that all the value resides in the consciousness of pleasure.

Moore famously claims, by contrast, that: 'The value of a whole must not be assumed to be the same as the sum of the values of its parts' (p. 28). Hence Sidgwick's subtraction is not guaranteed to give the correct result.

Rather, Moore's method is first to consider the parts in isolation (as if they were the only occupant of the universe), and determine their intrinsic values (the intrinsic value of an entity is the value it has 'in itself', as opposed to any value it may have as a means to achieving something of intrinsic value (p. 21)). He then asks whether, in addition to the intrinsic values of the parts of the whole, there is a value to their combination. The intrinsic value of the whole is the sum of the intrinsic values of its parts plus the value of their combination.

Moore's general method is laid out on p. 214ff, where he considers, among other wholes, that of 'vindictive' or 'retributive' punishment. The wickedness of the crime is bad, but so is the pain of the punishment – so how are matters improved by the latter's imposition? In Moore's terminology, the improvement is due to the fact that the 'value as a whole' ('which arises solely *from the combination* of two or more things': sense (1) on p. 215) of crime followed by punishment is positive, where the value as a whole is to be distinguished from the value 'on the whole'. The latter is the sum of: the value of the crime plus the value of the punishment plus their value as a whole.

Moore's arithmetic is perhaps best explicated by numerical example. In the case of vindictive punishment (where $V(x)$ is the intrinsic value of x), suppose the intrinsic values of the parts are:

$V(crime) = -8$
$V(pain inflicted as punishment) = -5$

Moore's idea is that the value of the combination might be positive – say:

$V(combination) = +6 = value as a whole$

+6, then, is the value of the crime and punishment *as* a whole. Its value *on* the whole is given by the sum of the three values above:

$V(on the whole) = -8 + -5 + 6 = -7$

Note that $-7 > -8$, so the situation is better on the whole as a result of the addition of the negatively valued punishment.

Moore counts only the crime and the punishment as parts, hence the value of the whole is not equal to the sum of the values of its parts: $-7 \neq -8 + -5$.

If we take zero as the point of indifference, Moore preserves the intuition that although the addition of the punishment does improve matters (from -8 to -7), the overall situation is still bad (-7 < 0). And he also preserves the intuition that the punishment must be *bad* in order for it to be *punishment*.

However, there is a strike against Moore's position here when we look to his isolation test to determine the intrinsic value of the punishment. Moore asks us to consider in isolation the associated pain or other evil. But in isolation from the crime, the 'punishment' would be the infliction of, say, incarceration, for no reason – it would not be punishment.[2] Presumably Moore assumes that the prisoner will have all the same beliefs in the isolated case as in the real one, such as the belief that she has been imprisoned after a trial, otherwise the subjectively experienced pain of the incarceration would be significantly different. However, these beliefs are, of course, all false in the isolated case. Yet in other places (e.g. p. 197) Moore takes true belief itself to be of value. Hence the false beliefs themselves detract from the value of the incarceration in the isolated case.

The difficulty that the punishment cannot be truly assessed in isolation (the incarceration in the absence of the crime, as we noted, not being punishment) is an instance of what we shall dub the 'intentional problem', by analogy with Brentano's use of the term 'intentional' (the crime here is analogous to the intentional object of a psychological state). As we shall shortly see, there are problem cases in which the use of the term is more than merely analogous – cases in which Moore actually does attempt to isolate psychological states from their intentional objects.

Lest there be doubt about our interpretation, we will now apply it to a few more of Moore's contentions. He claims, for example, that although the addition of pain as punishment for a crime makes for a state of the world that is '*always* better, *as a whole*, than if no pain had been there', yet matters 'may not be better *on the whole*' if the pain of the punishment 'be too intense, since that is a great evil' (p. 214). This can be illustrated by modifying our numerical example thus:

V(crime) = −8
V(pain inflicted as punishment) = −7 (cf. −5 above: here the pain is too
    intense)
V(combination) = +6
V(on the whole) = 6 − 7 − 8 = −9

−9 < −8, so the situation is *not* made better on the whole as a result of the infliction of such intense pain.

In our first illustration, matters are improved by the addition of negatively valued punishment but, since −7 is not greater than −5, we have not illustrated how

(C) 'the combined existence of two evils may yet constitute a less evil than would be constituted by the existence of either singly' (p. 215).

But that is easily done. Let:

V(crime) = −8
V(pain inflicted as punishment) = −5

V(combination) = +9 = value as a whole
V(on the whole) = 9 – 5 – 8 = –4

In this case 'there arises from the combination a positive good which is greater than the *difference* between the sum of the two evils and the demerit of either singly' (p. 215): the sum of the two evils is –13 and the difference between –13 and –8 is 5, that between –13 and –5 is 8, and 9 is greater than both these differences. That is: 9 > 13 – 8 and 9 > 13 – 5. Or, alternatively: 9 – 13 > –8 and 9 – 13 > –5, which is our illustration of (C). Thus we can see how it is that

> If it is true that the combined existence of two evils may yet constitute a less evil than would be constituted by the existence of either singly, it is plain that this can only be because there arises from the combination a positive good which is greater than the *difference* between the sum of the two evils and the demerit of either singly: this positive good would then be the value of the whole, *as a whole*. (p. 215)

Moore, it seems, must apply his method of absolute isolation to wholes as well as parts (the consciousness of pleasure is a case in point) – he could not determine the value of a combination as a whole by considering *it* in isolation from the parts of which it is a combination. Rather, it appears that one must consider the whole in isolation, and its parts in isolation, and then calculate the value of the whole minus the sum of the values of its parts to yield the value of the combination as a whole. (This procedure raises difficulties, which we discuss below.)

Applying this method to 'personal affections and aesthetic enjoyments', Moore concludes that these 'include *all* the greatest, and *by far* the greatest, goods we can imagine' (p. 189). Moore 'regard[s] it as indubitable that Prof. Sidgwick was so far right ... that ... mere existence of what is beautiful has value, so small as to be negligible, in comparison with that which attaches to the *consciousness* of beauty' (ibid.). But the main value does not reside in the mere consciousness. Moore (p. 197) 'imagine[s] the case of a single person, enjoying throughout eternity the contemplation of scenery as beautiful, and intercourse with persons as admirable, as can be imagined; while yet the whole of the objects of his cognition are absolutely unreal'. He 'think[s] we should definitely pronounce the existence of a universe, which consisted solely of such a person, to be *greatly* inferior in value to one in which the objects, in the existence of which he believes, did really exist just as he believes them to do'. Personal affections and aesthetic enjoyments, when valuable, comprise several constituents, and Moore sees three as particularly important in combination, though not singly (p. 199): the cognition of appropriate objects (beautiful objects, or worthy objects of affection such as admirable people (p. 198)), appropriate emotion toward these objects, and true belief in their existence. By themselves, these three have 'little or no value' (p. 199), but 'taken together [they] seem to form a whole of very great value' (ibid.). (Here we have another instance of the intentional problem: true beliefs in the existence of the appropriate objects, for example, presuppose the existence of the latter. Thus these beliefs cannot be assessed in isolation.)

Moore then proceeds to draw out a pair of consequences of these thoughts that he sees as constituting their chief importance (p. 199): (1) we can see why mere knowledge can seem so valuable (consider the claims of Plato and Aristotle in this regard): it is a crucial part of wholes of great value, though of 'little or no value by itself' (p. 199 – as with true belief, another instance of the intentional problem); (2) beauty and emotion can be greatly enhanced by the presence of true belief (p. 200).

This completes our initial summary of Moore's views on value. We have only discussed one difficulty for Moore's position, namely the intentional problem that besets the isolation test. But many other questions can be raised; for example:

Does Moore divorce value from reasons?

It is plausible to suppose that value is a mark of reasons: if some entity or state is of positive value, then there is reason to take a positive stance toward it – to admire it, approve of it, bring it about etc. And, correspondingly, if it is of negative value, then there is reason to take a negative stance toward it. Perhaps the link between value and reasons also runs in the reverse direction: if we have reason to take a positive stance toward something, then it is of positive value (*mutatis mutandis* for the negative case).

Jonathan Dancy (2004: 177; 2003b: 630–31) sees Moore as breaking this connection between value and reasons on the grounds that, on Moore's view, 'a part can contribute to the whole more value than it has actually got *there*' (2004: 177). Dancy considers Moore's discussion (Moore 1903: 35) of the value of the arm, in which Moore suggests that the intrinsic value of the arm is zero, yet '*as* a part of the body, it has great value'. He (Moore) goes on to say: 'To have value merely as a part is equivalent to having no value at all, but merely being a part of that which has it'. On Dancy's interpretation of Moore, the arm is contributing value to the whole (the body) that it has not got, yet '[s]urely we do have reason to protect the part *here*, if it is contributing value. So its presence is of value, it would seem, on pain of breaching the link between values and reasons' (Dancy 2004: 177).

Dancy is here relying on the thought that if we have reason to protect something, then it is of value: the presence of the arm is of value (*pace* Moore) because we have reason to protect it. He also 'will allow no value that is not essentially linked to reasons' (Dancy 2004: 172). Even if the Moorean attempts to reject the former thought, unless she also rejects the latter she still faces the following sort of problem that Dancy raises. Consider Moore's account of punishment: the punishment is bad, according to

Moore, but it 'contributes' a positive value to the whole of crime-followed-by-punishment (thus the addition of the punishment improves matters overall). Now if the punishment is bad, we have reason not to impose it, if we are not to sever the link from value to reasons. But, on the contrary, we surely *do* have reason to impose it.

How might Moore respond to Dancy's complaint? Dancy gives a 'contributory' interpretation of Moore on which each part of a whole has (potentially) two values associated with it: its intrinsic value (which it genuinely has), and its contributory value (which doesn't actually belong to it at all). We, on the other hand, favor an 'emergence' interpretation. Each part possesses only its intrinsic value. But when parts are combined into a whole, additional properties can 'emerge' that are properties of the whole but not of the parts individually. And these additional properties can confer value (either positive or negative) on the whole (Moore's 'value as a whole') beyond that of the parts. Thus, for example, a whole of positive value can be made up of parts each of which is valueless. Or in the case of the just punishment of a crime, it is not that the pain of the punishment has two values associated with it: intrinsic badness but contributory goodness. Rather the pain is bad, but the whole of crime and punishment bears the property of being just; and this justice, we are supposing, is a good that outweighs the bad of the pain of the punishment.

Does this interpretation sever the connection between value and reasons? If one insists that one only has reason to protect a part if that part itself is of positive value, then yes. But why buy this principle? The Moorean might have it that: one has reason to protect (or produce) a part if and only if that part is itself valuable or its presence increases value. In the case of a valuable whole made up of valueless parts, we have reason to protect the parts because they are necessary to the whole or for the whole to have the value it has. In the case of punishment, the pain of the punishment is bad, hence we have some reason not to impose it; but its addition increases the good, giving us stronger reason to inflict it than not. And, on this account, the criminal also has stronger reason to suffer the punishment than to avoid it – although, of course, he might well *think* that he has stronger reason to avoid it. (We are assuming that the Moorean denies that agent-relative positional considerations can play a role in practical reasons, thus she cannot maintain that the prisoner's reasons to escape differ in strength from our reasons to abet him.)

What of Dancy's own view? As we have seen, he maintains that one has reason to protect a part if and only if that part itself is of positive value. He distinguishes between the grounds of value and its enabling conditions. In explaining the value of the whole, appeal is made to the value of its grounds, but only to the presence of its enabling conditions: enabling conditions are 'required for the whole to exist … [so] they are of value (because we have reason to protect them). But that value is not contributed to the value of the whole. So, we might say, every necessary part of a valuable whole will be of value, though not all such parts contribute their value (or all their value) to the value of the whole. . . . Any part, then, that contributes value must have that value to contribute; but some valuable parts do not contribute their value to the whole, even though their presence is necessary for the whole to have the value it does' (2004: 180–81). Dancy, as we have seen, complains that on Moore's view, 'a part can contribute to the whole more value than it has actually got *there*' (2004: 177). Dancy disallows this, but allows that parts can have 'uncontributed value'.

Questions can be raised about this asymmetry, particularly around the issue of negative value. In the case of punishment, on Dancy's contributory interpretation of Moore, the pain of the punishment is bad, but it 'contributes' positive value to the whole of crime followed by punishment: recall that in the first numerical illustration above the value of the crime is −8, and value on the whole of crime followed by punishment is −7. On the one hand, the punishment is contributing more positive value than it has: it contributes +1, yet its value alone (as pain) is 6 fewer than this: i.e. −5. But alternatively described it is *not* contributing all of its *negative* value: it has 5 to contribute in a negative direction, but contributes 6 fewer than this in this direction: i.e. +1. Thus it has 6 negative units of 'uncontributed value'. The content of Dancy's dictum that parts cannot contribute more value than they have but can contribute less seems, then, at best unclear.

Another troubling aspect of Dancy's appeal to uncontributed value concerns the issue of context-free value. Dancy's position seems to be that a part can have value in a context but not contribute all its value in that context: 'It remains true that no feature contributes to the whole any value that it has not got in that context. But it is also true that some features that have value in that context do not contribute that value to the value of the whole' (2004: 181). The issue then arises as to whether a feature that possesses uncontributed value possesses that value outside the context in question. If the uncontributed value is not present outside the context where it fails to be contributed, then it would seem that it never could be contributed; but is value that could never make a contribution really value? We think not. So is Dancy committed to features that have context-free value (or, at least, 'trans-context' value)? He does discuss (2004: 181–82) the case of a dress that would be improved by the removal of diamonds. Of the diamonds, he says, 'in a case where something of intrinsic value [the diamonds] makes matters worse by its presence, what we should do is preserve it, but remove it from the present context [the dress]'. Here perhaps he implies that the diamonds have context-free intrinsic value. But then the question arises of how this is to be assessed.

To sum up: Dancy appeals to the notion of uncontributed value in order to combine (i) the claim that there can be parts of a valuable whole that, though necessary for its existence or for it to have the value it has, contribute no value to it, with (ii) the principle that one has reason to protect a part if and only if that part itself is of positive value. The appeal to the existence of uncontributed value at the least raises awkward questions, or so we have claimed. Better, in our view, to abandon it. One could still maintain that there are enabling conditions by hanging onto (i), but dropping (ii) and holding instead that (iii) one has reason to protect a part if and only if that part is itself valuable or is necessary for the presence or the value of a valuable whole. We see the Moorean as taking this option. On an emergence interpretation, Moore maintains that value beyond the sum of the intrinsic values of the parts may be conferred by new properties that emerge from their combination; thus there can certainly be parts of a valuable whole that, though necessary for its existence or its value, have zero intrinsic value themselves – indeed it is possible that a whole of positive value be made up entirely of parts with zero (or even negative) intrinsic value.

Varieties of value and the isolation test

There are aspects of Moore's views on value with which we are in sympathy – for example, the idea that one cannot determine the value of a 'whole' by looking only at its 'parts' in isolation. Yet Moore does appeal to isolation in determining intrinsic values, which leads to what we called the 'intentional problem'. And this is not the only problem. For example, depending on one's perspective, the isolation test may give rise to difficulties when it comes to generalization.

According to the isolation test, the intrinsic value of an entity or state is its non-instrumental value in a world where it is the sole existent. This value cannot, of course, vary. In particular, it does not change when the entity appears in a whole – for example, 'if it had no value by itself, it has none still, however great be that of the whole of which it now forms a part' (Moore 1903: 30). This entails that entities and states have their intrinsic values essentially or unconditionally – for instance, 'a judgment which asserts that a thing is good in itself ... if true of one instance of the thing in question, is necessarily true of all' (1903: 27). Moore's isolation test for intrinsic value, then, renders such value essential; and each instance of intrinsic value gives rise to a generalization: if X is intrinsically valuable here, then it is intrinsically valuable to the same degree wherever it appears.

What of those who find generalization implausible, such as extreme particularists? They reject Moore's isolationism on the grounds of their claim that no feature need have the same intrinsic value in every possible whole of which it is a part. But even those of a more moderate temperament (such as ourselves) might find Moore's degree of generalization excessive.

Moore's isolationism, then, results in over-generalization. But it also results in under-generalization. We find it plausible, for example, that justice can never be anything but intrinsically good (which is distinct from saying that being motivated by a sense of justice is always appropriate). But justice suffers the intentional problem: it cannot be isolated in Moore's sense – there could not be, we contend, a universe consisting solely of, say, a just act.[3] And given this it seems that Moore cannot assign it an intrinsic value.

Finally, even in cases that do not suffer the intentional problem, isolated evaluation seldom if ever makes much sense – how can one evaluate, say, the contemplation of a beautiful rose in a universe where it and its observer are the sole existents? To begin with, is the life of the observer short or long? Perhaps a longer life is better – but what about a long life spent only in the contemplation of a rose?

Given that the isolation test has (at the least) these problems, is it helpful? We doubt it. We claimed above that Moore must apply his method of absolute isolation to wholes as well as parts – in order to calculate the value of a combination as a whole, it seems one must consider the whole in isolation, and its parts in isolation, and then calculate the value of the whole minus the sum of the values of its parts. But why bother determining the values of the parts in isolation? Doing so does not help in working out the value of the whole 'on the whole', since this is the sum of the values of the parts *plus* the value of the whole 'as a whole' – and calculating the latter requires, as we have just seen, prior knowledge of the value of the whole 'on the whole'. Moore's evaluative procedure is, then, at best unhelpful.

Moore defines an organic unity (1903: 36) as a whole the intrinsic value of which does not equal the sum of the intrinsic values of its parts. And he takes recourse to organic unities lest the intrinsic value of a whole be mistakenly calculated by looking only to the isolated intrinsic values of its parts. However, we reject the isolation test, and once it is abandoned the notion of an organic unity in Moore's sense becomes subject to challenge. Why be committed to the existence of Moorean organic unities unless one is committed to the claim that the parts of a whole can be evaluated independently of that whole? There may be other potential methods for such independent evaluation apart from the isolation test, but we see little prospect for their success.

Moore avoids the mistake of calculating the value of a whole by summing the values of its parts in isolation. But there is an alternative picture that also forestalls this error. We contend that there are indeed wholes that have more to them than is evident from their parts taken by themselves.[4] But we do not conclude from this that the value of such a whole cannot equal the sum of the values of its parts. Rather we reject both Moore's isolation test and his account of organic unities. We claim, rather, that parts can only be evaluated in a way relevant to the whole of which they are a part if they are evaluated *in situ* (thus one cannot evaluate a whole by looking to its parts in isolation; this is one reason why we consider ourselves holists); and the value of the whole does equal the sum of the values of its parts.

We reject, then, Moore's version of holism; but what of Dancy's? As we saw above, Dancy endorses uncontributed value, thus although 'the value of the whole is identical to the sum of the values of the contributing parts', yet given that some parts do not contribute their value, 'the value of the whole is not identical to the sum of the values of all the parts' (2004: 181). On our picture there is no uncontributed value, thus the value of the whole is simply the sum of the values of its parts.

Where do we stand, then, on (i), (ii) and (iii) at end of previous section? Before addressing this question directly, we need to lay out more of our view.

We are sympathetic to the idea that you have overall reason to perform some act if and only if this act of yours and its consequences would be valuable. However, this does not entail that the strength of your reasons to φ always varies only with the value of your φ-ing – we contend that value is not the *only* mark of the *strength* of reasons: agent-relative positional considerations also play a role in certain reasons, such as reasons of friendship or reasons to pursue certain benefits for oneself (see, e.g. McNaughton and Rawling 2006). This complication aside, however, the strength of your reason to φ varies with, and only with, the amount of value that your φ-ing will produce, where this includes the value of your act itself, and may depend on what has happened in the past. The type of value here is value as an end, which we discuss below; and the object of evaluation is the state of affairs that your act produces, which includes the act itself. (We address below Scanlon's objections to attributing the values of actions solely to states of affairs.)

When it comes to practical reasons, then, the evaluative comparison of interest is that between states of affairs (we do not draw a distinction here between states of affairs and events) – these are the relevant wholes. And we shall take it that for purposes of evaluation their parts are also states of affairs. Consider, for instance, the state of affairs, S, of A committing a crime and subsequently being tried and imprisoned. S has as some of its parts: A committing the crime; A being tried; A being imprisoned; and A believing that he committed the crime, believing that he has been imprisoned because of this, and feeling remorse. There could have been a state of affairs, T, like S in that A is tried, imprisoned, has the same beliefs and feels the same remorse, but in which he did not actually commit the crime. T and S have some similar parts, then, but the values of these parts may be influenced by their surroundings. For example, A's feelings of remorse in S are of positive value but in T this is reversed. Or take the imprisonment of A. In S it is a case of punishment, and, let us suppose, justice, in which case it is of positive value. But in T it is not punishment (assuming that for the intentional infliction of pain to count as punishment it has to be in retribution for an offence), and is unjust, and thus of negative value (we are assuming that A's imprisonment in T does not have some unmentioned beneficial side-effect).

Every action, then, results in a state of affairs, which may be broken down into parts, each of which is another state of affairs. Care must be taken when evaluating these parts, since one and the same part can be picked out by differing descriptions[5] – and these descriptions can make reference (either implicit or explicit) to other parts of the same whole: A's imprisonment in the case above can be re-described as just punishment in state S but not in state T. Also, when summing the values of parts, the catalogue of parts must be mutually exclusive and exhaustive lest the whole be over- or under-valued (there will in general be more than one way to carve up the whole into such a catalogue).

The descriptions true of a state of affairs may, as it were, pull in different directions vis-à-vis its value. Consider again A's just imprisonment. On some views the pain of the imprisonment is a bad to be weighed against the good of the justice. But there aren't two different states of affairs here, one bad and one good. There is one state of affairs with two different descriptions (the intentional infliction of pain, the imposition of justice), and in determining whether it is better to imprison A rather than not, the good must be weighed against the bad. We are supposing that the good outweighs the bad here, so we have more reason to impose the punishment than not. (The prisoner, on our view, may have more reason to escape rather than not, but this is because of agent-relative considerations that we are leaving aside here.)

Vis-à-vis (i), (ii) and (iii) at end of previous section, we are inclined to adopt (i): there can be parts of a valuable whole that, though necessary for its existence or for it to have the value it has,[6] are not themselves valuable as ends – indeed, we see it as possible that there can be such parts of a valuable whole that have negative value. But we adopt neither (ii) nor (iii). These both make reference to the idea of having reason to protect a part, but we reject this possibility. When you act you produce a state of affairs. You cannot simply replace or protect a part of a whole without creating a new whole. And all we are committed to is the claim that you have reason to produce such a whole if and only if that whole is valuable. Parts of wholes have values; the value of a whole is the sum of the values of its parts; you have reason to produce a whole if and only if it's valuable.

What of the case above of the diamonds on the dress? The three states of affairs to compare are (a) that of the dress being decorated with the diamonds; (b) that of the dress being devoid of the diamonds, the latter being held ready for a more appropriate use; and (c) that of the dress being devoid of diamonds, the latter being destroyed. We are supposing that the middle state of affairs is the most valuable. The diamonds themselves are not a state of affairs, and although we have no objection to speaking of their value as objects (in some context), that value is not relevant here. But we do have reason to preserve them: since the middle state is the most valuable, we have most reason to remove the diamonds from the dress and hold onto them.

The value of a state of affairs with which we have been concerned is its value as an end. How does this relate to intrinsic value? We reject Moore's isolation test, and with that rejection goes, of course, rejection of Moore's account of intrinsic value. Moore restricts value to only two varieties:

intrinsic and instrumental (value as means[7]). And intrinsic value is, for Moore, identical to all of the following: value in itself (see, e.g. 1903: 21), value as an end (see, e.g. 1903: 24), and (as far as we can tell) value for its own sake (see, e.g. 1903: 87). Also, as we have seen, intrinsic value is, on Moore's account, held essentially.

Is there an alternative account of intrinsic value that does not appeal to the isolation test? Part of the intuitive appeal of the isolation test rests on the thought that intrinsic value should not depend on extrinsic features. For example, suppose that a state in which a beautiful object exists is increased in value by the arrival of an appreciative observer. Is the *intrinsic* value of the former state increased by this arrival? It seems not. Or to take another example, a red helleborine may be made more valuable by its rarity, but its rarity (since this is dependent upon the number of *others*) is not relevant to its *intrinsic* value. On this approach, the intrinsic value of an entity is dependent upon that entity's intrinsic features – but work would need to be done to spell out both the nature of an intrinsic feature and the nature of the dependence (see, e.g. Dancy 2004: ch. 10).

We do not propose to do this work. Rather, the important category for our purposes here is that of value as an end. And, *pace* Moore, two states of affairs might differ in their value as ends even though they have the same intrinsic value (because intrinsically similar). For example, suppose that in one state of affairs red helleborines are rare, but in another they are not. Each of these states of affairs has as a part the existence of some red helleborine. The intrinsic values of these two parts are identical, but their values as ends differ: the value as an end of the existence of the plant is greater in the state in which it is rare.

Value as an end is, of course, to be contrasted with value as means. But in addition to this distinction, there is also a fundamental/derivative distinction (and there may be more – see, e.g. Dancy 2004: ch. 10). Instrumental value is clearly derivative: the value of a means derives from the value of the end at which it aims. But there also seem to be cases of derivative value as an end, such as certain cases of constitutive value. For example, innocent enjoyment is valuable as an end, and watching cricket constitutes such a form of innocent enjoyment for David. It is not that watching cricket is a means to enjoyment in the way that driving to the cricket match is such a means, or in the way that surgery is a means to health: David's watching cricket *is* a form of innocent enjoyment. Watching cricket in this case is valuable as an end. But it is not fundamentally valuable: its value, on this account, derives from the fact that it is a form of innocent enjoyment. One way in which to distinguish the fundamental from the derivative is to consider the question 'Why is that valuable?' In the case of David's watching cricket, one answer is: 'because he enjoys it'. But if we ask, 'And why is enjoyment valuable?' we seem to hit bedrock – although enjoyment may not be valuable (if it is sadistic, for example), when it is valuable, there seems to be no further feature that confers its value. Thus, in this sense, watching cricket is derivatively valuable; it is the enjoyment that is fundamentally valuable, although both are valuable as ends.[8]

So much for our discussion of value as an end *per se*. But we have assigned it, in the case of actions, to states of affairs. We now turn to Scanlon's complaints against this approach.

Scanlon and the teleological account of value

Scanlon (2000, ch. 2) criticizes what he calls the 'teleological' account of value, according to which (as we read Scanlon) intrinsic value is assigned to, and only to, states of affairs (which he sees as entailing the claim that 'To be (intrinsically) valuable ... is to be "to be promoted"' (2000: 80)). We take it that Scanlon would see his criticisms as applying not only to this approach in the case of intrinsic value, but also in that of value as an end. The value (as an end) of an action is the value (as end) of the whole that it produces (which has its performance as a part). But what kind of entity is this whole? It is hard to see that it can be anything but a state of affairs (or, perhaps, an event – we do not see the distinction as important in the current context). Thus although the teleological view may not be generally true, when it comes to action it seems unavoidable – at least if that is read as claiming that the value of an action is the value of the state of affairs that arises as a result of its performance.

Two questions immediately arise:

(1) Does this entail, in line with Scanlon's claim above, that valuable actions are 'to be promoted'?
(2) What of Scanlon's arguments against a teleological account of value – do they weigh against our account?

(1) This question needs clarification. Some acts are more valuable than others, so even on a naïve consequentialist view, not all valuable acts are to be promoted if this means promoting them all equally. Presumably, on any sensible view, at most only the most valuable acts at a particular juncture are to be promoted at that time. Suppose one holds, as on certain consequentialist views, that (roughly) each of us should, on every occasion, maximize the good. Then each of us should so act on every occasion. If we should do what we have most reason to do (we actually deny this – see McNaughton and Rawling 2004 – but that discussion is not relevant here), then on some consequentialist views you always have most reason to perform the most valuable action within your power. We deny this – we claim above that the strength of your reasons to A may not vary only with the value of your A-ing. Perhaps this means that we do not see valuable actions as always 'to be promoted'. We're not sure. But in any case, we do not see that our view is inconsistent with assigning value to states of affairs when it comes to evaluating actions.

(2) Scanlon (2000: ch. 2) argues against a purely teleological account of value. As we have said, we have no quarrel with assigning value to entities other than states of affairs, except in the case of action. But in the case of action, we claim, they are its sole repository. Do Scanlon's arguments tell against this?

As far as we can tell, Scanlon offers three arguments against the purely teleological account of value. First, he attempts to undercut what he sees as one of the sources of the teleological notion of value: a purportedly mistaken teleological account of reasons (Scanlon 2000: 83–84). Second, he offers cases of value that, he claims, do not fit the teleological mould (e.g. 2000: 89, 100). And third, he seems to argue that the teleological account of value commits one to explaining practical reasons by reference to value in cases where the reverse direction of explanation is more plausible (e.g. 2000: 93). We address these arguments seriatim.

According to 'the purely teleological conception of reasons, ... since any rational action must aim at some result, reasons that bear on whether to perform an action must appeal to the desirability or undesirability of having that result occur, taking into account also the intrinsic value of the action itself' (2000: 84). But, Scanlon argues, 'many of the reasons bearing on an action concern not the desirability of outcomes, but rather the eligibility or ineligibility of various other reasons' (ibid.). Thus Scanlon distinguishes (pp. 50–51) between pro tanto reasons, which 'can be outweighed without losing their force or status as reasons' (2000: 50) and prima facie reasons, which may lack force altogether under certain conditions (2000: 51). We are not convinced, however, that Scanlon's analysis of the phenomenon he is pointing to is the correct one. And, more importantly for our current discussion, we do not see how his complaints against a teleological account of reasons have any bearing on a teleological account of value.

First, then, Scanlon's examples of 'non-teleological' reasons. There is the case of 'playing to win' (2000: 51–52). Suppose that playing to win a particular game is what you would most enjoy, and that no other relevant considerations weigh as heavily as this one. So you decide to play to win. Then, claims Scanlon, this decision renders irrelevant the fact that executing certain strategies will leave your opponent feeling 'crushed and disappointed' – you simply need not weigh this fact when determining which strategy to execute. However, while we might agree that when the time comes to decide upon a strategy you need not consider your opponent's feelings, this is not because they are irrelevant, but because you should already have taken them into account when deciding to play to win in the first place. The effects on your opponent's feelings were a relevant consideration at the time you decided on this, and remain so – but it is built into the case that they did not, and do not, weigh heavily enough to override your decision.

The other examples concern 'various formal and informal roles' (2000: 52) and deontological constraints (2000: 84–86). Concerning the former, Scanlon claims that being 'a good member of [say] a search committee ...

involve[s] bracketing the reason-giving force of some of your own interests which might otherwise be quite relevant and legitimate reasons for acting in one way rather than another' (2000: 52). On one reading, Scanlon's idea seems to be that reasons that arise from various interests of mine are silenced by my role as a search committee member. But this makes it appear that these reasons are still somehow present, but rendered inoperative. On the account we find more plausible, by contrast, if I am on the search committee then the fact that, say, Eve is a close friend of mine is simply no reason to vote for her – as opposed to being an 'ineligible' reason to do so. We have here an instance of the more general particularist point that a consideration that is a reason in one situation may lack that status in another: that Eve is in my friend may be a reason to favor her in another context, but not here.

Alternatively, perhaps Scanlon has in mind a counterfactual account of the non-teleological reason-giving force of my committee membership – something like the following: if I weren't on the search committee then the fact that Eve is my friend would be a reason to vote for her (even though, given that I am on the search committee, that fact is no reason to do so). The problem here, of course, is that if I weren't on the search committee I wouldn't have a vote. The fact that I'm on the search committee is not a non-teleological reason that 'bear[s] on whether to [vote for Eve]' (2000: 84 – cited above); rather it is a necessary condition for having a vote.

Do deontological constraints fare any better as an example of non-teleological reasons? Scanlon says the following:

> Consider, for example, the principle that one may not kill one person in order to save several others. Accepting this principle involves accepting a certain view of the reasons one has: that the positive value of saving these others does not justify killing a person. If this principle is correct, then one does not need to balance the value of abiding by it against the good to be achieved through its violation. Doing this would be flatly inconsistent with the principle itself, which holds that the good is not sufficient to justify the action in question. Someone who accepts this principle therefore does not need to appeal to the 'negative intrinsic value' of killing in order to explain why she does not do what is necessary to save the greater number. (Scanlon 2000: 84)

The relevant claim here is that a constraint against killing is not to be weighed against the disvalue of more deaths; rather it is built into the constraint that the weighing 'does not need' to be done. As Scanlon goes on to say, however:

> Of course there is also the question of whether one should accept such a principle to begin with. This is the question to which the claim that deontological prohibitions are 'paradoxical' is most plausibly addressed, and it obviously needs an answer. (2000: 85)

We side with the consequentialist here, and deny that there are constraints. That is something we argue elsewhere, however (see, e.g. McNaughton and Rawling 2006). For present purposes our complaint is that, on this account of constraints, it is not so much that the constraint against killing renders 'ineligible' the reasons that favor minimizing the loss of life (in the way that being on a search committee purportedly renders reasons of friendship ineligible); rather, on Scanlon's account of it, the constraint simply has built into it the claim that the reasons that favor minimizing the loss of life are ineligible. Scanlon seeks to avoid the thought that the constraint against killing is appealing to killing's undesirability. But, first, the constraint itself makes reference to the desirability of minimizing killing – as quoted above (2000: 84): 'the [constraint] holds that the good [of minimizing killing] is not sufficient to justify' one's own act of killing. And second, constraints, on Scanlon's account of them, dictate what is to count as a sufficient reason, so of course they are not to be weighed in the way that killing's undesirability is to be: just as the rules of evidence in a trial are not themselves evidence but dictate how it is to be weighed, so Scanlon's constraints are not, as he seems to claim, reasons, but, rather, dictate how they [the reasons] are to be weighed.

On a different account of constraints, that (say) by pulling the trigger I would be the killer of an innocent myself is to be weighed against the fact that by not doing so several innocents will be murdered by others. And the latter reason to pull the trigger is argued to be weaker than the former reason not to pull it. We disagree that such arguments work generally: although we acknowledge that there may be circumstances in which I shouldn't pull the trigger even to prevent the murders, we disagree that constraints are so weighty that they trump any consideration that might favor their violation – we disagree, for example, that you are generally forbidden to violate a constraint even to prevent more egregious violations by others. But at least this account of constraints brings positional reasons into play – that the killing would come about by *my* hand is seen as crucial.

On our view positional considerations are relevant to practical reasons, and they do not 'appeal to the desirability or undesirability of having [a particular] result occur' (2000: 84) – to this extent, then, they might be referred to as at least non-teleological components of reasons. For example, that something would bring *me* pleasure, or console *my* friend, gives me a reason to pursue it beyond its desirability. That I have certain pleasures is desirable; but no more or less desirable than, say, that you have those same pleasures. Similarly, it is desirable that my friend be consoled by me; but no more so than that your friend be consoled by you. However, on our view, I typically have more reason to pursue my pleasure or console my friend than to facilitate your pursuit of your pleasure or your consolation of your friend – and not merely because it is a more efficient use of my time.

To conclude, we agree with Scanlon to the extent that there are at least non-teleological components of reasons. But we disagree that his examples exemplify these; and, more crucially, we do not see how these non-teleological aspects of reasons for action tell against a teleological account of the *value* of actions. These non-teleological aspects count, as it were, alongside value, not as non-teleological components *of* value.

What, then, of Scanlon's cases that, he claims, do not fit the teleological mould? On p. 88 (2000) he considers the case of friendship. He makes various points, but his direct argument here against the purely teleological account of valuable action seems to run as follows. Friendship is valuable, but there are reasons of friendship that are not reasons 'to promote friendship (for ourselves or others)' (2000: 89). We agree. But we disagree with Scanlon's conclusion that therefore there are non-teleological values involved in reasons for action vis-à-vis one's friends. Rather, according to us, what this shows is that there are reasons of friendship that are not concerned with value. What I have reason to do for my friends involves producing valuable states of affairs, but there will be instances where, say, what I have most reason to do is help *my* friend (to produce the valuable state of affairs in which I aid her), even though I could produce even more value by doing something else. The positional consideration that she's my friend is a reason here – a reason that doesn't rest entirely on value. (Notice that we don't deny that states in which friends help friends are valuable; but if that value were the entire story then I would have no special reason to help my friends – the state in which I help my friends is no more valuable than the state in which you help yours, so I would have, ceteris paribus, as much reason to bring about the latter as the former. And such parity, we have argued elsewhere (in McNaughton and Rawling 2006, for instance), would undercut the very possibility of friendship.)

On p. 99 (2000) Scanlon offers the case of the value of music and art. Consider, say, Beethoven's late quartets. Scanlon wants to distinguish between the following questions: (1) how valuable is the experience of listening to them? (2) how should we value them? And he claims that the purely teleological view of value cannot handle (2). Again, we disagree. Question (2) is directed at the issue of 'what one should expect from [this music], and in what way it is worth attending to' (2000: 100). But we don't see why the teleological account of value can't handle this: there are states of affairs in which people attend to this music appropriately, and states of affairs in which they don't (when it is 'played in the elevators, hallways, and restrooms of an office building, for example' (p. 100)). The former are more valuable than the latter.

Scanlon wants to draw the same distinction regarding friendship (2000: 88 ff). We are more sympathetic here to the idea that teleological value misses the mark when it comes to the issue of how to value friends. But, as we argued above, this is not because there's anything amiss with the teleological account of value in the case, but rather that not all the relevant reasons are rooted in value. (The same point might also apply in the case of valuing music: it might be that each of us has special reason to attend to

Beethoven's late quartets appropriately *ourselves* – a reason that does not stem from the general value of all of us attending appropriately.)

Finally, we come to Scanlon's claim that the purely teleological account of value commits one to explaining practical reasons by reference to value in cases where the reverse direction of explanation is more plausible (e.g. 2000: 93). Scanlon claims, for instance, that 'we have good reason to be curious about the natural world and to try to understand how it works', (2000: 93) and that this explains the value of scientific knowledge, rather than the other way around. And he sees this as an argument against the purely teleological account of value.

It is unclear to us, however, how this argument is supposed to proceed. Suppose we agree that scientific knowledge is valuable because we have reason to be curious about the world (as opposed to claiming that we have reason to be curious because knowledge is valuable). Is this inconsistent with attributing value to states of affairs here? We think not. For instance, Scanlon himself adopts what he calls a 'buck-passing'[9] account of value according to which 'to call something valuable is to say that it has other properties that provide reasons for behaving in certain ways with regard to it' (2000: 96). So, on this account, to call the state of affairs in which I possess knowledge valuable is to say that this state 'has other properties [apart from its value] that provide reasons for behaving in certain ways with regard to it'. One of these properties is that it is a state in which my curiosity is satisfied – and on the view we are considering in this paragraph this state is valuable because I have reason to satisfy my curiosity. We see nothing inconsistent in such a view.

Concluding remarks

We see no problem, then, in claiming that the objects of value, when it comes to actions, are states of affairs (where the value here is value as an end). There will in general be more than one way to break a state into a mutually exclusive and exhaustive set of component states, but the sum of the values of the members of any of these sets will equal the sum of the values of the members of any of the others. And this sum is the value of the original state. This account of matters is not holist in Moore's sense, then, because the value of a whole is equal to the sum of the values of its parts. But it is holist in another sense: the value of a part is dependent upon the whole in which it appears.

Notes

1 We presented a version of this paper at the 2005 Bled Philosophy Conference on particularism. We benefited greatly from the feedback of the participants.
2 Thanks to Anthony Price at the Bled conference for this point.
3 The Moorean might respond by claiming (1) that only agents can exhibit justice; and (2) that there could be a universe consisting solely of a just agent. We are

dubious of both claims. But even if they were substantiated, could the value of a just agent be realized if she were the only presence?

4 These parts do not include their combination as an additional part – to do so would not only be misleading, but probably lead to regress: would we include the combination of [the basic parts and their combination] as itself a further part?

5 cf Davidson (e.g. 1980: 59) on the redescription of actions.

6 See Dancy (2004: 172) for discussion of such necessary conditions.

7 Note that one and the same feature may be both intrinsically and instrumentally valuable: health, for example, might be intrinsically valuable and valuable as part of the means to, say, some achievement.

8 Setting aside the isolation test, this distinction between fundamental and derivative value, if adopted by a Moorean, might help in her defence against certain complaints. For example Scanlon (1998: 88–89) claims that because Moore adopts a purely 'teleological' account of value (see below), he (Moore) cannot give a satisfactory account of his own claim that friendship is a good. Scanlon implies that Moore's teleological account of value commits him to the view that 'the primary reason to be loyal to one's friends is ... that this is necessary in order for the friendship to continue to exist' (1998: 89). We take Scanlon to be attributing to Moore the following line of reasoning: loyalty is not fundamentally valuable, hence it must be instrumentally valuable – valuable as a means to continuing friendships. But a modified Moorean position has available the following possibility: loyalty is not a means to continued friendship; rather it is partly constitutive of friendship. On this account, loyalty is both valuable as an end and derivatively valuable – its value derives from the value of the friendship. We do not think that this will save the Moorean account of friendship, but we do not share Scanlon's account of why it should be rejected. Scanlon rejects a teleological account of value; we accept it (at least as far as acts are concerned). We reject the Moorean account of friendship not because of objections to its account of value, but because we take it that a Moorean account of reasons would entail that the strength of your reasons to act always varies only with the value of your so acting. And we deny this: we claim that positional facts can also play an ineliminable value-independent role in certain reasons, such as reasons of friendship (see, e.g., McNaughton and Rawling 2006).

9 We remain neutral on the issue of buck-passing about value: the buck-passer maintains that value is not itself a reason, but that to say something is valuable is to say that there are reasons to, say, promote it. On occasion people do express matters by saying that there is reason to do something because it's good – and this locution might be taken as implying that value is a reason. We have no objection to this provided that double-counting is avoided, unless done uniformly. When something is valuable, there are reasons for its value, and these might also be reasons for action (or perhaps some attitude). The danger is that if one then contends that the value is an additional reason, the reasons for that value get counted twice, as it were. There is, perhaps, a way of keeping things kosher here: one can uniformly double-count and thereby give all objects of evaluation equal advantage.

11 Particularism and pleasure

Anthony W. Price

Reasons for an act (a possibility) derive from what will be, if the act is performed, good-making features of an action (a reality). We give reasons by stating facts. Particularists hold either (very strongly) that any fact that is a reason to φ in one situation would cease to be a reason to φ – or even become a reason not to φ – in some other situation, or (rather weakly) that this is not excluded by the very concept of a reason, or (most likely) something betwixt and between.[1]

This claim goes with two distinctions that have been advanced by Jonathan Dancy: between reasons and enablers or disablers, and between reasons and intensifiers or attenuators.

Being able to act is a universal enabler: I have no reason to do what I cannot possibly do; yet it would be unintuitive to count my being able to do a thing as already a reason in favour of doing it (Dancy 2004: 40). Someone's having stolen a book disables his having lent it to me from counting as a reason for my returning it to him, though that would normally have amounted to a good reason (Dancy 1993: 60).

Dancy gives as an example of a reason (1) 'She is in trouble and needs help', and of an intensifier (2) 'I am the only other person around'. He says that (1) is a reason already, whereas (2) isn't 'another reason, on top of the first one' (Dancy 2004: 41). Yet it isn't clear why he insists that (2) strengthens (1) without there being a more complex reason of which each is a part. Why shouldn't (1) be *both* a reason in itself, applying to anyone present, however many are present, *and* part of a more imperative reason applying only to myself? (Indeed, these reasons aren't independent: one couldn't add them together to make a *yet* stronger reason.)

A clearer example of a reason *plus* an intensifier might be derived from Saki's 'The Story-Teller'. Take the 'deplorably uninteresting story' that the aunt tells to three small children about 'a little girl who was good, and made friends with every one on account of her goodness, and was finally saved from a mad bull by a number of rescuers who admired her moral character'. The eldest child asks, 'Wouldn't they have saved her if she hadn't been good?' to which the lame answer is 'Well, yes, but I don't think they would have run quite so fast to her help if they had not liked her so much.'

It is indeed implausible that her being good should be either a reason, or part of a reason, to rescue her; but one might try to defend the aunt by counting it as an intensifier. Certainly a failure to save a saint, if not a prig, would be an intelligible cause of extra regret.

One may feel that Dancy neglects variations between the contexts within which one ascribes or excludes reasons. What is often an enabler or absence of a disabler, or an intensifier or absence of an attenuator, may on occasion constitute a plausible reason, either in context, or for doing one thing *in preference to another*. Thus, that I am the only person around may be a reason for stopping to offer help even when a large lecture audience is awaiting my arrival, or for helping A rather than B when there are others available to help B, but not A. The fact that the lender didn't steal the book may be part of my reason for returning it if I live in an environment where most books are acquired by theft; it may also be my reason for returning a book to him rather than returning a different book to someone else who did steal it, when I haven't time to do both. And perhaps, if I can only save one of two children, a permissible, if optional, reason for saving A rather than B might be that A is a good child.

However, Dancy's distinctions may be intuitive, so long as we apply them with a sensitivity to context. And particularism needs at least to separate a reason for action from the presence of enablers and absence of disablers: if one was permitted, or required, to incorporate such things within the reason, particularism about reasons would become implausible. For it would become committed to the claim that, however finely we discriminate circumstances, it will always be possible to imagine a further complication that would cancel or reverse valence (generating no reason to φ, or even a reason not to φ, out of what was previously a reason to φ). Yet it is not credible that our practical sensibilities should be infinitely fine-grained, so that there could never be an end of drawing relevant further distinctions; nor has any argument been offered, at least by Dancy, for supposing otherwise.[2]

But then the label 'variabilism' seems apter than 'particularism'. It is in part because the fact providing a reason is left pretty *general* (as opposed to specific) that it may plausibly vary between favouring, or failing to favour, or even disfavouring (i.e. being a reason for, or no reason for, or a reason against) the very same action.

One generalist response is to distinguish *primary* from *secondary* reasons: if fact *A* may count either for or against φ-ing, or neither, depending on other features of the situation, this must be because it leaves open whether another fact obtains, *B* say, which can only count either for φ-ing, or against φ-ing. Thus, that someone has lent me a book may contingently be a reason to return it, depending on whether he lent it to me rightfully; but *that* would necessarily be a reason (though not necessarily a decisive one).[3] Yet it is not a feasible strategy in general to try to derive all variant reasons from invariant ones. Take the instance of lying: generally speaking, that it would be a lie to assert that *p* is a reason against it; being a lie is generally a bad-making feature of an action. But there are white lies (though we should be sparing of them), and lies told when under unjust or hostile interrogation, and lies told when playing the game 'Diplomacy', etc. etc.[4] We may well speculate that there is some underlying and unifying *point* to veracity which is lacking in such cases; but identifying this is difficult, and would require the most intelligent ethico-philosophical reflection. It would seem a mistake to lay down that the *real reason* against telling a lie in an ordinary situation is not that it is a lie, but that it offends against that elusive value. For we expect reasons to be accessible to agents and citable by them; justification is a public and articulate practice.[5] It makes better sense to claim that what is really *good-making* about most cases of telling the truth is that they preserve the point of veracity. We might say this: that asserting that *p* would be telling a lie is a reason against it in contexts where lying would be contrary to the point of veracity; but we needn't identify the *reason* against it with its being contrary to the point of veracity – the reason, in an ordinary case, is just that it would be a lie.

Against any generalist appeal to a distinction between primary and secondary reasons, the particularist might also try to identify a feature with variable valence that would appear to yield a primary reason if anything does. Such might be *enjoyment*: that I would enjoy φ-ing is surely a plausible candidate for a primary and non-derivative reason for φ-ing. Yet the valence of enjoyment appears to be variable: Dancy remarks, 'Pleasure at a wrong action compounds the wrong' (Dancy 1993: 60), by which I take him to mean that enjoying acting wrongly makes the action worse. It is this issue that I want especially to discuss here.

In such cases, it is plausibly necessary that the agent enjoys not just an act which is morally bad, but whatever constitutes its badness: then the pleasure is bad not just in its source, but in its focus.[6] However, for the converse case of a pain that loses its disvalue in context, Dancy cites extracting a sea-urchin from one's daughter's foot, proposing that, if there is no alternative, the physical pain caused does not tell *at all* against the action taken (Dancy 1993: 55–56). Here there is nothing inappropriate about the cause of the pain: anyone, however impeccable their character, would find it painful to undergo such an operation. Does the pain really lose its *pro tanto* disvalue in context, in view of the necessity? This seems implausible to me: the father can surely say sincerely to his daughter, 'I'm terribly sorry to be doing this'; and surely anaesthetics were not invented solely for *un*necessary operations.

Analogous cases may involve pleasure. We are told that Nero fiddled as Rome burned, doubtless for fun; did not his aesthetic pleasure become bad in context? This raises two questions. First, was he taking an innocent pleasure in playing the fiddle, but at the wrong time, or a perverse pleasure in playing the fiddle inopportunely? (I presume that it was not from absence of mind that he felt like fiddling *then*.) Secondly, *if* the first was the case, should we say that, in context, the pleasure itself became simply bad, or that, though still mildly good *in itself*, it became very bad *in context* as unfitting to the occasion?

Take other instances. In Saki's story 'The Boar-Pig', Matilda force-feeds her cousin Claude upon raspberry trifle, so that no one can say again that, unlike her, he has never taken too much. Suppose that, at least initially, he can't prevent himself from enjoying the taste, as any child would. Would that not be even a *pro tanto* compensation, however insufficient?[7] Cruel Frederick in Heinrich Hofmann's *Struwwelpeter* provides a more complex case. He meets his come-uppance after whipping the good dog Tray: Tray bites him in the leg, and he ends up in bed, taking nasty physic too. We may suppose that his sufferings are double: (1) he dislikes his sore leg and the nasty physic, as *any* boy would; (2) he resents his inability to carry on tearing off flies' wings, and the like, as only a *naughty* boy would. I incline to count the pain of (1), though not that of (2), as a *pro tanto* evil.

Of course, some may disagree: if Frederick got what he deserved, perhaps the pain of (1) was even a *pro tanto* good.[8] We might count one's daughter's pain, as one extracts the sea-urchin, as a *pro tanto* evil, although it was necessary, but Frederick's physical sufferings as a *pro tanto* good, because they were deserved. This would be an attitude, perhaps common enough, which is intermediate between mine, which may be over-compunctious, and Dancy's, which strikes me as factitious. It might be held that retributive punishment in general fits Dancy: the pain of incarceration, say, is perhaps not *pro tanto* bad when it is deserved, even when this is the pain of a general loss of liberty, and not the pain of an inability to be actively bad (a pain which surely tells not at all against incarceration). This would seem to be a case where moral disagreement may have philosophical implications. I find such a view of retribution elegant but chilling. For surely we value humanity towards prisoners. Consider this: if the restraint that is part of incarceration is not bad at all if the incarceration is merited, then St Leonard, the patron saint of prisoners, was wasting his time when he visited the guilty (though not when he visited the innocent). But few of us would wish to draw that inference. And we would surely think a parent who told Frederick 'You have got what you deserved' excessively severe if he not only *said* that, but imposed the nasty medicine for its taste as well as its effect, and denied him any salve on his leg.

Aristotle is relevant: he takes the view that the value of a case of enjoyment is a function of the nature of its object: 'Since activities differ in respect of goodness and badness, and some are worthy to be chosen, others to be avoided, and others neutral, so, too, are the pleasures; for to each activity there is a proper pleasure. The pleasure proper to a worthy activity is good and that proper to an unworthy activity bad' (*EN* X 5, 1175b24–28). This is not a piece of free-floating moralism, but a plausible inference from a central principle within his account of pleasure, which is, as he then restates it, that 'as activities are different, so are the corresponding pleasures' (b36). Once we have described some good and enjoyable mode of activity sufficiently to identify *what* pleasure is taken in it by the agent, that pleasure will have invariant valence: it will be a good, and count in favour, most obviously, of the activity itself. If the activity is by nature bad, then any pleasure proper to it will be characteristic of a bad agent, and make it worse. Aristotle goes so far as to claim that pleasures of a reprehensible kind may make it preferable not to be alive (*EE* I 5, 1215b25–26).[9]

In a way, this suits Dancy: it is good to enjoy acting well, bad to enjoy acting badly. However, why not then suppose that the value, negative or positive, inheres in the determinate pleasure, so that no value attaches to pleasure as a determinable? If so, it isn't the *thing* that varies in valence; rather, 'pleasure' is a general term that applies mostly to desirable experiences, but also (though in Aristotle's view only secondarily and qualifiedly)[10] to undesirable experiences of enjoying being bad (*EN* X 5, 1176a10–29).

In regard to the relation of good-making, we might go still further and say that the value of an instance of enjoyment depends upon the *concrete* (or maximally determinate) nature of the activity, and degree of engagement of the agent, on that particular occasion. And surely this should count as 'particularism' if anything does, since it takes what is good-making to be, in reality, unrepeatable.[11] However, if the facts that constitute reasons need to be predictable and articulable, this would not be plausible as a view of reasons. We might still only allow good species of pleasure to supply favouring reasons. Yet we may be willing to concede that 'Because it would be fun' can, in some cases, state a perfectly adequate and intelligible reason for doing something. It seems to me plausible to allow that a thing's being fun does *something*, in innocuous cases, to make it good. (Of course we must then avoid double counting: in weighing up alternatives, we mustn't *add* the generic value to the specific value.)

If we prefer to maintain something closer to Dancy's position, about *both* good-making *and* favouring, we would seem to have two alternatives:

(a) The *default* position is that pleasure is good.[12] However, if what is enjoyed is bad, the pleasure becomes itself bad, making the whole worse. We could say: innocent pleasure is good. But, when a pleasure is innocent, its being innocent is not part of what makes it good: rather, there is then missing something whose presence would make it bad. (Thus, in these cases, non-innocence is a disabler; innocence is not a component of what is good.) When one enjoys acting well, the value of the pleasure is enhanced.

(b) Human activity (at least) is naturally a good: i.e. it is good unless something corrupts it.[13] Pleasure is a function of its object, both in its nature and in its value. Enjoying acting *enhances* value when one is not acting badly. Enjoying acting well enhances acting well, whereas failing to enjoy acting well (when enjoyment would be in place, as it is, say, with giving a present if not with dying in battle) attenuates the value of acting well. Enjoying acting badly intensifies its disvalue.

(a) would assign a basic and default value to pleasure, though this is only realized when the pleasure is innocent. Enjoying acting well will then count as being enhanced in value by the extra value of acting well over acting innocently. However, this hardly establishes any objective demarcation between reasons and intensifiers: when one has a choice between enjoyable activities, the nature of the pleasure can surely be *part* of one's reason for preferring one to another.

(b) equally applies Dancy's concept of an intensifier. Again, it must be questioned whether there is any objective demarcation between reasons and intensifiers. Very occasionally, that an activity is good just *qua* being an activity may give one reason to pursue it: 'Why are you doing that?' 'Well, doing something is better than doing nothing.' But one may choose an activity, otherwise only minimally good, *because* it is enjoyable, citing the enjoyment as one's reason, and not as an intensifier of one's reason.

One might try applying the notion of a default valence to (b) as follows: human activity (at least) has a default valence which is positive; no positive extra is needed in a situation to *make* it good; and yet, when it is gravely bad in some way, its valence gets reversed. Is this plausible? Hardly. The credible claim is that human activity (at least) is good if it isn't bad; it makes no sense to say that an activity's being a case of *activity* usually makes it good, but on occasion (when the activity is bad) makes it worse. So if Dancy is to justify the application of the notion of a default valence to such cases, he needs to argue *independently* in favour of (a) and against (b).

It is also unpromising to attempt an objective demarcation between some features that make an action *good*, and others that make it *still better* (which would be a species of enhancing). For the distinction is often relative to context. If I have already described a piano recital as consisting of Beethoven, I may add that it was also given by Brendel, which enhanced it. But I might equally have said, in one breath, that it was Brendel playing Beethoven.

I end with these general suggestions about reasons and good-making features. Facts constituting reasons are by their nature general, and this may give rise to what may aptly be called 'variabilism'. One may take what might aptly be called a 'particularist' view of good-making as maximally determinate; or we can count general features as good-making, and these may indeed be subject to enabling, disabling, enhancing, and attenuating – all within the varying contexts of choice and conversation.[14]

Notes

1 Dancy (2000b) is open-minded about the proper strength of his position.
2 This is an objection to Richard Holton's 'supersession argument', which he offers to variabilists, and states as follows (2002: 196–97): 'Given any action whose features are described in non-moral terms, and a principle that says that an action having those features will be good, we can always think of some further feature which is such that, were the action to have that feature too, it would

become a bad action.' Dancy's position, which is variabilist about reasons, but not about reasons *plus* conditions, is not implausible in this way.

3 Thus Roger Crisp distinguishes 'ultimate' from 'non-ultimate' reasons (2000: 37).

4 Perhaps consciously stating a falsehood during a game, even to deceive a fellow player, is not *lying*. But consider this in Foot (2001: 77–78): 'I think it especially ludicrous to suggest, for instance, that those fighting with the Resistance against the Nazis should not if necessary have *lied* through their teeth to protect themselves or their comrades' (my italics).

5 This invites further discussion, as Ursula Coope has pointed out to me. Successful communication is a matter not only of what a speaker succeeds in articulating in what he says, but what he thereby conveys to his audience. Two people who belong to the same cultural community may communicate quite specific meanings in an allusive manner that would leave them a mystery to an intelligent but alien observer. However, it remains counter-intuitive (I think) to make the *real* reason for making an assertion that counts as telling the truth, in an ordinary situation, something that *no one*, perhaps, has yet succeeded in precisely putting a finger upon. (I am indebted here to a brief remark made at Bled by Mark Lance.)

6 It would be further restrictive to demand that the agent enjoy not just what constitutes the badness, but the badness that this constitutes. But I do not believe that pleasure only makes a bad activity worse when the pleasure is diabolic.

7 Those who like more grown-up examples may look up a regrettably unforgettable one in Dover (1978: 36, n. 18).

8 On the other hand, as a variabilist is free to distinguish, perhaps the death of Harriet, who played with matches and burnt to death, was not good *at all*, since as a penalty it was disproportionate.

9 I take this from a fuller discussion of Aristotle's relation to particularism in Price (forthcoming).

10 This may strike us as counter-intuitive. Wholly intuitive, however, would be the same claim about what is *enjoyable*. The perverted or brutish activities that Aristotle elsewhere describes (*EN* VII 5) are not such as *we* would label as 'enjoyable'.

11 Of course, one may specify an imaginary twin earth as one where the *exact* pleasure is repeated, evidently with no change of value or disvalue. No particularist would go so far as to claim that the individual identity of some instance of value is essential to the value that it has.

12 On the notion of a default valence, cf. Dancy (2004: 184–87), and, more recently and positively, 'Defending the Right' (unpublished). The idea of generalizations that are not exceptionless, and yet are explanatory *as they stand*, is valuably explored in recent work by Mark Lance and Margaret Little.

13 This goes back to Aquinas; see Foot (2001: 76). It is endorsed by Foot: 'The principle "good if not bad" is one that should be seen as unexciting and unexceptional when applied to an operation of a living thing.' (ibid.) It is applied to things in general, and to actions in particular, by Anscombe (2005: 234–35): 'Good and bad are not equal and opposite characteristics. A thing is good, and so is an action, if and only if there is *nothing* bad about it, as that kind of thing, or as a human action. It is bad if there is *something* wrong with it.' Such an extension from actions to things in general would appear to express a distinctively religious outlook.

14 I do not discuss here whether certain general features of acts, notably those designated by terms for virtues or vices, may have an invariable valence, for all their generality. My claim is not that a sufficient degree of generality is *sufficient* for plausible variance, but that it is *necessary*.

12 Laughter and moral ambiguity
Particularist reflections on the ethical dimensions of humour

David Bakhurst

Humour is a phenomenon that has been poorly served by philosophers, who for the most part have neither helped us understand it, nor made us laugh.[1] Philosophy's neglect of humour is unfortunate, since laughter is so evidently a distinctive aspect of the human condition. No philosophical anthropology could be complete without attending to the smiling side of our nature. Moreover, humour raises specific issues of importance in a number of philosophical fields, especially ethics. Humour often excites disapproval, and sometimes moral condemnation. When I was a child, my parents would habitually switch off the television, to my great irritation, when comedy programmes became too 'smutty' (or 'near the knuckle' as my father would say). Today, fewer people are embarrassed by sexual humour, but there remain many forms that regularly cause offence.

Consider someone – call him Ernest – who is distressed by the nastiness of so much humour. Ernest is impressed by Henri Bergson's famous essay 'Laughter', which establishes a strong connection between laughter and cruelty. For Bergson, the aim of laughter is to 'intimidate by humiliating' (1900: 188); it thus requires 'an absence of feeling', 'a momentary anaesthesia of the heart' (63–64). Bergson admits that this is 'not very flattering to ourselves' (188), but argues that laughter is justified by its social purpose, which is to restrain 'eccentricity' (73): laughter serves to ridicule us when we behave 'absent-mindedly' – that is, like things or automata whose actions are dictated by causes rather than flowing from free intellectual activity (see 117, 145).

Ernest applauds Bergson's recognition of the cruelty in humour, but disagrees with his rationalization of it. Ernest doubts that the project of humiliating through mockery is a noble one whatever it serves to achieve. But in any case, Ernest challenges Bergson's account of the function of laughter. Ernest thinks that laughter has many purposes, not one, and he is sure that some among them are morally problematic. It is no coincidence, Ernest feels, that laughter is often directed against the powerless – women, ethnic minorities, homosexuals, the disabled – as well as the weak, the lonely, the ignorant, the ugly and so forth. If laughter is targeted at eccentricity, it is the 'eccentricity' of those who depart from the social norms by which those who have power and status define themselves. Ernest contends that humour often serves not just to ridicule folly, but to perpetuate humiliating images of those who are socially disadvantaged, thereby contributing to their subordination.

To his credit, Ernest disputes Bergson's idea that laughter always aims to mock and humiliate, for he recognizes that we sometimes laugh with joy, delight or amusement. However, for Ernest, this raises a further problem about the moral status of humour. Ernest observes that in many examples of comedy, we are invited to find amusing actions and situations that would normally warrant moral condemnation. 'Bad-taste jokes' about rapists or serial killers provide graphic examples, but Ernest claims that this is equally, if less spectacularly, true of numerous cases of seemingly benign humour. Take two examples from celebrated 'vintage' British television comedy. In *Steptoe and Son*, father and son Albert and Harold Steptoe are rag-and-bone men yoked together in a miserable existence. Much of the humour derives from how the Steptoes manipulate each other and from the petty spite of their exchanges. And *Fawlty Towers* is funny for the contemptible behaviour of the outrageous hotelier Basil Fawlty, including his exploitation of the hapless Spanish waiter, Manuel. A great deal of humour, traditional or alternative, pedestrian or brilliant, gets its laughs from portrayals of people mistreating one another.[2]

Ernest recognizes that, just as humour is sometimes a vehicle of oppression, it can also be a weapon of resistance: in some cases we laugh at wrongdoing in order to express our dislike of it. Thus in parody, we employ ridicule to cut vice down to size. However, Ernest notes that though parody sometimes features in the comedies cited above, the laughter they provoke does not simply function to express disapproval. In many cases, we positively enjoy, even revel in, the spite, cruelty, or small-mindedness that is portrayed, and this seems somehow to implicate us in it. Thus Ernest cannot trust the protestations of those who claim that in laughing at a character like Alf Garnett or Archie Bunker, they are expressing their disdain for bigotry rather than their enjoyment of it.[3] Ernest protests that their laughter, although not an explicit endorsement of bigotry, nonetheless makes them complicit in it.

1 Taking Ernest seriously

Ernest's concerns about the cruelty of laughter, and its role in the oppression of disadvantaged groups, are comparatively familiar. I therefore propose to concentrate on his more unusual claim that there is something morally dubious in itself about laughing at depictions of morally dubious behaviour.

Let us consider a more detailed example of the kind of humour that upsets Ernest. Consider *Rising Damp*, a notable situation comedy made in the 1970s. Central to the humour is the relation between the scheming landlord, Rigsby, and Philip, a black African student lodging in Rigsby's house. Rigsby sees Philip as a savage who cannot be trusted to behave properly in a civilized society. Rigsby's racism is supposed to make him ridiculous, since Philip is evidently a well-educated and pleasant person, far more civilized than Rigsby himself. Nevertheless, it is hard to see the show today without detecting in it a certain moral ambiguity, for we are intended to laugh not just at the folly of Rigsby's racism, but at the racist remarks themselves. We are supposed to find talk of savages, cannibals and jungle-drums humorous, but to recognize the absurdity of associating such things with the erudite Philip. Thus, even when we laugh at Rigsby, and laugh at him for being a racist, we are expected to find his racist remarks amusing. Ernest sees this as revelling in wrong.

We may be persuaded by Ernest's view of *Rising Damp*, yet feel he is wrong to suspect there is a general problem about laughing at depictions of morally dubious behaviour. How should we decide which cases are problematic?

1.1 Questions of harm

It is tempting to suppose that the issue turns exclusively on whether our laughter causes harm. Thus it might be argued that the problem with humour that is racist or sexist, or mocks people for their looks or their loneliness, is that people are directly or indirectly injured or offended by it. This could be said about *Rising Damp*: there are elements of racism in its humour and racism is a harmful thing. But in the vast majority of cases where we laugh at portrayals of morally dubious behaviour no one is harmed. After all, in comedy we are often dealing with the machinations of fictional characters, who cannot actually harm or be harmed. The question is whether any real person is injured or offended by the depiction of these fictional goings-on, and often no one is.

This argument will not move Ernest. He will respond that it is uncertain that no one is harmed by this kind of humour, for the fact that nobody objects to it may be a feature of a moral ineptitude that makes us all worse off. For him, the important question is not whether people *are* offended by such humour, but whether they *ought to be*. Moreover, Ernest denies that whether some form of humour is morally reprehensible depends exclusively on its consequences. The problem Ernest takes *Rising Damp* to illustrate is not that our laughing at Rigsby serves to legitimate racial oppression (though this might be a concern), but that where we laugh at vice with anything other than derision, we are somehow guilty of failing to take it seriously. Indeed, we are deriving pleasure from vice and this is wrong.

1.2 Absurdity and unreality

It might be suggested against Ernest that the events depicted in a great deal of comedy cannot be taken seriously from a moral point of view because they appear so unreal and artificial. This is particularly obvious where the humour is absurd (or 'zany' or 'wacky', as Americans say). It is true that *Monty Python's Flying Circus* invites us to laugh at numerous examples of violence, abuse, deception and so on. Moreover, the intention of such humour is not usually to make a moral point. But our laughter is innocent because the events are depicted so absurdly that they are emptied of moral significance.

As is often remarked, much humour derives simply from incongruity, from 'inversions' of sense and nonsense, the expected and the surprising, the possible and the impossible. Since morality serves to define right and proper behaviour, it is no surprise that acts that are morally incongruous are a source of humour.[4] When a frustrated customer shoots an unhelpful bank clerk, or a sales assistant in a menswear shop salaciously inquires about his customer's sexual activities, we laugh primarily because the behaviour is ridiculous and outrageous. We do not thereby endorse the depicted acts.

Ernest will respond, however, that it remains unclear why the absurdity of some depicted act enables us to be indifferent to its moral dubiousness. Of course, if laughter is a mere reaction to incongruity, the explanation might seem plausible: we are not laughing at the wrong, we are laughing because we find wrong where right should be. However, in such cases our laughter is rarely that of the infant playing 'peek-a-boo'. To learn to appreciate absurd humour, particularly that as radical as *Monty Python*, involves the cultivation of sensibilities that, if not exactly sophisticated, are hardly juvenile. We learn to delight in the inversion of sense and nonsense, good and bad. But the moral status of relishing the latter inversion remains questionable. Their absurdity may be among the reasons why the depicted events strike us as funny, but this does not explain why laughter is morally appropriate. We might imagine a culture whose members thought that, say, a portrayal of someone being dismembered or gratuitously killed was morally incomprehensible, however silly the depiction. Appealing to the absurd does not show why they would be mistaken.

Anyway, Ernest will continue, by no means all the problematic species of humour exploit absurdity in the relevant sense. Many derive their effect from the verisimilitude of the behaviour they portray. In *Steptoe and Son*, the Steptoes' mutual abuse is all too realistic. The absurdity of their predicament is Beckettian, not Pythonesque, and there is no sense in which their actions are not candidates for moral appraisal. We are supposed to see them as wrong and also find them funny. Moreover, even where humour does present actions in a way that is absurd and unreal, the purpose is frequently to direct attention to behaviour, motives or character types which are utterly familiar. The target of absurd humour is often real phenomena.

1.3 The depiction and the depicted

The appeal to the absurd does draw attention to one obvious fact: the mode of presentation of a joke is of critical importance to whether it is funny. In comedy, we often laugh as much at the depiction as at what is depicted. We might wonder whether Ernest is conflating the moral status of depicted events with the moral status of their depiction. Though at times the former can infect the latter – as when the lewdness of the behaviour portrayed makes the portrayal itself lewd – the moral status of depictions of behaviour is usually different from the status of the acts depicted. There can be inoffensive depictions of offensive acts and offensive depictions of inoffensive acts. This distinction appears to allow us to say that where we laugh at depictions of morally contemptible behaviour, the pleasure our laughter expresses is not derived from the dubious behaviour so much as from its depiction, and the depiction itself need not be morally contemptible.

Ernest will respond that humour is not *all* in the telling. Our taking pleasure in some comic portrayal usually depends on our finding what is portrayed funny. Thus the claim that the pleasure we take in laughing at a comic depiction of cruelty is pleasure in the portrayal and not in the cruelty depicted has to reckon with the fact that the source of the pleasure is nonetheless a depiction of *cruelty*. The event is depicted as cruel and this, it seems, is partly what amuses us. The issue remains whether that source of pleasure is morally problematic.

We can take stock of Ernest's position by considering his favourite analogy: screen violence. He observes that many people enjoy graphic depictions of violence on film and television. In their defence, they argue that what they enjoy is 'only a depiction'. The events are acted, not real, and the objects of enjoyment are *depictions* of violence, and not violence itself.

Ernest points out that, as with humour, the morality of screen violence is often taken to depend on questions of harm. Its opponents usually argue that exposure to fictional violence numbs our sensibilities to the real thing; we become habituated to viciousness and cease to care as much about it. Ernest takes this objection to be a good one, but he also worries that there is something morally contemptible simply in enjoying depictions, albeit fictional, of people being vicious to one another. It may be obvious that enjoying scenes of fictional violence is not as bad as enjoying scenes of actual violence, but that does not show that the former pastime is innocent. It will not do, Ernest argues, simply to point to the fact that the events portrayed are only fictional, for the power of fiction, indeed its very possibility, derives from the fact that the reader or viewer becomes absorbed in the work. In some genres, works aspire to absorb us totally: the medium of depiction is designed to be transparent. In so far as a work engrosses us in this way, we cannot remain morally neutral to the events portrayed, for our feelings are engaged as we sympathize with the characters. Thus we cannot think of what occurs there as just not mattering. Even though its mattering does not consist in real harms done to living persons, our failure to respond to the morally significant characteristics of the world depicted is, Ernest argues, a genuine failure of our moral sensibilities.

Ernest believes that the horror that violence merits ought to make it impossible for us to enjoy graphic depictions of it. Comic portrayals of vice, he suggests, represent a similar, if less conspicuous, cause for concern. For here too pleasure is derived from the representation of nastiness.

Ernest admits, of course, that where our imaginative identification with fiction is less intense, we do not find ourselves relating to characters as if they are real and our usual moral responses are sometimes lessened or suspended. It is interesting that Quentin Tarantino's violent film *Pulp Fiction* is described as a 'dimestore thriller', thus acknowledging that the work self-consciously casts itself in a genre renowned for a tenuous grip on reality. This self-referentiality serves to remind us that what we see is a pretence, and thereby attenuates the outrage that we might feel about its violence. Likewise, comedy often involves one-dimensional or 'stock' characters with exaggerated behaviours, who inhabit limited and artificial worlds. Since we are all too aware that this is not for real, we do not sympathize when nastiness befalls them (see Bergson 1900: 150–57).

Ernest maintains, however, that even if certain ways of depicting events suggest that our normal moral sensibilities need not be engaged, this does not show that the depictions in question are morally innocuous. He claims that the fact that we are unmoved by the fate of fictional characters with whom we do not identify is related to the fact that in reality we care less about those at a distance from us. One does not have to believe that the moral point of view requires us to have equal concern for all persons to admit that the fact that our concern for others typically diminishes in proportion to their remoteness is an aspect of moral psychology that warrants critical self-reflection. Perhaps, Ernest suggests, the way in which our forms of comedy or drama encourage us to distance ourselves from the events that befall their characters ought to be an object of moral concern. He finds it disturbing that we are indifferent to, or even relish, the destruction of minor characters (think of the numerous deaths of faceless henchmen and innocent bystanders in action movies) and the humiliations of comic figures. What, Ernest asks, does that reveal about our moral sensibilities?

2 Judgement and complexity

Disconcertingly, it has so far proven difficult to quieten Ernest's concerns. Having admitted that there are cases where laughter at depictions of morally dubious behaviour would be problematic, we sought to distinguish those from similar cases where we feel laughter is harmless. We considered some quick responses that appealed respectively to considerations of harm, to the absurdity of many comic depictions, and to the fact that we often laugh at the depiction as much as at what is depicted. Although these features seemed somehow relevant, they were not enough to silence Ernest, who continued to detect a certain sinisterness in our familiar forms of comedy. How should we proceed?

It may be instructive to dwell in more detail on factors relevant to deciding whether laughter at some depicted situation is indeed morally appropriate. Someone laughs at a joke or comic depiction; Ernest objects. What considerations should we take into account to determine whether the objection is a good one? In some situations, it is evident why someone is offended by another's laughter, or why laughter is not a possible response to some state of affairs. But what is at issue in 'hard cases'?

First, it is important to consider what exactly the laugher is laughing at. While this is sometimes clear, it is not always so. Laughter can be amorphous, directed vaguely towards some generally funny situation. And laughter can 'snowball': we begin laughing at some well defined joke or comic situation and then find ourselves continuing to laugh at jokes or situations where it is much less clear what is funny. The amorphousness of laughter is fuel to Ernest's fire since it allows him to suggest that when we laugh at representations of wrongdoing, part of our laughter is laughter at the wrong's being done. This suggestion obviously needs careful scrutiny case by case.

Relevant also is the *kind* of laughter at issue, for whether laughter is appropriate will depend not just on the subject matter of the joke, but on the character of the laughter it provokes. So far our discussion has not reflected much on laughter itself. Laughter is an intriguing phenomenon, situated, as it were, at the intersection of the 'realm of law' and the 'space of reasons'. In its simpler forms, laughter is an involuntary reaction elicited by some state of affairs. But as we mature, we learn to see laughter as *appropriate* to certain situations, and we cultivate our senses of humour, coming to appreciate certain kinds of humour and to disparage others that used to amuse us. Such normative talk of 'appropriateness' is precisely what makes Ernest's worries possible – he urges that we have developed our senses of humour in a way that does not befit us – and since the emergence of senses of humour is clearly an aspect of our enculturation, so Ernest sees our propensity to laugh at depictions of wrong as an indictment of our culture.[5]

It is crucial, however, that as our senses of humour develop, so we learn many different kinds of laughter each appropriate to different situations – ironic chuckling, naughty giggling, joyous guffawing, mischievous cackling, and so on. Ernest is perhaps guilty of an unduly bipolar view of laughter, where laughter ultimately expresses either approval or disapprobation. In fact, each of the many kinds of laughter may, in context, express different sentiments and emotions – from glee to resignation, spite to delight. Indeed, a single laugh can express more than one emotion and form a response to features of a situation that are humorous in different ways.

So where humour concerns matters moral, we need to consider what kind of laughter is being elicited and what that laughter expresses. In turn, the genre of humour in question may also be important, for different genres, in their distinctive ways, call for distinctive kinds of laughter. Our discussion has focused on situation comedy, sketches and jokes, but the problem of the moral standing of humour is an issue in numerous other genres, from cartoons to satire.

In addition, the moral status of humour may depend in part on the intentions of those who would make us laugh, and why those who laugh with us laugh as they do. Moreover, the standing of any joke, and of our response to it, may hinge on the circumstances of its telling, the wider narrative of which it is part, or considerations about the social context in which the joke is told.

Thus, to take a simple case, when I laugh at Harold Steptoe calling his father 'a dirty old man', my laughter may be prompted by several different features of the situation. I laugh at Harold's abusiveness, at the way the insult is delivered and the actor's mode of delivery, I laugh at his father's response to the insult, and more generally I laugh at the whole desperate setting of their lives. My laughter is also prompted by the familiarity of the incident: the insult is a 'catch phrase', its occurrence stylized and predictable. Whether it is appropriate to laugh in these ways at some or all of these things depends on how they are made funny, the broader context of the narrative of which they are part (What is the outcome of the Steptoes' nastiness to one another?), and the role of this kind of depiction in our culture at large (Does the comedy foster contempt for the poor, the ill-educated, the working class?). Whether such humour is morally problematic will surely rest on the configuration of factors such as these, and whether my laughter is appropriate will depend on how and why I laugh as I do.

It seems, then, that in hard cases we form judgements about the moral status of humour by weighing a complex multitude of factors. Such a situation looks ripe for treatment in broadly intuitionist terms. Here we can draw inspiration from the account of moral judgement that has emerged over the last three decades in the writings of thinkers sometimes described as 'British Moral Realists', such as John McDowell, David Wiggins and Jonathan Dancy. On their account, we come to determine which properties are the morally relevant ones, and how morally relevant features combine to determine the moral standing of some action or state of affairs, by a process akin to perceptual judgement.[6] Moral judgement is a matter of the deliverance of a sensibility, exercised by attending carefully to the features of cases, and not by the formal application of moral rules to particular circumstances. In the present case, where we are concerned with the moral dimensions of humour, the intuitionist will see this as a matter of the relation of two (sets of) sensibilities: first, those of morality and, second, those of our 'sense(s) of humour'. The two sensibilities are importantly related. Possession of a well-developed sense of humour is itself a vital ingredient of the good life.[7] In addition, while moral considerations can serve to moderate or silence laughter, a sense of humour is a significant mediating influence in moral consciousness, contributing to the ability to 'keep things in proportion'. Yet though they often act in consort, the deliverances of the two sensibilities will sometimes conflict. Moreover, there will be cases where we are uncertain whether there is conflict or what the appropriate response to it should be. Here it is doubtful that the character of the conflict and its resolution can be defined by appeal to rules or principles. It will be a matter of attending carefully to the features of the case and of making considered judgements in light of them. In some cases, we shall come to see that the moral features of the case ought rightly to suppress our laughter, or to cause us to lose our sense that the situation was funny at all. Here reflection aims not to formulate an argument to the conclusion that a particular piece of humour is morally dubious, but to arrive at a satisfying way of seeing the humour so that its moral standing strikes us. We ask ourselves: How might this be viewed so as to appear either offensive or innocuous? Which 'way of seeing' the situation carries greater conviction? Such an account seems to fit well our actual practice of the moral assessment of humour, in which the outcome of our reflections is not so much an argument, as an expression of the response we deem appropriate. We find ourselves saying, 'It's in bad taste', 'It's not offensive, just outrageous', 'I didn't care for the way he laughed', 'The humour was deliciously wicked', and so on. These expressions are not low-grade substitutes for argument, but gestures towards those features of the situation that strike us as warranting a moral response of a certain nature.[8]

This approach does not promise to give us a litmus test to decide which instances of humour are morally offensive, or if, when we laugh at depictions of morally dubious behaviour, we are in fact relishing wrong and whether it matters if we are. Rather, moral assessment here might be seen on a par with problems of an aesthetic nature.[9] No formula will tell us whether something constitutes a work of art, and if it does, how successful the work is. No procedure will dictate how to complete some musical composition, or to design the interior of a building. We must simply reflect thoroughly on our practices and attend carefully to the features of particular problem cases. In some cases, we may see our judgement as a response to a perception of necessity (we have seen how the work *must* be completed); in others, we perceive a range of alternatives within which we may choose. So too with the perception of the moral status of actions. Arguments will turn on whether our moral responses are appropriate to their objects, whether our view of those objects is sufficiently nuanced, our sensibilities suitably refined.

Thus we can represent the deliberative framework in which controversies over cases will be contested with the likes of Ernest. This framework presupposes the possibility of objective judgement: we strive to discover which responses are merited or required by their objects. Yet even though the terms of debate may presuppose realism about value, there is every reason to believe that many judgements will be highly, if not essentially, contestable. Through critical reflection and discussion, we can improve our terms of moral discrimination and thereby further hone the sensibilities those terms facilitate, suggesting a further refinement of terms, and so on. But this dialectic will contain no promise of closure. There will be no privileged vantage point from which the philosopher can resolve disputes.

3 Moral particularism

The view that sound moral judgement is best understood as issuing from sensitive appreciation of the nature of particular cases, rather than the application of rules, has found powerful expression in Jonathan Dancy's 'ethical particularism'. I propose, therefore, to look in some detail at whether Dancy's position can illuminate our problems about the moral status of humour.

The point of departure of Dancy's position is a critique of a familiar 'generalist' view of morally relevance (see Dancy 1993: esp. chs 4–6). This view divides morally relevant considerations into two broad classes: those that serve to make actions or situations right or good ('right- or good-making characteristics'), and those that go to make actions or situations wrong or bad ('wrong- or bad-making characteristics'). The former include properties such as promoting pleasure, being the keeper of a promise, as well as kindness, considerateness, fairness, generosity, and so on; the latter properties include causing harm, being a lie or a deception, as well as cruelty, spite, duplicity, and so forth. It is usually assumed that each such property is always morally relevant wherever it appears and that it always matters in the same way. Each property has a certain moral weight, of positive or negative 'valence', which it contributes to situations where it is present. Thus wherever an action promotes pleasure it is the better for it; that it promotes pleasure is a reason to bring it about. It may be that the action in question also has further wrong-making characteristics (e.g. it involves lying) that serve to eclipse the pleasure it brings and make it wrong overall. Nevertheless, that it promotes pleasure continues to feature as a morally positive aspect of the action, even though it does not suffice to make it right.

On this generalist view, morally relevant properties have a value that they bring with them to particular cases and that determines the way they contribute to the overall value of the particular case. The view has its attractions. First, it engenders a seemingly plausible account of moral principles. The fact that an action that is a lie is the worse for it, generates the principle that 'Lying is wrong, prima facie'; that is, wrong just in case there are no further right-making characteristics of the action which make it right overall despite its being a lie.[10] Second, generalism fits well with a plausible view of moral concepts. When someone has a concept, φ, their knowledge is general in kind; it is knowledge they bring to particular cases and which enables them to identify whether these cases fall under the concept. We want to say that when someone has the concept of cruelty, they know something general about the nature of cruel actions. They know what characteristics an action has to have to be cruel, and they know what kind of disvalue cruelty lends the action. Third, as we already observed, generalism represents the moral standing of particular cases as the outcome of the contribution made by the respective value of its moral features. The value of any particular action is a consequence of the value of the different moral properties present in it, value which those properties possess antecedently to their appearance in this case. These attractive features of generalism account for its prevalence in moral philosophy.

Dancy attacks the central tenet of this generalist picture: the idea that properties are morally relevant in the same way wherever they appear. That some feature figures as a right-making characteristic in one case does not mean that it makes a similar contribution whenever it appears. It is not just that a property that is a very strong right-making feature of some action may have a less positive influence elsewhere. Rather, Dancy maintains that a feature which is here right-making may elsewhere prove morally irrelevant, or may even serve to make an action wrong. Dancy's position is a form of holism, according to which the moral relevance of some property is not something it possesses prior to its entering into relation to other properties in particular cases. How much some property matters, indeed whether it matters at all, follows from the relation it bears to other properties of the case.[11]

Dancy's position has some striking consequences. It undermines the standard philosophical conception of moral principles outlined above, and it complicates and enriches our understanding of the exercise of moral judgement. To determine the overall value of some action, we cannot bring to bear principles that set out in advance what contribution the individual moral features of the situation make to its overall value. We need to determine just what contribution each property is making in virtue of its relation to other properties. We must do more than ascertain how various antecedently relevant aspects combine to give the action value, we need to establish what is relevant in the first place. Moreover, Dancy delineates a variety of ways in which considerations can matter to the constitution of reasons. Some considerations directly favour or disfavour some action, and these are the kinds of factors that we cite as our reasons. Other considerations are not themselves reasons, but act as 'enablers' (i.e. they make it possible for some other consideration to act as a favourer), 'disablers' (i.e. they prevent some property acting as a favourer) or 'intensifiers'/'attenuators' (they increase/decrease the reason-giving force of some consideration). Discerning how such features are at work in some situation demands an exercise of judgement that resists codification. While we may operate with 'principles' that alert us to the kinds of properties that are often morally significant, these are manifestly insufficient to determine our judgements in particular cases. We must simply attend to the peculiarities of the particular case, opening ourselves to the special way its relevant features interact there.

4 Particularism as applied to humour

Dancy's position enhances the intuitionistic picture of moral judgement I earlier suggested fitted an honest view of how we deliberate about morally problematic instances of humour; namely, an account of moral judgement as an exercise of sensibility. Moreover, Dancy's holism about moral reasons immediately illuminates the kind of concerns that we put into Ernest's mouth. The particularist can grant that there are many cases of humour that are morally problematic for the reasons Ernest spelled out. Some jokes are the worse for being cruel, scornful, mocking or contemptuous, or for the way in which they ridicule people or groups, whether their targets are real people or fictional characters. And sometimes, when we laugh at such jokes we are thereby complicit in those qualities that make them morally reprehensible. It does not follow from this, however, that we can move from the recognition of what is problematic in such cases to establish informative moral norms governing the moral status of humour. Indeed, if the particularist is right, Ernest's protestations do not even succeed in identifying certain morally relevant features of humour that are always influential in the same way. His remarks often presuppose that there are such features, but he does not establish this.

It is open to the particularist to argue that, although the fact that a joke is cruel sometimes makes it morally reprehensible, a joke will sometimes be the better for being cruel – in a case, for example, where its target is a legitimate object of contempt. In the latter case, it is not that the wrongness of the joke's cruelty is overridden by some other factors: cruelty is precisely what is called for. Moreover, there will be further cases where the potentially negative moral significance of the cruelty involved in some joke will be disabled by other considerations, including perhaps that the joke is just so funny. When my daughter's teacher claims to 'have a deep love of Canadian history' and some wag quips back, 'It's a shame his love is unrequited', the joke is funny enough to eclipse its cruelty and the point it makes would not have been the better for being less cruelly made. Of course, that one might hurt the teacher's feelings might be a reason to suppress the remark (a reason that is never relevant where the targets of humour are fictional characters), but there is cruelty in the remark whether or not it is ever heard by its target and its moral significance (or lack of it) is well served by a particularist account.

The fact is that we do not confront a simple dichotomy: either humour is the worse for being cruel or its cruelty is somehow legitimate because its target deserves to be scorned. Things are far more complicated. How cruelty figures in the case and how its figuring matters morally, if it does, depends on a wealth of factors. As I noted above, these may include considerations about how successful the joke is, but there will be many other contextual factors including considerations about the joke's audience and how they will understand its point, and what the telling of the joke will reflect about its teller. None of this can be anticipated by principles. We have to use judgement.

Some of Dancy's technical apparatus can assist us in illuminating such complexities. For example, many jokes that deploy ethnic stereotypes are morally reprehensible for so doing. But sometimes a joke that would be morally problematic if told by someone who was not a member of the ethnic group in question would be perfectly innocuous if told by someone who was a member. There is plenty of Jewish humour that is morally problematic in the mouths of people who are not Jewish, but fine – indeed wonderful – when told by Jews. Similar remarks can be made about jokes about the Irish and the Scots, and so on and so forth. Can we formulate a principle to govern such cases? Clearly it will not do to declare that Jewish jokes are innocuous if told by Jews, because we can envisage many counterexamples to this principle. We have to take into account the nature of the joke, the character of the teller, the context of its being told, the sensibilities of the audience, and so on. Even if we could somehow regiment all this and more into a principle, there would need to be so much room for discretion in its application that it would not amount to much more than the injunction to exercise judgement in light of the interplay of an open-ended list of factors. Surely it is better to say, as Dancy permits us to, that in certain circumstances, considerations about the identity of the teller can disable the moral relevance of features that would otherwise make the joke morally problematic. This view has the advantage of addressing the problem without putting the identity of the teller into the reasons why a joke is morally permissible (or, for that matter, into the reasons why it is funny), and this seems correct.

Dancy's particularism also sheds interesting light on the role of the so-called 'thick' moral concepts. It is possible that Ernest's view is prompted by a popular conception of the relation between 'thick' moral properties (cruelty, kindness, duplicity, etc.) and the responses they evoke. It is often argued that such thick properties are each tied to specific responses or attitudes, so that no one could possess the concept of some particular thick property unless he or she was 'party to the attitude' in question, as Wiggins puts it (1991: 199). This might suggest that a necessary condition of identifying the presence of the property is actually experiencing in its presence the response that constitutes the engagement of the appropriate attitude. Thus Ernest concludes that no one could see an action as cruel without feeling the indignation appropriate to cruelty, and that this indignation must surely quell any propensity to laugh. But a more nuanced account of the relation between moral properties and the attitudes or responses appropriate to them is surely necessary. All we should require is that someone who possesses a thick moral concept recognize that this is a property of a kind that usually merits a certain response or responses (a property might be tied to a plurality of responses, not just one). Indeed, such a view seems necessitated by Dancy's particularism, for the particularist cannot tie the identification of moral properties to the presence of a felt response in the identifier when the question of what response is appropriate is something to be ascertained only when the contribution of other properties is evident. If we can recognize the presence of cruelty, and acknowledge the responses it typically calls from us, without being struck by an immediate felt response, it is easier to see how laughter and other expressions of emotion might coexist with our awareness of the presence of wrong.

Perhaps Ernest, irritated by such philosophical digressions, may grant all this. It was never really his intention, he might say, to make some grand point about the moral standing of comedy *per se*, or about the relation of the real and the depicted. He was simply trying to draw attention to the fact that there is something less than innocent about our laughter at certain comic depictions we take to be benign. And this insight, Ernest will maintain, is not threatened by anything said so far. To return to *Fawlty Towers*, we might grant that were the events portrayed real they would still strike us as funny. But even if we would laugh in the real case as we do at the depiction, we must surely concede that our laughter would be significantly different. For although in the real case we might laugh from amazement, embarrassment or contempt, we would not laugh at the mistreatment itself. In the depiction, however, Fawlty's abuse of Manuel is made funny. We even laugh at Fawlty beating Manuel, at Manuel cringing as Fawlty makes to strike him, and so on. Admittedly, the abuse is represented in a cartoonish manner but, Ernest insists, we are nevertheless making a spectacle of cruelty and deriving pleasure therefrom.

I think we must concede to Ernest that we do find ourselves laughing overtly at Fawlty's mistreatment of Manuel in a way we could not in the real case. But, we might continue, this must be seen in its proper context. Fawlty's misbehaviour is, of course, only part of what we are laughing at when we take in the whole comic situation. We laugh at many aspects of Fawlty's preposterousness, and at the ludicrous conspiracy of events that have brought his plans to nought, and so forth. If we are to appreciate the humour in all of that, it is crucial that the wrongness of Fawlty's behaviour is treated light-heartedly, otherwise it would occlude the features that the comedy is designed to reveal. Thus there is a sense in which we *are* encouraged to laugh at Fawlty's misdemeanours in a way that invites us to enjoy his moral failings, but this is a precondition of appreciating the comedy as a whole that does not condone Fawlty's weaknesses. Indeed, the point is to hold them up to ridicule.

Ernest is not yet silenced, however, for he will argue that if comedy must often portray wrongdoing in a light-hearted manner, this ensures it is always at least potentially morally ambiguous. A character like Basil Fawlty may be an embodiment of type, but so perceptive and engaging is the portrayal of this character that we find ourselves identifying with him. This is why the character is compelling and effective. We laugh at ourselves through him, at our own vain pretensions, inhibitions, petty thirstings for power, and so on. In this way, Ernest will admit, the humour can be morally educative. But there is a cost for the fact that Fawlty encapsulates elements of ourselves heightens our propensity to enjoy his shortcomings, to delight in his rudeness and at his power over Manuel. It is easy for us to find our laughter somehow endorsing the view that there is something hilarious at being 'from Barcelona'. (The repetition of this catch phrase trades on the bigotry it is supposed to unmask, hinting that there is something strangely funny about being from Barcelona.) In this way, Ernest suggests, the Fawlty character may serve to domesticate, rather than expose, our failings. And comedy of this kind will always be prey to such problems.

5 Conclusion

We have to give Ernest his due. He has succeeded in identifying a source of moral ambiguity in comedy, ambiguity that should force us to reappraise such celebrated comedies as *Fawlty Towers* and *Rising Damp*. In addition, his concerns draw attention to the fact that we are peculiar beings whose powers of representation enable us to externalize our imaginations and countenance fictional characters as if they were real. When philosophers talk about the pros and cons of 'experience machines', they imagine us retreating into solipsistic worlds of private experiences. Yet our real world is littered with fragments of 'virtual realities', in the form of literary, cinematic and other representations, which are matters of public assessment and criticism, notwithstanding the personal meaning they may have for us. Ernest is right that the attitudes we take to such worlds and their inhabitants tell us a lot about ourselves. It may be better to enjoy screen violence than the real thing, but it is an interesting, perhaps sad, fact about us that we are drawn to representations of violence at all. This is true even when the violence is meant to be funny, as in the familiar antics of cartoon characters. As our forms of comedy grow harsher, it is important that we should ask ourselves what it is we are laughing at and why.

However, if the particularism that has informed this discussion is correct, there will be no easy way to move from cases where we find attempts at humour morally problematic because, say, of the way in which the joke involves cruelty to statements of general norms that define just those cases in which cruelty-involving humour is wrong. Philosophical analysis can illuminate the structure of controversies in this area and the nature of the judgements we make to resolve them, but it cannot provide recipes for how we should judge. Insight can only come from critical self-reflection on our practices, reflection of a kind that Ernest's concerns, however humourless they may seem, force upon us.

That particularism leaves us here seems to me to represent a strength rather than a weakness of the position, for here is exactly where we are.[12]

Notes

1 Philosophers who have pronounced on laughter include Plato, Aristotle, Hobbes, Kant, Schopenhauer, and Bergson (whom I discuss briefly below). See Morreall (1987). More recent writings include Ted Cohen (1999).

2 For the uninitiated, copious details of the various television programmes discussed in this paper can be found on the web. The following is an excellent site: *www.bbc.co.uk/comedy/guide/articles*. All the shows mentioned are still broadcast as 'classics' and are available on DVD.

3 Alf Garnett is the bigoted 'hero' of the BBC's *Till Death Us Do Part*, the American version of which was *All in the Family*, in which the Garnett character became Archie Bunker.

4 Bergson claims that crude examples of 'moral inversions' are a hallmark of English comedy. He writes, 'To express in reputable language some disreputable idea, to take some scandalous situation, some low class calling or disgraceful behaviour, and describe them in terms of the utmost *"respectability"* is generally comic. The English word is here purposely employed, as the practice itself is characteristically English' (Bergson 1900: 142).

5 Those interested in the relation of reasons and causes might do well to reflect on phenomena like laughter. Philosophers often draw a sharp distinction between, on the one hand, the causal influence on and of our bodies and, on the other, actions conceived as issuing from an appreciation of reasons. Laughter seems to fall somewhere between these cases. Where we laugh because laughter is merited, it is not that laughter is best seen as following from the cognition that there is reason to laugh (or as the outcome of some 'comic syllogism'), it is rather as if we open ourselves to the humorous features of the situation and allow them to elicit laughter from us. The moral philosophers discussed later in this section often represent our moral reactions as elicited in similar fashion, though no one has really dwelt on what we might learn from this about the relation of the causal and the normative, despite the relevance of the latter issue to the work of several of the thinkers in question, especially John McDowell.

6 Dancy describes his position as 'a recognizable successor to the intuitionistic tradition' of Ross and Prichard in his *Moral Reasons* (Dancy 1993: ix), and Wiggins refers to himself as defending a form of 'new intuitionism' in the postscript of the second edition of *Needs, Values, Truth* (Wiggins 1991). McDowell is an exception, but he is reluctant to characterize his position with any '-ism'. The term 'intuitionism' expresses what unites these thinkers better than either 'realism' (which does not suit Wiggins) or 'cognitivism' (with its psychological associations). The designation is out of favour because ethical intuitionism was so long unimaginatively criticized on the grounds that intuition is, at best, a kind of mystical route to knowledge and, at worst, something which could not amount to knowledge at all. But if we deploy 'intuition' to mean a kind of rational receptivity to reasons, as the perceptual model of moral judgement would suggest, the term seems apt.

7 We should observe, however, that this was not always taken to be the case. The entry on humour in *The Oxford Companion to the Mind* notes 'a long period of history, finishing not so far back, when laughter was not so universally prized. In the eighteenth century, Lord Chesterfield, writing to his son, said " ... there is nothing so illiberal, and so ill-bred, as audible laughter;" and others have said of laughter that it is "the mind sneezing" (Wyndham Lewis), "the hiccup of the fool" (John Ray), and that it "(speaks) the vacant mind" (Oliver Goldsmith). In the 1930s Ludovici argued that humour was a principal cause of the decadence of the times; and, for him, laughter was sinister behaviour' (320).

8 This is not to say that vagueness of such judgements does not betray a certain inarticulateness. Greater articulateness, however, would be attained, not so much by representing these judgements as the product of argument, but by pointing out more clearly, and more self-consciously, what features of the situation warrant the response in question. The desired clarity will often only be attained by a refinement of our forms of expression themselves.

9 Dancy invokes an analogy between moral and aesthetic judgement at 1993: 112–13. See also McDowell (1978: 21).

10 The concept of prima facie duties is of course owed to W.D. Ross (1930). Dancy criticizes the notion at Dancy (1983) and (1993: ch.6).

11 For Dancy, this is even true of so-called 'thick' moral properties such as cruelty, kindness, generosity, etc. Dancy originally stated his view as one about the role of non-moral properties in the constitution of moral reasons. In opposition to non-cognitivists such as Hare, Dancy argued that if we make a moral judgement in virtue of certain natural features of some case, we are not committed to the view that those natural features always make the same moral difference wherever they appear. However, Dancy also maintains that thick properties can vary their moral significance from case to case and are even capable of changing their 'valence'. This makes his position especially radical.

12 This paper grew out of discussions with Jonathan Dancy, who also provided penetrating criticisms of an earlier draft. I am most grateful to him for his help and encouragement. I am also indebted to Christine Sypnowich, and to audiences at Keele and Oxford, for insightful comments.

References and bibliography

Anscombe, G.E.M. (2005) *Human Life, Action and Ethics*, Exeter: Imprint Academic.

Aristotle (1894) *Ethica Nicomachea (EN)*, I. Bywater (ed.), Oxford: Clarendon Press.

—— (1984) *Rhetoric*, in J. Barnes (ed.), *The Complete Works of Aristotle*, vol. 2, Princeton: Princeton University Press.

—— (1985) *Nicomachean Ethics*, trans. T.H. Irwin, Hackett.

—— (1991) *Ethica Eudemia (EE)*, R.R. Walzer and J.M. Mingay (eds), Oxford: Clarendon Press.

Audi, R. (1993) *The Structure of Justification*, Cambridge: Cambridge University Press.

—— (1995) 'Acting from Virtue', *Mind*, 104: 449–71.

—— (1997) *Moral Knowledge and Ethical Character*, New York: Oxford University Press.

—— (2003) 'Intrinsic Value and Reasons for Action', *Southern Journal of Philosophy*, suppl. vol. XLI: 30–56; reprin. in T. Horgan and M. Timmons (eds) (2006) *Metaethics After Moore*, Oxford: Clarendon Press, pp. 79–106.

—— (2004) *The Good in the Right*, Princeton: Princeton University Press.

Bach, K. (1984) 'Default Reasoning: Jumping to Conclusions and Knowing When to Think Twice', *Pacific Philosophical Quarterly*, 65: 37–58.

Baier, A. (1985) 'Theory and Reflective Practices', in her *Postures of the Mind*, Minneapolis: University of Minnesota Press, pp. 207–27.

Barnard, B. and Horgan, T. (2006) 'Truth as Mediated Correspondence', *The Monist*, 89 (1): 000–000.

Beauchamp, T. and Childress, J. (2001) *Principles of Biomedical Ethics*, New York: Oxford University Press.

Bergson, H. (1900) 'Laughter', in W. Sypher (ed.) (1980) *Comedy*, Maryland: Johns Hopkins Press, pp. 59–190.

Bird, A. (1998) 'Dispositions and Antidotes', *Philosophical Quarterly*, 48: 227–34.

Blackburn, S. (1992) 'Through Thick and Thin', *Proceedings of Aristotelian Society*, suppl. vol. LXVI., pp. 285–99.

Blum, L.A (1991) 'Moral Perception and Particularity', *Ethics*, 101: 701–25.

—— (1994) *Moral Perception and Particularity and Other Essays*, Cambridge: Cambridge University Press.

Bonjour, L. (1998) *In Defense of Pure Reason: A Rationalists Account of A Priori Justification*, Cambridge, MA: Cambridge University Press.

Brandom, R. (1994) *Making It Explicit*, Cambridge, MA: Harvard University Press.

Broad, C.D. (1930) *Five Types of Ethical Theory*, London: Routledge and Kegan Paul.
Bromberger, S. (1992) *On What We Know We Don't Know*, Chicago: University of Chicago Press.
Brower, B.W. (1988) 'Virtue Concepts and Ethical Realism', *The Journal of Philosophy*, 85 (12): 675–93.
—— (1993) 'Dispositional Ethical Realism', *Ethics*, 103: 221–49.
Brown, H.I. (1988) *Rationality*, London: Routledge.
Cargile, J. (1991) 'Real and Nominal Definitions', in J.H. Fetzer, D. Shatz, and G.N. Schlesinger (eds) *Definitions and Definability*, Dordrecht, Boston, London: Kluwer, pp. 21–50.
Churchland, P.M. (1996) 'The Neural Representation of the Social World', in L. May, M. Friedman and A. Clark (eds) *Mind and Morals*, Cambridge, MA: MIT Press, pp. 91–108.
Clark, A. (1996) 'Connectionism, Moral Cognition, and Collaborative Problem Solving', in L. May, M. Friedman and A. Clark (eds) *Mind and Morals*, Cambridge, MA: MIT Press, pp. 109–28.
Cohen, T. (1999) *Jokes*, Chicago: University of Chicago Press.
Crisp, R. (2000) 'Particularizing Particularism', in B. Hooker and M. Little (eds) *Moral Particularism*, Oxford: Clarendon Press, pp. 23–47.
Cuneo, T. (2001) 'Are Moral Qualities Response-Dependent?', *Noûs*, 35: 569–91.
Dancy, J. (1983) 'Ethical Particularism and Morally Relevant Properties', *Mind*, 92: 530–47.
—— (1986) 'Two Conceptions of Moral Realism', *Proceedings of the Aristotelian Society* suppl. vol. 60 (1986): 167–87; reprin. in J. Rachels (ed.) (1997) *Moral Theory*, Oxford: Oxford University Press, pp. 227–44.
—— (1993) *Moral Reasons*, Oxford: Basil Blackwell.
—— (1995) 'In Defense of Thick Concepts', in P.A. French, T.E. Uehling, Jr., and H.K. Wettstein (eds), *Midwest Studies in Philosophy, Volume XX: Moral Concepts*, Notre Dame: University of Notre Dame Press, pp. 263–79.
—— (1999a) 'Can the Particularist Learn the Difference between Right and Wrong?', in K. Brinkmann (ed.) *The Proceedings of the Twentieth World Congress of Philosophy, Vol. 1: Ethics*, Bowling Green: Philosophy Documentation Center, pp. 59–72.
—— (1999b) 'Defending Particularism', *Metaphilosophy*, vol. 30: 25–32.
—— (2000a) *Practical Reality*, Oxford: Clarendon Press.
—— (2000b) 'The Particularist's Progress', in B. Hooker and M. Little (eds) *Moral Particularism*, Oxford: Clarendon Press, pp. 130–56.
—— (2003a) 'What Do Reasons Do?', *Southern Journal of Philosophy*, suppl. vol. XLI, pp. 95–113; reprin. in T. Horgan and M. Timmons (eds) (2006) *Metaethics After Moore*, Oxford: Clarendon Press, pp. 39–59.
—— (2003b) 'Are There Organic Unities?', *Ethics*, 113: 629–50.
—— (2004) *Ethics without Principles*, Oxford: Clarendon Press.
—— (2005) 'Moral Particularism', in E.N. Zalta (ed.) *The Stanford Encyclopedia of Philosophy (Summer 2005 Edition)*. Available HTTP: http://plato.stanford.edu/archives/sum2005/entries/moral-particularism/ (accessed 6 January 2006).
—— (forthcoming) 'Defending the Right', *Journal of Moral Philosophy*.
D'Arms, J. and Jacobson, D. (2006) 'Sensibility Theory and Projectivism', in D. Copp (ed.) *Oxford Handbook of Ethical Theory*, Oxford: Oxford University Press, pp. 186–219.

Davidson, D. (1980) *Essays on Actions and Events*, Oxford: Clarendon Press.

Donagan, A. (1977) *The Theory of Morality*, Chicago: University of Chicago Press.

Dover, K.J. (1978) *Greek Homosexuality*, London: Duckworth.

Doyle, B. (2000) 'The Joy of Sexing', *The Atlantic Monthly*, March 2000: 28–31.

Dreier, J. (1997) 'Humean Doubts about the Practical Justification of Morality', in G. Cullity and B. Gaut (eds) *Ethics and Practical Reason*, Oxford: Clarendon Press, pp. 81–100.

Dreyfus, H. and Dreyfus, S. (1992) 'What is Moral Maturity? Towards a Phenomenology of Ethical Enterprise', in J. Ogilvy (ed.) *Revisioning Philosophy*, Albany: SUNY Press.

Dummett, M. (1973) *Frege, Philosophy of Language*, Duckworth: London.

Dworkin, G. (1995) 'Unprincipled Ethics', in P.A. French, T.E. Uehling, Jr., and H.K. Wettstein (eds) *Midwest Studies in Philosophy, Vol. XX: Moral Concepts*, Notre Dame, Indiana: University of Notre Dame Press, pp. 224–39.

Eklund, M. (2004) 'What are Thick Concepts?' was available on author's web page in 2004.

Evans, G. (1985) *Collected Papers*, Oxford: Oxford University Press.

Feldman, F. (1992) *Confrontations with the Reaper: A Philosophical Study of the Nature and Value of Death*, New York: Oxford University Press.

—— (1997) *Utilitarianism, Hedonism, and Desert: Essays in Moral Philosophy*, New York: Cambridge University Press.

Fischer, J.M. and Ravizza, M. (1998) *Responsibility and Control*, Cambridge: Cambridge University Press.

Fodor, J. (1983) *The Modularity of Mind*, Cambridge: MIT Press.

—— (2001) *The Mind Doesn't Work That Way: The Scope and Limits of Computational Psychology*, Cambridge: MIT Press.

Foot, P. (2001) *Natural Goodness*, Oxford: Clarendon Press.

Garfield, J.L. (2000) 'Particularity and Principle: The Structure of Moral Knowledge', in B. Hooker and M. Little (eds) *Moral Particularism*, Oxford: Clarendon Press, pp. 178–204.

Giaquinto, M. (1998) 'Epistemology of the Obvious: A Geometrical Case', *Philosophical Studies*, 92: 181–204.

Gibbard, A. (2003) 'Reasons Thin and Thick', *The Journal of Philosophy*, vol. C, no. 6, pp. 288–304.

—— (1992) 'Thick Concepts and Warrant for Feelings', *Proceedings of Aristotelian Society*, supp. vol. LXVI., pp. 267–83.

—— (forthcoming) 'Moral Feelings and Moral Concepts', forthcoming in R. Shafer-Landau (ed.) *Oxford Studies in Metaethics*; available on author's web-page http://www-personal.umich.edu/%7Egibbard/OSME06moral-feelings.pdf

Goldman, A.H. (2002) *Practical Rules: When We Need Them and When We Don't*, Cambridge: Cambridge University Press.

Goldman, A.I. (1979) 'What is Justified Belief?', in G. Pappas (ed.) *Justification and Knowledge*, Dordrecht: Reidel, pp. 1–23.

—— (1993) 'Ethics and Cognitive Science', *Ethics*, 103: 337–60.

Greco, J. (2000) *Putting Skeptics in Their Place*, Cambridge: Cambridge University Press.

Gregory, R. (1987) *Oxford Companion to the Mind*, Oxford: Oxford University Press.

Haidt, J. (2001) 'The Emotional Dog and Its Rational Tail: A Social Intuitionist Approach to Moral Judgment', *Psychological Review*, 108: 814–34.

Hare, R.M. (1952) *The Language of Morals*, Oxford: Clarendon Press.
—— (1963) *Freedom and Reason*, Oxford: Clarendon Press.
—— (1981) *Moral Thinking*, Oxford: Clarendon Press.
Harman, G. (1977) *The Nature of Morality*, New York: Oxford University Press.
Hawthorne, J. (2002) 'Deeply Contingent A Priori Knowledge', *Philosophy and Phenomenological Research*, 65: 247–69.
Heller, M. (1995) 'The Simple Solution to the Problem of Generality', *Noûs*, 29: 501–15.
Henderson, D. and Horgan, T. (2001) 'Practicing Safe Epistemology', *Philosophical Studies*, 102: 227–58.
Herman, B. (1993) *The Practice of Moral Judgment*, Cambridge, MA: Harvard University Press.
Holton, R. (2002) 'Principles and Particularisms', *Proceedings of the Aristotelian Society*, suppl. vol. 76: 191–209.
Hooker, B. (2000a) *Ideal Code, Real World*, Oxford: Oxford University Press.
—— (2000b) 'Moral Particularism: Wrong and Bad', in B. Hooker and M. Little (eds) *Moral Particularism*, Oxford: Clarendon Press, pp. 1–22.
—— (2002) 'Intuitions and Moral Theorizing', in P. Stratton-Lake (ed.) *Ethical Intuitionism*, Oxford: Oxford University Press, pp. 161–83.
—— (2003) 'Dancy on How Reasons are Related to Oughts', *Southern Journal of Philosophy*, suppl. vol. XLI, pp. 114–20.
Hooker, B. and Little, M. (eds) (2000) *Moral Particularism*, Oxford: Clarendon Press.
Horgan, T. (1991) 'Metaphysical Realism and Psychologistic Semantics', *Erkenntnis*, 34: 297–322.
—— (1998) 'The Transvaluationist Conception of Vagueness', *The Monist*, 81: 313–30.
—— (2001) 'Contextual Semantics and Metaphysical Realism: Truth as Indirect Correspondence', in M. Lynch (ed.) *The Nature of Truth*. Cambridge, MA: MIT Press, pp. 67–95.
—— (2002) 'Replies', *Grazer Philosophische Studien*, 63: 303–41.
Horgan, T. and Potrč, M. (2000) 'Blobjectivism and Indirect Correspondence', *Facta Philosophica*, 2: 249–70.
—— (2002) 'Addressing Questions for Blobjectivism', *Facta Philosophica* 4: 311–21.
—— (forthcoming a) 'Abundant Truth in an Austere World', in Greenough, P. and Lynch, M. (eds) *Truth and Realism: New Debates*, Oxford: Oxford University Press.
—— (forthcoming b) *Austere Realism*, Cambridge, MA: MIT Press.
Horgan, T. and Tienson, J. (1996) *Connectionism and the Philosophy of Psychology*, Cambridge, MA: MIT Press.
Horgan, T. and Timmons, M. (2002) 'Conceptual Relativity and Metaphysical Realism', *Philosophical Issues*, 12: 74–96.
Irwin, T.H. (2000) 'Ethics as an Inexact Science: Aristotle's Ambitions for Moral Theory', in B. Hooker and M. Little (eds) *Moral Particularism*, Oxford: Clarendon Press, pp. 100–129.
Jackson, F. and Pettit, P. (2002) 'Response-Dependence without Tears', *Philosophical Issues* (suppl. to *Nous*), vol. 12, pp. 97–117.
Jackson, F., Pettit, P. and Smith, M. (2000) 'Ethical Particularism and Patterns' in B. Hooker and M. Little (eds) *Moral Particularism*, Oxford: Clarendon Press, pp. 79–99.

Johnson, M. (1993) *Moral Imagination*, Chicago: University of Chicago Press.

Johnston, M. (1993) 'Objectivity Refigured: Pragmatism without Verificationism', in J. Haldane and C. Wright (ed.) *Reality, Representation and Projection*, New York: Oxford University Press, pp. 85–130.

Kagan, S. (1999) 'Equality and Desert', in L. Pojman and O. McLeod (eds) *What Do We Deserve?* New York: Oxford University Press, pp. 298–314.

Kant, I. (1961) *Groundwork of the Metaphysics of Morals*, H.J. Paton (trans.) London: Hutchinson & Co.

—— (1797) *The Metaphysics of Morals*, reprin. in M.J. Gregor (trans. and ed.) (1996) *Practical Philosophy*, Cambridge: Cambridge University Press, pp. 37–108.

Kirsh, D. and Maglio, P. (1992) 'Reaction and Reflection in Tetris', in J. Hendler (ed.) *Artificial Intelligence Planning Systems: Proceedings of the First Annual International Conference AIPS 92*, San Mateo: Morgan Kaufman.

Kripke, S. A. (1972) *Naming and Necessity*, in D. Davidson, and G. Harman (eds) *Semantics of Natural Language*, Dordrect: Reidel, pp. 253–355.

Lance, M. and Little, M. (2004) 'Defeasibility and the Normative Grasp of Context', *Erkenntnis*, 61(2–3): 435–55.

—— (2006a) 'Particularism & Anti-Theory', in D. Copp (ed.) *The Oxford Handbook of Ethical Theory*, Oxford University Press, pp. 567–94.

—— (2006b) 'Defending Moral Particularism', in J. Dreier (ed.) *Contemporary Debates in Moral Theory*, Oxford: Blackwell, pp. 305–21.

Lance, M. and O'Leary-Hawthorne, J. (1997) *The Grammar of Meaning*, Cambridge: Cambridge University Press.

Lewis, D. (1983a) 'Attitudes De Dicto and De Se', in *Philosophical Papers. Volume I*. Oxford: Oxford University Press, pp.133–59.

—— (1983b) 'Scorekeeping in a Language Game', in *Philosophical Papers. Volume I*. Oxford: Oxford University Press, pp. 233–49.

—— (1989) 'The Dispositional Theories of Value', *Proceedings of the Aristotelian Society*, suppl. vol. 63: 113–37.

Little, M. (2000) 'Moral Generalities Revisited', in B. Hooker and M. Little (eds) *Moral Particularism*, Oxford: Clarendon Press, pp. 276–304.

—— (2001) 'On Knowing the "Why": Particularism and Moral Theory', *Hastings Center Report*, 31(4): 32–40.

Lockhart, T. (2000) *Moral Uncertainty and Its Consequences*, New York: Oxford University Press.

MacDonald, S. (1991) 'Ultimate Ends in Practical Reasoning', *The Philosophical Review*, 100: 31–66.

McDowell, J. (1978) 'Are Moral Requirements Hypothetical Imperatives?', *Proceedings of the Aristotelian Society*, suppl. vol. 52: 13–29.

—— (1979) 'Virtue and Reason', *The Monist*, 62: 331–50.

—— (1981) 'Non-Cognitivism and Rule-Following', in S. Holtzman and C. Leich (eds) *Wittgenstein: To Follow a Rule*, London: Routledge and Kegan Paul, pp. 141–62.

—— (1988) 'Values and Secondary Qualities', (first published 1985 in T. Honderich (ed.) *Morality and Objectivity*, London: Routledge.), reprin. in G. Sayre-McCord (ed.) *Essays on Moral Realism*, Ithaca and London: Cornell Univiversity Press, Ithaca, pp. 166–80.

—— (1998) *Meaning, Value, and Reality*, Cambridge, MA: Harvard University Press.

McKeever, S. and Ridge, M. (2005a) 'The Many Moral Particularisms', *Canadian Journal of Philosophy*, 35: 83–106.

—— (2005b) 'What Does Holism Have to Do with Moral Particularism?', *Ratio*, 18: 93–103.

—— (2006) *Principled Ethics: Generalism as a Regulative Ideal*, Oxford: Clarendon Press.

McNaughton, D. (1988) *Moral Vision*, Oxford: Blackwell.

—— (1996) 'An Unconnected Heap of Duties?', *Philosophical Quarterly*, 46: 433–47.

McNaughton, D. and Rawling, P. (2000) 'Unprincipled Ethics' in B. Hooker and M. Little (eds) *Moral Particularism*, Oxford: Clarendon Press, pp. 256–75.

—— (2004) 'Duty, Rationality, and Practical Reasons', in A.R. Mele and P. Rawling (eds) *The Oxford Handbook of Rationality*, Oxford: Oxford University Press, pp. 110–31.

—— (2006) 'Deontology', in D. Copp, (ed.) *The Oxford Handbook of Ethical Theory*, Oxford: Oxford University Press, pp. 424–58.

Mill, J.S. (1863, [2000]) *Utilitarianism*, London; [Orchard Park: Broadview Press, 2000].

Millgram, E. (2002) 'Murdoch, Practical Reasoning, and Particularism', *Notizie di Politeia*, 18: 64–87.

Miščević, N. (1998) 'The Aposteriority of Response-Dependence', in Menzies, P. (ed.) *Secondary Qualities Generalized*, *The Monist*, 81: 69–84.

—— (2005a) 'Is Apriority Context-Sensitive?', *Acta Analytica*, v. 20 (1): 55–80.

—— (2005b) 'Empirical Concepts and A Priori Truth', *Croatian Journal of Philosophy*, V(14): 289–315.

—— (forthcoming) 'Devitt's Shocking Idea and Analyticity Without Apriority', *Croatian Journal of Philosophy*, vol. VI (16).

Moore, G.E. (1903) *Principia Ethica*, Cambridge: Cambridge University Press.

Morreall, J. (1987) *The Philosophy of Laughter and Humour*, New York: SUNY Press.

Murdoch, I. (1970) *The Sovereignty of Good*, London: Routledge and Kegan Paul.

Nisbett, R.E. and Wilson, T.D. (1977) 'Telling More Than We Can Know: Verbal Reports on Mental Processes', *Psychological Review*, 84: 231–54.

Nussbaum, M. (1985) 'Finely Aware and Richly Responsible: Moral Attention and the Moral Task of Literature', *Journal of Philosophy*, 82 (10): 516–29.

—— (2000) 'Why Practice Needs Ethical Theory: Particularism, Principles, and Bad Behaviour', in B. Hooker and M. Little (eds) *Moral Particularism*, Oxford: Clarendon Press, pp. 227–55.

O'Neill, O. (1996) *Towards Justice and Virtue*, Cambridge: Cambridge University Press.

——(2001) 'Practical Principles & Practical Judgment', *The Hastings Center Report*, 31(4): 15–23.

Parfit, D. (forthcoming) *Wrongness, Rationality, and Reasons*.

Pietrowski, P. (1993) 'Prima Facie Obligations, Ceteris Paribus Laws in Moral Theory', *Ethics*, 103: 489–515.

Plantinga, A. (1993) *Warrant: The Current Debate*, Oxford: Oxford University Press.

Potrč, M. (2000) 'Justification Having and Morphological Content', *Acta Analytica*, 24: 151–73.

—— (2003) 'Transvaluationism, Common Sense, and Indirect Correspondence', in Horgan, T. and Potrč, M. (eds) *Vagueness: From Epistemicism to Transvaluationism*, Dettelbach: Roell, pp. 101–19.

Potrč, M. and Strahovnik, V. (2004) *Practical Contexts*, Frankfurt: Ontos Verlag.

Price, A.W. (forthcoming) 'Was Aristotle a Particularist?', *Proceedings of the Boston Area Colloquium in Ancient Philosophy.*

Raz, J. (1999) 'The Truth in Particularism', in *Engaging Reason*, New York: Oxford University Press, pp. 218–46, reprin. in B. Hooker and M. Little (eds) *Moral Particularism*, (2000) Oxford: Clarendon Press pp. 48–78.

Reicher, M. (2002) 'Ontological Commitment and Contextual Semantics', *Grazer Philosophische Studien* 63: 141–55.

Ross, W.D. (1930) *The Right and the Good*, Oxford: Clarendon Press.

—— (1939) *The Foundations of Ethics*, Oxford: Oxford University Press.

Ryle, G. (1949) *The Concept of Mind*, Chicago: The University of Chicago Press.

Sainsbury, M. (1990) 'Concepts without Boundaries', Inaugural Lecture, King's College, London; reprin. in Keefe, R. and Smith, P. (eds) *Vagueness: A Reader*, Cambridge: MIT Press, 1996, pp. 251–64.

Salmon, W.C. (1967) *The Foundations of Scientific Inference*, Pittsburgh: University of Pittsburgh Press.

Scanlon, T.M. (1998) *What We Owe to Each Other*, Cambridge, MA: Harvard University Press.

—— (2003) 'Thickness and Theory', *The Journal of Philosophy*, v. C, no. 6: 275–87.

Schiffer, S. (2003) *The Things We Mean*, Oxford: Clarendon Press.

Sellars, W. (1956) 'Empiricism and the Philosophy of Mind', in H. Feigl and M. Scriven (eds) *The Foundations of Science and the Concepts of Psychoanalysis*, *Minnesota Studies in the Philosophy of Science, Vol. I*, Minneapolis: University of Minnesota Press, pp. 127–96.

Sherman, N. (1989) *The Fabric of Character: Aristotle's Theory of Virtue*, Oxford: Clarendon Press.

Sidgwick, H. (1907; 1981) *The Methods of Ethics*, 7th edition, London: Macmillan; Indianapolis: Hackett.

Sinnott-Armstrong, W. (1999) 'Some Varieties of Particularism', *Metaphilosophy*, 30: 1–12.

Smith, H.M. (1988) 'Making Moral Decisions', *Noûs*, 22: 89–108.

Smith, M. (1994) *The Moral Problem*, Oxford: Blackwell.

Stich, S. (1993) 'Moral Philosophy and Mental Representation', in M. Hechter *et al.* (eds) *The Origin of Values*, New York: Aldine de Gryuter, pp. 215–28.

Stratton-Lake, P. and Hooker, B. (2006) 'Scanlon versus Moore on Goodness', in T. Horgan and M. Timmons (eds) *Metaethics After Moore*, Oxford: Clarendon Press, pp. 149–68.

Stroud, S. (2001) 'Moral Commitment and Moral Theory', *Journal of Philosophical Research*, 26: 381–98.

Sunstein, C. (2005) 'Moral Heuristics', *Behavioral and Brain Sciences*, 28: 531–42.

Van Inwagen, P. (1990) *Material Beings*, Ithaca, New York: Cornell University Press.

Väyrynen, P. (2004) 'Particularism and Default Reasons', *Ethical Theory and Moral Practice*, 7: 53–79.

—— (2006a) 'Moral Generalism: Enjoy in Moderation', *Ethics*, 116: 707–41.

—— (2006b) 'Ethical Theory and Moral Guidance', *Utilitas*, 18: 291–309.

—— (unpublished) 'A Theory of Hedged Moral Principles', typescript.

Wiggins, D. (1991) *Needs, Values, Truth*, 2nd edn, Oxford: Blackwell.

Williams, B.A.O. (1985) *Ethics and the Limits of Philosophy*, Cambridge, MA: Harvard University Press.

—— (1996) 'Truth in Ethics', in B. Hooker (ed.) *Truth in Ethics,* Oxford: Blackwell, pp. 1–18.

Williamson, T. (2003) 'Understanding and Inference', *Proceedings of Aristotelian Society,* suppl. vol. 77: 249–93.

Wright, L. (1999) 'Reasons and the Deductive Ideal', in P.A. French and H.K. Wettstein (eds), *Midwest Studies in Philosophy, Vol. 23: New Directions in Philosophy.* Malden, MA: Blackwell, pp. 197–206.

Index

Lightning Source UK Ltd.
Milton Keynes UK
UKOW031919050912

198555UK00005B/12/P